THE HOUSE BY THE THAMES

and the people who lived there

GILLIAN TINDALL

PIMLICO

Published by Pimlico 2007

10 9

Copyright © Gillian Tindall 2006

Gillian Tindall has asserted her right under the Copyright,
Designs and Patents Act 1988 to be identified as the author of this work

This book is a work of non-fiction. The author has stated
to the publishers that the contents of this book are true.

First published in Great Britain in 2006 by
Chatto & Windus

Pimlico edition 2007

Pimlico
Random House, 20 Vauxhall Bridge Road,
London SW1V 2SA

www.randomhouse.co.uk

Addresses for companies within The Random House Group Limited can be
found at: www.randomhouse.co.uk

The Random House Group Limited Reg. No. 954009

A CIP catalogue record for this book
is available from the British Library

ISBN 9781844130948

The Random House Group Limited supports The Forest Stewardship
Council (FSC), the leading international forest certification organisation.
All our titles that are printed on Greenpeace approved FSC certified paper
carry the FSC logo. Our paper procurement policy can be found at:
www.rbooks.co.uk/environment

Mixed Sources
Product group from well-managed
forests and other controlled sources
www.fsc.org Cert no. TT-COC-2139
© 1996 Forest Stewardship Council
FSC

Printed and bound in Great Britain by Cox & Wyman Ltd, Reading, Berkshire

PIMLICO

770

THE HOUSE BY THE THAMES

Gillian Tindall is well known for the quality
of her writing and the meticulous nature of
her research. She is a master of miniaturist
history, making a particular person or situation stand for a much larger picture. She
began her career as a prize-winning novelist
and has continued to publish fiction, but she
has also staked out a particular territory in
idiosyncratic non-fiction that is brilliantly
evocative of place. Her *The Fields Beneath:
the history of one London village*, which first
appeared almost thirty years ago, has rarely
been out of print since; nor has *Celestine:
voices from a French village*, published in the
mid-1990s and translated into several
languages, for which she was decorated by
the French government. Her two most
recent books are *The Journey of Martin Nadaud*
('haunting and moving ... impossible not to
love for its humanity and integrity' *The
Times*) and *The Man Who Drew London:
Wenceslaus Hollar in reality and imagination* ('a
book that is both elegant and thoughtful'
Sunday Telegraph), also published by Pimlico.
Gillian Tindall lives with her husband in
London, in a house that is old – though not
as old as the house by the Thames that forms
the centrepiece of her present book.

Contents

List of Illustrations

The testimonial presented to Edward Perronet Sells I in 1852. Photograph © Nick Hale, 2003. Courtesy of Andrew Sells.

Edward Perronet Sells II. Courtesy of Andrew Sells.

Edward Perronet Sells III. Courtesy of Andrew Sells.

View of Barges on the Thames. Wash and ink by William Luker jnr. © Guildhall Library, Corporation of London. Courtesy of the Luker family.

Bankside 1927. Etching by Grace Golden. © Museum of London. Courtesy of Colin Mabberley.

The quay in front of number 49 Bankside in 1911, with power station chimney behind. Courtesy of the London Metropolitan Archives.

The same stretch of Bankside in 2004, with rebuilt chimney (now part of the Tate Modern). Photograph © Richard Lansdown.

Anna Lee at home in number 49 (1936). Courtesy of the late Anna Lee.

Buildings looking towards Southwark Bridge (1946). Wash and ink by Albert T. Pile. © Guildhall Library, Corporation of London. Courtesy of Cordelia Stamp.

Bankside power station, from across the river (1946). Courtesy of Southwark History Library.

Bankside 1970. Oil painting by Trevor Chamberlain. Courtesy of Alan Runagall.

Maps by Martin Collins.

Land is like old vellum . . . a document that has been
written on and erased over and over again.

O. G. S. Crawford, archaeologist and aerial photographer
(1886–1957)

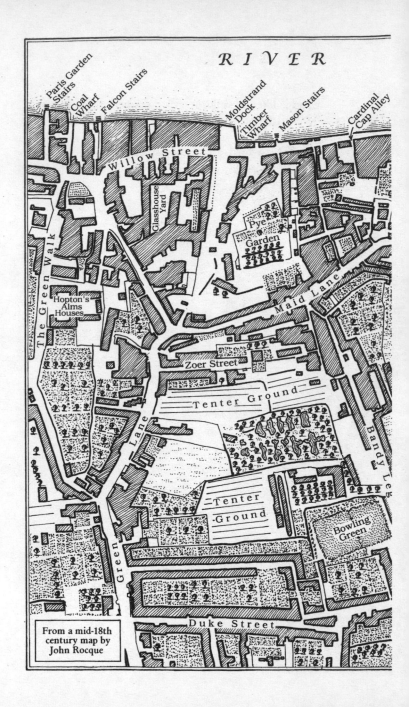

RIVER

Paris Garden Stairs

Coal Wharf

Falcon Stairs

Moldstrand Dock

Timber Wharf

Mason Stairs

Cardinal Cap Alley

Willow Street

Glasshouse Yard

Pye Garden

The Green Walk

Hopton's Alms Houses

Maid Lane

Zoer Street

Tenter Ground

Green Lane

Bandy Leg

Tenter Ground

Bowling Green

Duke Street

From a mid-18th century map by John Rocque

THAMES

Goat Stairs

New Thames
Street Stairs

Bankside

Horseshoe Alley

Stairs

Bank End
Stairs

Skin
Market

Daris's Coal Yard

Maid Lane

Globe Alley

Mr.
Rushe's

Vinegar
Yard

Burying
Ground

Stonecutters
Yard

Tenter Ground

Walk

Queen Street

Red Cross Street

St Saviour's
Burying
-Ground

MC

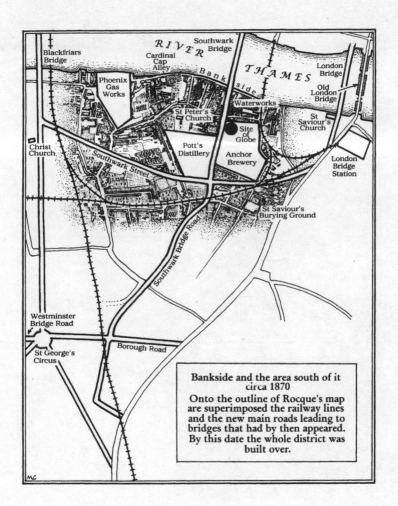

Bankside and the area south of it circa 1870

Onto the outline of Rocque's map are superimposed the railway lines and the new main roads leading to bridges that had by then appeared. By this date the whole district was built over.

Chapter I

IN WHICH WE FIND THE HOUSE

You can reach the house a number of different ways. It will still be the same, an inconspicuous but remarkable survivor in a landscape where almost everything else has changed. And changed. And changed again.

You may approach it from London Bridge, as people did when it was a new house, because that was then the only route from the opposite bank of the Thames, on foot, on horseback or on wheels. There was already a bridge there under the Roman occupation, and a later one was constructed in wood on the remains of the Roman stone work. The song that is still sung in our nurseries today commemorates this wooden bridge: it was burnt down in the Danish wars about a thousand years after the Roman invasion. Subsequent bridges on the site also suffered from fire, or were broken down by gales and flood tides. *'Sticks and stones will wash away . . .'*

Then, in the last quarter of the twelfth century, another stone one was constructed, a triumph of engineering with nineteen arches. This bridge, with intermittent accidents and modifications, carried Londoners back and forth for the next six hundred and fifty years; till the time came when accumulating complaints about its antique inconvenience, followed by decades of discussion, finally decided the Corporation of London to replace it.

Shortly before Victoria became Queen, when the new London Bridge was at last opened with flags, fire-works, balloon ascents, royalty and massed bands, the house across the water from St Paul's was one hundred and twenty years old already.

You could also take a route a little further west, over Southwark, Blackfriars or Waterloo Bridges. The house saw all these built too. From any of these bridges you can walk to the house along the river, where today a continuous, broad pedestrian path has superceded the old quays. What you cannot readily do, however, since the quays were swept away along with their many mooring points and water stairs, is what people did for hundreds of years: reach Bankside by crossing from the north shore in a boat.

Bankside, where the house stands, derives its name from being one of the earliest pieces of embanking done on the edge of the sprawling Thames, providing a solid shore for men and goods to land in a low-lying, marshy area. But today Bankside's long and intimate working relationship with the river seems to be over. The Thames, which throughout history has bound London and Southwark informally together, linking the north and south banks in waterborne commerce, is now little more than a great, airy space which separates them, a ribbon of changing light, a view.

To counteract this separation one more very recent bridge has been built, with the declared intention of linking Bankside to the heart of London. The Millennium Bridge, the footway on the axis of St Paul's cathedral, now crosses the water to meet the almost equally large bulk of the Power Station-turned Tate Modern on the other side. But a bridge at this point, usually a full-scale traffic one, has been hanging ghostly in the air for more than three hundred years. First suggested soon after the Restoration, the idea was revived at intervals through the eighteenth century but never quite got carried out. In the year of the Great Exhibition, in the mid-nineteenth century, it was proposed again with much fervour, and continued to be intermittently during the decades that followed. It nearly got itself built in the years just before 1914, but the Great War supervened and by the

1920s the sheer cost of the enterprise, including the amount of compensation that by then would have had to be paid to City property owners, meant that the plan lapsed again. This was fortunate, for the St Paul's Bridge as dreamed by its most enthusiastic promoters was a massive affair, complete with a winged goddess driving a two-horse chariot, and double pedestrian staircases surmounted by turrets at either end. Whatever social cachet its construction might have imparted to the warehouses and wharves which by then crowded on Bankside, one thing is sure: built where the present airy, slim pedestrian bridge now spans the river, St Paul's Bridge would have caused the destruction of a broad swathe of riverside buildings including the house which we are now approaching. As things are, by one of those chances which obliterate so much and yet sometimes idiosyncratically preserve, the newest bridge across the river misses the house but leads to within fifty yards of its door.

Viewed from the footbridge today the house, and the two smaller rebuilt ones adjoining it, look like miniatures that have strayed into the wrong construction-model. The house is three storeys high, plus an attic, but the modest scale of this quintessential English domestic architecture is dwarfed by two giants. On one side of it stands the industrial pile of the ex-Power Station, and on the other the reconstructed Globe Theatre with its combination of Disneyland fantasy and genuine sixteenth-century building methods. These two exceptional buildings are strange company for the house to keep. Long ago, it was one of a whole line of houses, many of them rather like itself or at any rate built to the same dimensions. Then, people would have passed it by without a second glance.

Now, as it stands almost alone in its white-stuccoed traditionalism, the guides on the passing tourist boats single it out:

'– And on your left,' the loud-speakers proclaim, 'we are just passing the house that was lived in by Sir Christopher Wren while he was building St Paul's, directly opposite.' Heads swivel, cameras snap, starting images of the house on

3

journeys to the ends of the earth, promulgating the myth. It is not actually true. Wren can never have watched the dome of his cathedral take shape from those twelve-paned windows, since the house was not built till about 1710 when only the final touches remained to be put to St Paul's and Wren himself was nearing eighty. It is true that the present house stands in the footprint of a much older one; but where Wren may actually have lodged for a while in the 1670s was a house further west, whose dust now lies, along with so much else, under the block of flats on the far side of the Power Station.

But today, we want the surviving house to be Wren's. Today, the decent one-time ordinariness of 49 Bankside, rendered unique in that place by time and chance, has become emblematic of an entire world we have lost. Perhaps the fantasist who, shortly after the Second World War, noticed a Wren commemorative plaque on a wrecked wall further along Bankside and appropriated the idea to his own house, was achieving something more important than a bogus claim. On the new plaque he placed by the front door of number 49, he also made the far more implausible claim that Catherine of Aragon stopped for the night in 1502. Even if we assume that this refers to a night spent in an inn that is known to have stood on that site before the present house was built, it remains a fantasy. Catherine of Aragon was Henry VIII's first and longest serving-wife, till she was eventually rejected in favour of Anne Boleyn. She had been married previously to his elder brother, Arthur, who died after a year. Her original landfall was in Plymouth, and from there she made the slow overland journey eastwards, finally to spend a night in Lambeth Palace before processing along the south bank and making her entry to London proper over the Bridge. Spanish princesses, let alone future queens, do not stay in waterfront inns.

In any case, the probability is that in 1502 even the Cardinal's Cap (or Hat) Inn lay in the future and the site where it would be built later in the century was vacant ground. No matter. We clearly need number 49 today to represent for us not only the rebuilding of London after the Great Fire and the coming Enlightenment associated with Wren and his contemporaries. We also need it to symbolise a much older world, in which a gabled Tudor inn might be supposed to cater for queens and bishops and prostitutes on the same night, Shakespeare dropped in for a drink, bears were baited near by and boiled heads leered from poles on top of London Bridge, all conflated in some dateless Olden Time.

People passing the house on foot, treading the brief stretch of cobbles, now hemmed in by the walkway, that is the remaining vestige of the Bankside quays, stop to look at the plaques. If you sit in the house's first-floor front room, the room where Wren is said to have gazed out on his works, the sound of the words being read aloud and commented on in a variety of tongues reaches you from below. After several hundred years of resounding to the noise of laden wheels on cobbles, this river bank has been returned to the era of the footstep and the human voice.

Occasionally strangers will be brave enough to tug the ancient bell-pull, which jangles a bell within on the end of a wire, and enquire if the house is a museum that can be visited. They are politely turned away.

Before the door is shut again they will get a glimpse of a panelled room and an arched doorway, rugs and a longcase clock, perhaps a whiff of logs smouldering on a pile of soft ash in an open fireplace. Here, surely, is the past, on which the door has fleetingly opened? But there is no automatic admittance to the past. A way has to be found.

You may try to reach London's past through Wren, or the Adam brothers, or the builders Cubitt, significant creators of the idea of townscape within which we still live today. Or you may reach further back, through kings and queens and bishops, whose palaces and orchards are ground to powder beneath wharves, offices and by-passes, but whose much-encumbered lives have at least left tough parchment evidence behind them. You may reach it through the letters preserved in a few great families, or through the personal accounts of Pepys and John Aubrey, John Evelyn and Boswell; or through a procession of nineteenth-century commentators from Charles Dickens to Charles Booth, who felt a moral mission to record what they saw around them.

But the vast mass of men and women in every time do not leave behind them either renown or testimony. These people walked our streets, prayed in our churches, drank in our inns or in those that bear the same names, built and lived in the houses where we have our being today, opened our front doors, looked out of our windows, called to each other down our staircases. They were moved by essentially the same passions and griefs that we are, the same bedrock hopes and fears: they saw the sun set over Westminster as we do. Yet almost all of them have passed away from human memory and are still passing away, generation after generation –

'Rich men furnished with ability, living peacefully in their habitations.

'. . . And some there be, which have no memorial; who are perished, as though they had never been; and are become as though they had never been born; and their children after them.

'But these were merciful men, whose righteousness hath not been forgotten . . .'

Witness to the living, busy, complex beings that many of these vanished ones were tends to be limited to fleeting references on pages of reference books that are seldom opened. At the most, there may be a handwritten note or a bill, perhaps a Will, a decorative trade-card, a few lines in a local newspaper or in a report from a long-obsolete committee, possibly an inscription on a tomb. There may perhaps be a relevant page or two in an account of something quite other, or a general social description which seems to fit the specific case.

Scant evidence, you may say, of lives as vivid and as important to the bearers as our own are today to us. But by putting these scraps together, sometimes, with luck, something more coherent is achieved. Pieces of lost lives are genuinely recovered. Extinct causes clamour for attention.

Forgotten social groups coalesce again. Here and there a few individual figures detach themselves from the dark and silence to which time has consigned them. They walk slowly towards us. Eventually, we may even see their faces.

Chapter II

LONDON'S OTHER TOWN

L ondon is an odd capital city by European standards and therefore by those of other cities round the world that have inherited the European urban tradition. In Paris, as in Rome, Washington or St Petersburg, a prime site on a river bank opposite the centre of the town and its celebrated cathedral would not be occupied by a small piece of three-hundred-year-old private property. It would long since have been selected as a suitable location for a large governmental building, institute, university or opera house. Such plans have indeed been mooted for sections of London's south bank at various times, and one or two of them have actually been built a little further up river, but Bankside itself has remained untouched by grandiose urbanism.

One reason for this is that, till the 1960s, the Pool of London below London Bridge was a working port and the entire stretch of the south bank up as far as Westminster Bridge and Lambeth acted as a necessary back-up area of wharves, docks and warehouses. But to state this is already to beg a question: how was it that, in the seventeenth, eighteenth and nineteenth centuries, when London was consolidating the shape it still has today, the south bank had such ample space available for lowly commercial uses? The north bank, too, was fringed with wharves, but these had to compete with the demands of City institutions, livery halls, the Inns of Court, the aristocratic houses in the Strand, the

Palace of Westminster, and later with government offices and with the new embankment laid out with prestigious public gardens. Yet the first and almost the only grand administrative building to be located on the south side of the river, and that in a deliberate attempt to colonise suitably the site opposite the Houses of Parliament, was the 1922 County Hall (now turned to other, piecemeal uses). Even when London was in the throes of visionary planning after the blitz damage of 1940–44, and the Festival of Britain was celebrated in the ruined spaces by Waterloo Bridge, what got rebuilt immediately across the river from St Paul's? A smoking industrial plant whose chimney stack rose as high as Wren's dome. It was as if the south bank, though physically only a couple of hundred yards from the nexus of the City's power and prestige, was perceived as somewhere far more remote, indeed hardly visible.

Cities are formed not only by what happens but also by what fails to happen, by the force or inertia of tradition, and by the almost random decisions of individuals which sometimes have unthinkably long consequences. Historically, the south bank has always avoided becoming part of London. As late as the 1830s the parishes on the south of the river were fighting a rearguard action to be allowed to form a township separate from the capital (a true 'Borough') with its own corporation, magistrates and judges. They were hauled protesting into the London system only by the establishment of the Metropolitan Board of Works in 1855, and finally by the creation of a new County of London in 1888. Till well into the twentieth century, long after the London County Council had carved Southwark and its eastern district into two London boroughs of Southwark and Bermondsey – casually splitting the ancient and cohesive area of greater Southwark down its central spine of London Bridge and Borough High Street – the whole area south of the Thames was still known as 'the Surrey side'.

Yet some sort of settlement on the Surrey shore, at the south end of London Bridge, goes back almost as far as London itself. By the second century AD there was a Roman suburb there, where leather was made, and glass (two riverside activities we shall meet again) and possibly golden ornaments too. A couple of Roman bodies have been found, pottery, and fragments of mosaic paving under a nineteenth-century brewery. The building of the Jubilee line in to London Bridge station in the late 1990s turned up an oil-lamp in the shape of a sandalled foot, a tiny breath of fantasy and elegance from the lost time.

Like much of Roman creation, that suburb was abandoned, along with London Bridge, in the ages we call 'dark', but it had been resettled again by the time of the Viking invasions in the eighth and ninth centuries. Essentially, it was formed as a fortification for the southern entry to London, and in spite of episodes of destruction by fire and sword it prospered, survived the arrival of the Norman rulers, and grew.

Being outside the walled city but so near at hand, it became a convenient place for the establishment of religious houses. A little later it was where lords both spiritual and temporal built themselves mansions. Edward II had a summer residence there in the early fourteenth century, on the riverfront a little to the east of London Bridge – its foundations, complete with cloisterlike central garden and a landing-stage for boats, briefly became visible again during re-development of the site in the 1990s. A hundred-odd years after Edward, a different grand house built on the same site was bought by a Sir John Fastolf, who is generally said to have been the original of Shakespeare's Falstaff. Both before and after the Reformation church dignitaries had houses in Southwark, in addition to the principal episcopal palace of the Bishop of Winchester, which was west of London Bridge on Bankside itself.

Already, by the Middle Ages, Southwark had become what has been described as 'an administrative jungle'. It consisted of five separate manors, each with its own privileges and rules. In addition, it was split into a number of parishes which were not necessarily coterminous with the manors. St Mary Overy's very ancient church (later to become St

Saviour's parish church) had been refounded in Norman times as an Augustinian priory. A tiny church called St Mary Magdalene, built against its wall, ran a parish for commoners living immediately near by, but the main parish was based, until the Reformation, in a church called St Margaret's half way down the High Street. This parish covered a large area westwards from London Bridge, which included Bankside. Further south, the land on that side was in the parish of St George's; that church stood where its successor stands today, where the pilgrim road to Canterbury forked eastwards.

On the eastern, Bermondsey, side of Southwark was the parish of St Olave's. Its small church stood guardian of the bridge as St Magnus's did on the northern shore. Much rebuilt over the centuries, it survived on the edge of the river till it was destroyed by a combination of commercial and municipal vandalism in the 1920s.

To complicate matters further, the priory of St Mary Overy's had acquired a substantial stake on the Bermondsey side of the High Street also, when St Thomas à Becket's hospital for the sick and poor, which had been founded within the priory, was transferred after a fire in 1212 to the other side of the street. There it remained for six hundred and fifty years, a separate fief occupying a substantial tract of ground, and eventually joined by Guy's Hospital alongside, till the demands of the railway age forced it off to another site in nearby Lambeth.

As time went on, there were added to these overlapping administrative parcels various smaller fiefs, notably the prisons of the King's Bench and the Marshalsea, in the control of the Crown, and the Surrey County Gaol under the Sheriff of Surrey. Other aspects of life in Southwark, particularly those to do with the trade guilds, were inevitably monitored by the City, as was the traffic on the river. There were rows about Southwark activities being in unfair competition with City trade, but grievances that were essentially economic were often dressed up as moral issues. There were long-running battles about who had or had not the right to sit as a magistrate in Southwark, and how far the Lord

Mayor might intervene on that side of the water. Being outside the jurisdiction of London, Southwark became something of a haven for wrongdoers. In fact the Templars, and after them the Knights of St John, who owned what became known as the 'Paris Garden' manor, made it into a sanctuary. Here criminals from London could shelter from arrest among rather boggy willow groves, reed beds and ditches full of 'hedgehog grass' for 6d. a night.

Naturally the City and the Crown did not look particularly favourably on all this unauthorised activity across the water. However, at the same time, Southwark was useful to them, in the time-honoured way of out-of-town areas, as a location for hospitals, prisons, almshouses and brothels. There were plans in the fifteenth century, under Richard III, to build a wall right round Southwark matching the walls on the City side and so make it indisputably part of London, but these plans were never carried out. At the Reformation Henry VIII had the opposite idea; he acquired a good deal of land in Southwark, including the priories and Paris Garden, and planned to build a palace and a hunting preserve there, but this did not happen either. Come Dissolution of the monasteries, Reformation, regicide, Commonwealth, Restoration and through a variety of ground landlords including the Crown, Southwark continued to function, more or less, in its own anarchic, fragmented way.

The only administrative areas that really concern Bankside are the Paris Garden and Winchester Park, both originally within the parish that started as St Margaret's and then became St Saviour's after the Reformation. Winchester Park was also known as the Liberty of the Clink ('Liberty' implies an autonomous jurisdiction) from the nickname given to the Bishop of Winchester's private gaol underneath his palace on the riverfront. 'Clink' means a latch or other fastening device. The Clink never seems to have been as large or important as the other Southwark lock-ups, so why, for later centuries, it should have bestowed its name as a general slang-term for prison anywhere is a small mystery. Today, the Bishop's prison has a mythical afterlife in the 'Clink Museum' near St Saviour's, which serves as a sort of general touristic compendium of Bad Old Prisons anywhere. Although it is situated not far from the ruinous vestiges of the palace, it has no connection with the ruin but occupies the basement of a Victorian commercial building by a railway viaduct.

The name Paris Garden, however, is lost as if it had never been, though it was applied for centuries to a tract of land on Bankside just west of the Bishop of Winchester's holding. The name seems to come from a very early lessee, Robert de Paris; presumably this origin was forgotten, as later maps sometimes give it the more likely-sounding but misleading names of Parish or Palace Garden. It disappears finally from the records in the early nineteenth century, under glass-works, timber-wharves, and the work yards of the Rennie family, bridge builders.

Paris Garden and Winchester Park both have a rural sound. Rural indeed they were for centuries, while London became ever more densely built on the opposite shore. Houses did spread from St Saviour's church and the Bishop's palace westwards along Bankside, but only gradually and in a piecemeal fashion. For the other fact about the south bank, and a fundamental reason why it took so long to become part of London, is that much of it was low-lying and unpropitious for building.

Bankside itself seems to have been built in the early thirteenth century as a causeway leading from the Bishop of Winchester's quays and tide-mills near St Saviour's, west round the shore line. Initially it would have been constructed in an attempt to keep the river water from invading the meadows, pastures and gardens of the Bishop's park. But incidentally it served as a landing-stage for boats and thus became a useful location for building. There are indications in early documents that the owners or tenants of the houses that gradually appeared overlooking the water were personally responsible for maintaining the section of causeway fronting their own properties. No doubt, over the course of time, more earth and gravel were heaped on the bank and there was more timber shoring to keep the flood tides at bay: the causeway became higher and more substantial. It was extended further, along the shore line of the Paris Garden and beyond towards Lambeth: that section became known as Upper Ground, presumably a description of its contour, the name it still bears today. After several centuries, according to the earliest 'road map' of Southwark, which was drawn in 1618 as part of a legal wrangle about access, Bankside was said to be wide enough to accommodate two carts abreast.

Another part of the thirteenth-century flood works, that was to become an enduring feature of the landscape and determine later road-contours, was a substantial drainage ditch like a small stream. This was cut roughly parallel with Bankside but further south, through both the Bishop's Park and the Paris Garden, and looping round at the west end to flow out into the Thames. Other ditches were added later, but the problem was never entirely solved: there were major floods at intervals on the south bank till the nineteenth-century arrival of proper sewers. The Paris Garden end of the parish was particularly vulnerable, since much of the land on that side originally lay several feet below the high water when it lapped at Bankside. Earlier names for the manor referred to withies and willows, and the memory of this was preserved long after, in the eighteenth century, when the western part of the Bankside was known as Willow Street.

By Elizabeth's time the Knights of St John had been dispossessed: the willows no longer provided a secure refuge for criminals, but the area remained a popular, if marshy place for clandestine encounters and a kind of pleasure garden was established there. It was said that the tree-cover was so dense that even on moonlit nights 'one man cannot see another' and that this created 'a notable covert for confederates to shroud in'. The words are those of a City of London lawyer, writing of secret political meetings in the Paris Garden between the French Ambassador and the Bishop of Ross – possibly on the matter of Mary, Queen of Scots. Paris Garden stairs, the access point for boats along that part of the Bankside, was, of course, easily reached from any of the Whitehall stairs a little further up river on the opposite shore. Indeed, the Royal Barge was kept on the south side of the river, in what sounds to have been a rather grand building complete with glass windows and gilt decoration.

Today, in spite of all the bridges, Bankside seems spiritually further from Westminster than it was in the days when the Royal Barge House lay at its western end. However, the trees have returned. Not willows, but rather similar silver birches, they are planted in a grove in front of the Tate Modern-Power Station. Paris Garden sleeps, fathoms deep, beneath the Blackfriars Bridge Road. The Barge House survived, derelict, till the mid-eighteenth century, but by the early nineteenth century it lay beneath a timber yard and a soap works. Only the water-stairs at that point continued to bear the name, which still survives today in a side road behind the Oxo Tower.

Further east, the medieval Bishops of Winchester solved their excess water problem perhaps more successfully by channelling it into fish ponds. Fish were of major importance in the days when the Church ordained many meatless days but the well-to-do, whether ecclesiastical or lay, still expected to eat lavishly. With ponds, the fish that swam in plenty in the Thames could be coralled, and fattened for the table as required. What could be nicer than a fat pike stuffed with oysters and roasted, basted with claret? After the Dissolution the lands and fish ponds were sold; but by the time of Elizabeth we find some of them apparently restored to the Church and some under Crown control. The mid-sixteenth-century map usually known as the 'Agas' map shows three large rectangular fish ponds on the land opposite Mason stairs, where Bankside veered away a little from the shore. This was, I think, 'the Great Pike Garden' which had its own elaborate entrance. A little further east, among the newly built bull-and bear-baiting pits, was another set of ponds; these constituted 'the Queen's Pike Garden' or, after the accession of James I, 'the King's'. These ponds were leased from the Crown under James, but some of the fish was kept for the royal table. When they were seized again under the Commonwealth, they were said to consist of a wharf and four fish ponds stocked with a hundred pike and eighty carp. Further east again, nearer the Bishop of Winchester's palace, the Agas map shows us a third garden which was 'the Bishop's Pike Garden' for his own use.

These ponds were the original Bankside 'stews'. The word comes from the old French word *'estuve'*, a containment place for fish, and they had given their name to Bankside from the days when there was little else but ponds on that shore. Because, at a later period, 'the stews-bank' was also associated with brothels, much ink has been expended trying to make out that the brothels were called 'stews' because they were heated bathhouses. No evidence for this exists, and plenty of general indications to the contrary. With one or two famous exceptions, the Tudors did not wash much at all. The bathhouse culture that developed in the eighteenth-century Turkish baths of Covent Garden was characteristic of an entirely different era with sophisticated new comforts.

The fish ponds themselves disappear from maps during the seventeenth century, but hints of their presence continued for a long time. At Mason stairs, where the entrance to 'the Great Pike Gardens' had been, there stood till near the end of the eighteenth century a large, old, double-fronted house, apparently Tudor, with twin gables and a cart-entrance in the middle. Its upper walls were decorated with plastered carvings in high relief of dolphins, pikes and other fish. At the top, in the centre, Neptune rode in a shell-chariot drawn by sea horses and attended by Tritons. When this wonderful 'Fish house', as it had come to be called, finally disappeared, 49 Bankside had co-existed with it for about seventy years.

49 Bankside had another, more intimate relationship with the vanished ponds. When it was built about 1710, an area just behind it to the east that was used as a garden, and later as a wood yard, was known as 'the Pye Garden'. Evidently,

by then, the fishy associations of this had passed from memory and people no longer knew this was the last remains of the King's Pike Garden. It finally disappeared under a lane of cheap tenements with the name 'Pond Yard', and this name survived till the site was flattened in the Second World War by a German bomb.

By the mid-sixteenth century, between the fish ponds and the river, there was a whole run of houses along Bankside, though they had spaces between them. A picture of the Coronation procession of the short-lived boy king Edward VI, in 1547, shows the houses, seen across the water, backed by trees. They look modest and countrified compared with the high-gabled City houses in the foreground. But in-filling evidently continued during the rest of the century; the relative prosperity and peace of Elizabeth's reign provided the conditions for a sustained building boom. John Stow, the first committed London antiquarian, who was writing near the end of Elizabeth's reign, remarked, as if it were a new phenomenon, that 'On the [south] bank of the river Thames there is now a continual building of tenements, about half a mile in length to the bridge.' This is corroborated by a St Saviour's record of church rates paid in what had become known as the Clink parish in 1600. There were stated to be five hundred and sixty householders. One of these householders, occupying one of the new tenements referred to by Stow, was the proprietor of the Cardinal's Cap – or Hat – Inn, on the exact plot of ground where, later, 49 Bankside would stand.

The new inn was built in 1579, apparently by a London lawyer called Hugh Browker who also made the alley alongside. He had done well in property development during these fat years and was later to buy the Paris Garden and erect some buildings there. He owned several inns in Southwark, including large ones in the Borough High Street where inn-keeping was now a major Southwark trade: it remained so until the coming of the railways. However, the inns and ale-houses strung by then along Bankside too were not for the accommodation of travellers so much as for the pleasure and convenience of Londoners coming over by water from the other side.

But which cardinal is commemorated in the name 'Cardinal's Hat' and why? Because the Bishop of Winchester had his extensive palace on Bankside for centuries, and because a fragment of this palace still survives today, poignantly visible once more since the warehouses that engulfed it have been cleared, there have been attempts to find a cardinal from the palace to fit. Cardinal Beaufort, who was Bishop of Winchester and died in 1447, has been suggested, and so has the redoubtable Cardinal Wolsey, who was briefly Bishop of Winchester in 1529–30 just before he fell from Henry VIII's favour. But neither of these can realistically be supposed to have inspired the name of an inn not built till 1579, and in any case why should a prosperous entrepreneur like Browker, living under the reformed Anglican regime, have wanted to single out a discredited prelate in this way?

An obvious conclusion would be that Browker simply rebuilt a previous inn on the same site, but, if so, the existence of this early Cardinal's Cap/Hat is rather shadowy. If there was a medieval inn there of that name it had disappeared by 1470, over a hundred years before Browker's construction, since the plot was then described as 'a void piece of ground near the steweside'. In 1533, when the plot was sold on, no mention was made of a building on it. This sale was by one fishmonger to another. We know that plot of land was just by one of the Pike Gardens. Since the fish ponds were run like fresh fish farms today, with live fish netted and killed as customers came and asked for them, it seems extremely likely that the fishmongers' presence was related to this trade. Possibly the empty plot on Bankside was used as a weighing and sales point for the fish, the place from which assistants were sent off to get a pike or carp of the requested size.

Yet evidence that there was a house thereabouts on Bankside, called the Cardinal's Cap or Hat, before the time when a vacant piece of land was noted there in 1470, is clear. The first Englishman was made a cardinal in 1310 and his image became a popular sign. Variants such as 'le Cardinalishatte' crop up on Bankside in 1361, 1447 and as late as 1468, two years before the plot was described as empty. It looks as if, in naming his inn a hundred-odd years later, Browker or his tenant (John Raven) was simply reviving an old tradition, a half-forgotten tale. So present-day 49 Bankside is linked with the very distant past not through something as material as foundations or re-used timbers: these form connections at a later period. What has persisted through six and a half centuries is a distinctive name. As well as its street number, the house has the name 'Cardinal's Wharf' lettered in plaster above its front door. Cardinal Cap Alley obviously took its name from Browker's inn; but without the persistence of the alley, which has survived when most of Bankside's narrow cross-lanes have been obliterated, the name of the inn would have passed away as all the others have.

The fact that the earliest house on the site was known by a sign does not necessarily mean that it was an inn. In that pre-literate era all houses were commonly known by reference to signs – 'You may find me at the sign of the Cross Keys . . . next the Green Lion . . . two doors from the Red Cross . . .' people would say. What the medieval Cardinal's Hat *may* have been, however, was a brothel.

Chapter III

OF WINCHESTER GEESE, BIRD'S-EYE VIEWS AND SHOW BUSINESS

Everyone likes hearing about ancient vice: it is not surprising that the long-ago brothels of Bankside have taken on a posthumous, mythic life of their own. Our vanished ancestors, with their strongly hierarchic society, their literal belief in Heaven and Hell, their brutal sports and punishments and their lack of what we would regard as cleanliness, seem closer to us when we think of them in their most private and instinctual functions. Casual sexual encounters are, you may say, among the most transient of human relations, intended as they are to be without consequences and rapidly dismissed from the individual memory. Yet in the collective memory the idea of all that male energy expended on Bankside, and all those anonymous women of pleasure who received it, touches us with some message about the frailty and impermanence of human beings which is, in itself, timeless.

John Stow was responsible for the belief ('heard of ancient men, of good credit') that the 'single women' of the Bankside houses, being disbarred by their sinful profession from burial in consecrated ground, were given their own separate graveyard away from both St Saviour's and St Margaret's churches. There is no evidence to corroborate this, but the idea has taken root in Southwark consciousness and is still current today. Near the beginning of the twenty-first century an attempt to build over a one-time local graveyard, the

Cross Bones ground, was vigorously opposed, as it had been several other times over the last hundred and fifty years. The supposition that this is the ground where lies the dust of all those despised medieval women is a potent modern argument against its obliteration.

Let us return to a few facts. The false trail connected with the fish ponds has led some commentators to claim a brothel whenever the term 'stew' or 'stewside' is mentioned in a record. To take just one example: the fact that the household accounts of the fifteenth-century Duke of Norfolk (who later died at the battle of Bosworth) contain an item about a sum of twenty-two shillings having been lent to him 'when he lay at the stews' probably indicates no more than that the Duke was spending that night on the Surrey side of the river for which 'stewside' was a current term. The Duke's secretary would hardly have left an official record of his master having slept in a brothel. It is, however, indisputable that the stewside was also a location for brothels, and that, by a natural transfer – aided, no doubt, by knowing fishy jokes and puns – the term 'stews' did come to be applied to the brothels as well.

But then the realities of medieval brothel-keeping do not quite seem to fit the highly coloured images of 'bawds' and lascivious fun and games that today get imagined – the 'buxom wench' genre of historical evocation. We are amused that apparently the Bankside whores were known as 'Winchester geese' from the fact that no less a grandee than the Bishop of Winchester himself reaped revenue indirectly from their activities. We assume there was something covert and corrupt in this situation. But the truth seems to be that, far from illicit, the whorehouse trade on Bankside was a conscious attempt by the City of London to recognise human nature for what it is. The City did not want the problem within its own walls, but, acknowledging the inevitability of prostitution 'for the repair of incontinent men and like women', it tolerated brothels on its doorstep, across the water. It also laid down guidelines about their good conduct. The medieval period was a time of assiduous regulation (or attempted regulation) in matters of social conduct, perhaps for the very reason that violence, anarchy and natural disasters were never far below the surface of life.

The lodging houses permitted on Bankside for single women seem to have been rather low-key, genteel establishments, not so much like our modern idea of a brothel as like the *maisons tolérées* of France up to 1946. Or perhaps not even that, since the women were apparently independent, but more like discreet private boarding houses, where women lodgers were allowed to bring men visitors provided certain rules were observed. Yet at the same time it was supposed to be obvious from the women's dress that they were in some sense set apart from respectable society: they were not to wear aprons like ordinary housewives, and for a while they were told to wear striped hoods. These differences were meant to signal to a censorious world that – unless they repented and became washer-women instead – these women's souls were bound for the fires of Hell and their mortal flesh for banishment to the unconsecrated ground where Red Cross Street now joins Union Street. It also appears from a fourteenth-century document that many of the women were not initially citizens of London but were 'frows of Flaunders' – Flemish women, foreigners, and therefore the classic marginalised outsiders who tend to appear in all cities, in every era, employed in the sex trade.

It is true that by then Flemings, many of them in the weaving trade, had begun to settle in Southwark, but this leads one to wonder if a number of the women were merely the friends and consorts of the weavers rather than brothel-inmates in a strictly defined sense. The intermittent moral fervours of the Middle Ages tended not to distinguish between actual prostitution and simple concubinage or loose living, and this further confuses an already confused record.

We owe our knowledge of the rules that are said to have regulated brothels to John Stow, who listed them in a later era in his *Survey of London* (1598). Some of them seem admirably designed to protect the women's own liberty to come and go and not be exploited or ill-treated by the 'stew-holders'. Others were designed to protect society's fabric – women of religion, married women, and 'any woman that hath the perilous infirmity of burning' (i.e. gonorrhoea) were not to be given lodging. Pregnancy was another reason for barring women, though this seems illogical given that this was the natural result of their permitted way of life. Several rules seem aimed at making the brothels as quiet and respectable as possible: convivial gatherings were not encouraged, for no food or drink was to be sold, men were not to be 'enticed' inside, the premises were to be inspected every week and were not to be open on holy days. There is too an interesting implication that the women of Bankside were offering something more than just quick relief – 'No single woman to take money to lie with any man, but she lie still with him all night till the morrow.'

How far these rules were kept is not clear: certainly everyone knew about the Bankside brothels, and they suffered periodic assaults from a people eager to escape the fires of Hell themselves by punishing sin elsewhere. They were attacked and burnt during the Peasants' Revolt of 1381, and again by Jack Cade's rebellious mob in 1449, when some of the houses were fired and the women 'reviled'. (They looted the Bishop's palace at the same time, for good measure, let the prisoners out of the Clink, and lynched several unpopular City dignitaries.) Stow says the brothels were closed again for a year near the beginning of the next century by Henry VII, and that their number was reduced after that from eighteen to twelve. They were clearly a target for troublemakers: there is a record from Henry VIII's reign of a party of drunk young men from good families, including Thomas Wyatt the younger, going out on the river at night and shooting with catapults at 'the queenes at the Bank'. A few years later the King had the houses 'put down' in a repressive gesture that Stow seems to think was final.

It is significant that Stow was writing half a century after this, when accurate memories of these licensed brothels must have been fading, even in the minds of 'ancient men of good credit'. The second half of the sixteenth century was one of those periods when life moved at great speed, with the dismantling of the religious fabric of society and the traumatic changes of regime and official faith, as the fanatically Protestant boy Edward was succeeded by Catholic Mary and then by Elizabeth. In the 1590s, when Stow was compiling his *Survey*, the time before the Reformation must already have seemed quaintly antique: an old world before modernity set in, when Bankside had no theatres or animal shows, and only the few houses scattered among trees that are shown in the picture of Edward's coronation.

Furthermore, some of what Stow recounts goes back almost a century before his own time, to the moment when Henry VII reduced the brothels from eighteen to twelve – 'These allowed stew houses had signs on their fronts, towards the Thames, not hanged out but painted on the walls, as a Boar's head, the Cross keys, the Gun, the Castle, the Crane, the Cardinal's hat, the Bell, the Swan, etc.'

It is a striking image, these black signs painted on whitewashed walls to be visible across the river, prefiguring the much later practice of printing the names of wharves large and clear on the walls for the same reason. When I was researching I found one interested party convinced that he had actually seen a painting depicting the houses with their signs, though diligent research has not revealed any such picture. However, it is clear that Stow was not recounting what he had seen with his own eyes but giving a general, vivid word-picture of what he had been told. So, when he lists the Cardinal's Hat among the names, this is an interesting indication but it is hardly conclusive evidence that the site of 49 was a functioning brothel at the beginning of the sixteenth century – especially in view of the plot having been described as 'void' twenty years before and not apparently rebuilt till much later. I suspect that Stow was simply taking assorted names from his own day of the inns on Bankside – which was by then, according to the playwright Dekker, 'one long ale-house' – and ascribing them to the notable houses of a hundred years before as a general illustration. So between them, John Stow, who evoked bygone days, and Hugh Browker, who bestowed on his new inn an old and possibly nostalgic name, were already contributing to the process of mythologising the past, a tendency which continues, with interludes of forgetting, to our own day.

Admittedly, some unofficial prostitution and generally 'licencious "behaviour' is likely to have continued on Bankside, what with all those ale-houses, later followed by the bear-pits and playhouses. But it seems to have moved two or three hundred yards westwards. By the time the Bankside brothels were shut down by Henry VIII, the old manor house in Paris Garden was rented by a local Southwark man. He attempted, once again, to deal with the chronic flooding problem, and established a gaming place there, with card tables and bowling alleys. By and by one of the Elizabethan theatres, the Swan, was also built on that ground. The place sounds to have been rather like the later riverside pleasure gardens of Vauxhall and Ranelagh and, like them, it acquired over the decades a louche reputation. It became known by the odd name of Holland's Leaguer, after a tenant of the one-time manor house, a Mistress Holland, who was charged with being 'an incontinent woman'. In 1632, a decade before the rise of Puritanism under Cromwell would close down much of the Bankside entertainment industry, a contemporary commented on the Paris Garden, with the relish usual in those castigating sin: 'This may better be termed a foule dene than a faire Garden . . . here come few that either regard their credit, or losse of time, the swaggering Roarer, the cunning Cheater, the rotten Bawd, the swearing Drunkard, and the bloudy Butcher, have their rendezvouz here.'[1] During the Commonwealth, much of the grounds were used for the bleaching and fulling of cloth, a long-term Southwark activity due to the abundance of water on hand. On eighteenth-century maps the land is still marked as being in this use ('Tenter grounds'). The one-time manor house, still with the remnants of a medieval moat around it, was finally pulled down in the 1760s to make way for the approach to 'Pitt's Bridge', which became Blackfriars Bridge.

The Agas map, and several others from the later sixteenth century, are all formalised bird's-eye views of London, all taken from a notional and shifting vantage point somewhere above Southwark – as if the Tudors possessed hot-air balloons but failed to record this interesting fact for posterity; or as if the artist-cartographer had been standing on a non-existent small mountain in the south located roughly at the Elephant and Castle. Such was the general convention of the times for views of towns and cities. This tells one something about the limits of accuracy in these early maps, since their creators were depicting what they knew to be there rather than what they could actually see: they did not hesitate to foreshorten certain features and exaggerate others to create a satisfying whole, and the scale does not diminish significantly in the perspective of distance. It also tells one something about the unbuilt nature of most of Southwark then and for some time to come. In these early maps of London and its suburbs, the ribbon of housing down Southwark High Street (the Borough) is cut off by the foot of the map, since it is clear that all around it still lay fields, not townscape to be mapped. Even the best part of a century later, in 1676, the first heroic, properly surveyed London street plan did not include the south bank at all.

Two other elaborate bird's-eye views from the first decades of the seventeenth century still observe the convention of the artist being suspended somewhere over Southwark and, by this happy chance, depict the townscape in the immediate foreground in greater detail than the body of London proper, which is the ostensible subject. Both views, by coincidence, were drawn and engraved by men who were not natives of London, who published respectively in Amsterdam and Antwerp, for the Low Countries were then the world centre for printing and map making.

Nicholas John Visscher was Dutch; his panorama appeared in 1616, though how well he knew London at first hand and how much he relied on other people's depictions is not clear. To make his view more comprehensive he shows the Thames running straight, as it does in many people's general image of London to this day but not in real life. This device allows him to depict a clear line of buildings along the south bank westwards from the Bridge. After St Saviour's (here under its old name of St Mary Overy's) comes the Bishop's palace (Winchester House), the great hall prominent with its stone tracery windows dating from a rebuilding about 1400. Then comes a bridge over a stream – St Mary Overie's Dock.[2] Then come the pointed backs of the Bankside houses, with their chimneys, their back lean-tos and their garden hedges. The Globe Theatre appears, with a cluster of cloaked and hatted people beside it, and so does the Bear Garden. Not shown are the Rose, the Hope and the Swan theatres, which were also there at the date of the map, leading one to think Visscher must have been working from earlier sources. A little west of the Bear Garden is a surviving pike pond. One of the row of gables just to the left of that must represent the back of the Cardinal's Hat Inn.

Wenceslaus Hollar's celebrated Long View of London was produced in Antwerp in 1648, but was based on drawings he made during a sojourn in England a few years earlier. A gifted Bohemian artist and pioneer etcher, Hollar was brought to London by Lord Arundel, and seems to have fallen in love with the place. Except for a few years in Amsterdam during the grimmest days of the Commonwealth, he spent the rest of his long life in his adopted city, and it is largely thanks to him, a foreigner, that we know what much of seventeenth-century London looked like. He never lived in Southwark, but it was the base for his views of London before and after the Great Fire. Unlike the other contemporary panoramas of London, his Long View manages to give the impression of being drawn from one identifiable vantage point: ostensibly this is the tower of St Saviour's/St Mary's, from which elevation Hollar had no doubt made sketches, but actually we are considerably higher up, as if Hollar were treading air like one of the baroque, celestial figures he places above the busy boats on the Thames.

One has the impression that Hollar embarked on this, his greatest work, with the intention of recording London on the opposite bank in the traditional manner, but got carried away by a naturalism and a passion for detail that changed the bird's-eye convention back into a genuine landscape study. The sweep of the south bank in the foreground, curving as in real life, predominates; one's eye is drawn to it as if this were the real subject and the City were a less important backdrop. We see right down into people's yards and gardens. There is a tide-mill near the bridge with sacks of grain on a platform and a deep bed of chaff, then a ferrymen's landing stage with oars laid out on the shore, then a large inn with a round-arched gateway from an alley behind and a rider just setting off. A little further is the dark water of St Mary Overie's Dock, with people walking on a built-up path beside it just as they do today where the *Golden Hind* is berthed. Then comes the very recognisable Winchester House, but with Hollar we are not being invited to admire the elevation but rather to take a walk in its carefully laid-out gardens where some people are already promenading two by two.

This is a final glimpse of the palace and its grounds near the end of its grandeur, for the Bishop was dispossessed under the Commonwealth and his palace was divided up for renting. At the Restoration the Bishop preferred to go elsewhere; the park was leased for building. The approximate spot where Hollar shows the people walking lies today beneath the railway viaduct from Cannon Street where it curves eastward towards London Bridge station.

Next in Hollar's View comes a huddle of houses with high, old roofs on which you can count the tiles. Several of them have small cabins tacked to the back of them, which I suspect of being 'necessary houses' placed over one of Bankside's many ditches. There is another large house with several chimneys right on the river, probably an inn, with another berthing place for ferries nearby. Then the Globe Theatre and the bear-baiting ring – whose names Hollar has transposed, no doubt because he was making his final drawing in Antwerp and could not check from there which building was which. He has the Globe nearer the river, whereas in fact it was the other way round. The building further from the river is the one with a roofed 'tiring house' on top, the actors' changing place, which a bear pit would not need. Horses graze in an adjacent meadow.

After this, the houses retreat along the shore line in diminishing perspective. We are no longer on top of them so cannot look down into their intimate world. If only Hollar had chosen a vantage point a little further west along Bankside. Then we could have seen with his wonderfully detailed, microscopic vision right into the back yard of the Cardinal's Hat with its barrels of beer, and its waterfront with boats tied up, and the narrow lane leading from one to the other just as it runs today.

It must have been quite a substantial building: Browker, who did business deals with the most respected citizens of Southwark, would hardly have erected anything shoddy, and we know from the house that sits in its footprint today that it had capacious cellars. Houses in the Elizabethan period were still constructed predominately of timber rather than stone or brick, but the new prosperity was favouring larger buildings in which there were more fixed fireplaces and therefore more chimneys. In the following century the Cardinal's Hat was assessed for hearth tax at seven hearths, which implies a good number of rooms – though not as many as the Falcon Inn up river, which was said in its heyday to have twenty-nine rooms. The Cardinal's Hat certainly would have had glass in its windows rather than the old-style coverings of horn or simply wooden lattice, for glass was now being produced much more cheaply, some of it to hand in Southwark, and windows were correspondingly bigger.

For reasons that will become clear when we enter 49 Bankside, I believe that the main door to the inn was probably from the side alley, so that customers came into the middle of the building facing the staircase, with the kitchen on one side and the dining and tap-room on the other side overlooking the river. If the inn let lodgings, which it apparently did, the furnishings would have been more comfortable than the old straw pallets and wooden benches of medieval and Tudor days: a late-Elizabethan cleric[3] noted that there were many more chairs and hangings than in his youth, and that chaff or wool mattresses or feather beds, previously 'thought meet only for women in childbed', were now much favoured. A decent inn's customers had pewter tankers now for their ale rather than horn ones and pewter plates rather than wooden trenchers, while wooden spoons were replaced with tin.

After John Raven's tenancy of the inn there was a John Powell and then a Thomas Mansell or Mansfield. After that, from 1627 to 1674 the place was continuously in the occupation of the memorably named Melchisedeck Fritter: it sounds as if he (like Dekker the playwright) was of Flemish origins, but by the seventeenth century the family was clearly well established in the parish. Fritter, like his predecessor Mansell, laid on dinners for members of the parish vestry, and he had the right to produce his own ha'penny tokens – in effect, to mint his own small change – which argues that he was a well-respected local citizen. We seem quite far here from 'the women of the stews'.

Because of the connection with Shakespeare, Bankside's identity as the place where Londoners went to the theatre tends to shine disproportionately large and bright in the panorama of remembered history. In reality, this phase was relatively brief; barely fifty years elapsed between the building of the first proper theatre and the suppression of all of them in 1642 in the run-up to the Civil Wars, and Shakespeare himself was only associated with the theatres for about fifteen years. Though the Wooden O of Shakespeare's *Henry V*, or the imaginary 'cloud capp'd towers and gorgeous palaces' of his *The Tempest*, is the way we like to think of the theatres at the turn of the sixteenth and seventeenth centuries, the truth is that the playhouses of Bankside were born out of the bull- and bear-baiting rings that were already well established before the theatres came, and which re-appeared there after the Restoration when the theatrical world had moved off elsewhere. On Bankside, the same building was sometimes used for both plays and bloodsports on separate days, and the most celebrated Bankside impresario of the time, Philip Henslowe, was just as keen to be recognised master of fights between dogs and bears as he was to give stage-room to Ben Jonson and Marlowe.

Shakespeare's Globe Theatre has been re-created by the riverside in our own day with loving care for authenticity, but I hardly think that an equally authentic ring in which blind bears were whipped or horses baited to death would be acceptable as an historical tourist attraction. Intimations of love or charity from the distant past still have the power to cheer us: in the same measure, the irremediable nature of long-ago cruelties of any kind weighs on our hearts. It comes as something of a relief to find that a sixteenth-century commentator too[4] thought that bear baiting was 'a full ugly sight' attracting 'most fools all' who could have put their pennies to better use, and that was over a hundred years before both Samuel Pepys and John Evelyn expressed a civilised disgust at the sport in their respective diaries. Foreign visitors usually settled for describing the whole experience deadpan, as they did the plays they saw: such entertainments were just another English curiosity, along with characteristic eating habits: 'They do not generally put fruit on the table, but between meals one sees men, women and children always munching through the streets, like so many goats, and yet more in the places of public enter-tainment.'[5] National quirks change surprisingly little over the centuries.

While the presence of this entertainment industry on Bankside must have increased business for the Cardinal's Hat, none of the four theatres (Rose, Globe, Hope and Swan) was immediately near it. Stow refers to two Elizabethan animal baiting rings on Bankside; one was on a site further east that carries the name Bear Gardens to this day. From the Agas map and from another reference it seems possible the other one was near the Great Pike Garden, a little to the west of the inn, but, if so, it later moved from there. This was probably just as well, since another foreign visitor to England at the end of Elizabeth's reign (Thomas Platter) remarked of the dog kennels adjoining the ring: 'And the place was evil smelling because of the lights and meat on which the butchers feed the said dogs.' The stench must have been strong to provoke a comment, for our ancestors walked through perpetual smells. Whiffs of fish would, for a long time, have been associated with the stewside, competing with the river breezes and the pleasant aroma of woodsmoke. Pig-keeping generated pungent scents, but general stable smells were not disagreeable – and they were so universally present in populated areas during the two-thousand-year dominance of the horse that few people would even have registered them. The same is probably true for human waste, some of which would have been consigned to underground cess-pits at this period, but much casually added to open manure heaps here, there and everywhere. Official attempts to keep it out of the drainage ditches that criss-crossed the south bank are a constant theme up to the nineteenth century, though the objection seems to have been not so much that faecal matter was unhealthy as that it choked the ditches and prevented water from running away.

'Shakespeare's Globe' (actually the creation of the actor-manager Richard Burbage) rises again today on the south bank. It is a near-unique example of the distant past returning, but its presence obfuscates detailed facts of that past. Descriptions and drawings of the original theatres are not numerous, but it is almost certain that the new Globe, conforming to modern ideas of safety and comfort, is both higher and more solid than the Elizabethan and Jacobean structures, since they could be dismantled and re-erected elsewhere rather as open-air concert arenas are today.

Nor is the new Globe on the site of the original, whose

exact location several hundred yards to the east was finally established in the twentieth century, and is marked today by a ring of distinctive cobbles in the courtyard of modern flats in Park Street. The new Globe is not, either, on the site of the Rose Theatre nearby, whose forgotten foundations right by Southwark Bridge Road were revealed by chance in 1989 when a Victorian warehouse was demolished. There lay hidden, sleeping, a perfect O, the original floor beneath layers of later dirt still strewn with the nutshells dropped by munching spectators.

This happy discovery gave further impetus to the actor Sam Wanamaker's campaign to resurrect the Globe. Indeed, so useful was the uncovered Rose for publicity purposes that the popular impression today is that the new Globe is built in the foundations of the old one, thus conflating two different theatres and three sites into one archetypal whole. So a pretend Shakespearean playhouse for our own time has now, by commemorating the original theatres, also superceded them. And for the first time ever the plot on which 49 Bankside sits finds itself with a playhouse right at its elbow.

Burbage's company, the Chamberlain's Men, was originally set up by his father, James, in Shoreditch which, like Bankside, was just outside the City jurisdiction. But, with no river to act as a barrier, it was uncomfortably close to the City and therefore subject to interference. The City Corporation disapproved of playhouses, which they regarded as the resort of undesirable people including thieves, horse-stealers, pimps, fraudsters and (rather oddly) rabbit catchers and those likely to commit treason. Actors were still by tradition 'rogues and strolling vagabonds', though a new generation of players, aristocratic patronage and fixed places for performance were making this designation obsolete. By 1598 James Burbage, a joiner by trade, was in dispute with the ground landlord, who was unwilling to renew the lease but was laying claim to the theatre's fabric. At Christmastide, while this City grandee was known to be celebrating the holy day in the country, the Burbage father and sons dismantled the theatre plank by plank, took all the material over on a series of boat-trips to the south bank, and re-erected it there as the Globe.

This location was no doubt influenced by the fact that the Rose was already on Bankside, erected there some ten years earlier by the moving spirit of the other leading company, the Admiral's Men. This was Philip Henslowe, theatrical manager, pawn broker, dyer, ruff-starcher, Groom of the King's Chamber, Master (after 1604) of the King's Bears, landlord, vestryman, and an emblematic Southwark citizen of his time. He later built a second Rose and the Hope Theatre, married his step-daughter to the leading actor, Edward Alleyn, and thus became indirectly part-responsible for the benevolent founding of Dulwich College (Alleyn's Gift). He was the son of a game warden of the Royal Ashdown Forest in Sussex: the family also had iron-ore mining and smelting interests in the forest. He came to London as an apprentice in the dyers' trade; evidently he knew how to make his mark, and when his employer died he married the widow. His busy and variegated life exemplifies the first period in London when entrepreneurial energy could win fortune and near-gentlemanly status, and Southwark, lacking the august dignitaries of London proper, was the ideal place for such a man to thrive. He stands as the first in a long line of them.

Because Henslowe wrote a wildly phonetic English, bought and sold second-hand clothes and lent money at interest to actors, later generations have tended to write him off as a vulgarian and a predator. However, his role with the actors was more like that of banker and he put up the money for production costs and costumes. It is clear that he was loved and respected by his son-in-law Alleyn, and was sufficiently honoured in his parish of St Saviour's to become a churchwarden and eventually one of the governors of the Free Grammar School. He had no children of his own, but tried to do his best by assorted orphaned nephews and nieces, not all of whom were grateful or as hard working as he was.

When he died in 1616 he was worth a substantial amount of money, and owned the leases of much property in Paris Garden and on Bankside, including some in the Great Pike Garden, and several inns.

It has sometimes been asserted that Henslowe owned the Cardinal's Hat. Documentation would suggest that he did not, nor even that he owned a lease on it, but one can tell from the addresses on family letters that both he and Alleyn and their respective wives lived on Bankside. One letter from 1592, before his Rose was constructed, indicates Henslowe ('hinslo') 'dwelling on the bank sid right over against the clink', which would suggest a house on the waterfront very near the Bishop's palace.But I think that later Henslowe or Alleyn or both may have moved much nearer to the Cardinal's Hat. In the Southwark archive collection is a nineteenth-century Deed of sale, plus earlier documents, relating to a parcel of land which, by then, represented numbers 44, 45 and 46 Bankside, plus a considerable amount of land to the back of them where other houses were built. The location of this sixty-six-foot frontage on the river, just two more house-widths east of number 49, is thus clear – by coincidence, it is roughly the stretch occupied by the Globe today. The oldest extant Deed in the bundle relating to this particular plot of land is dated 1698, but this one recapitulates, on durable parchment, the earlier history of the plot, going back to 1604, when a 'gentleman' called Devonish Rymen sold it to Philip Henslowe, complete with several 'messuages' (houses). The next sale occurred in 1616, which is the year Henslowe died.

So the Cardinal's Hat would have been conveniently near to hand, and that the family were good customers is undoubted. The year after Henslowe's death, Alleyn's engagement-diary-cum-accounts records several dinners there, one for local vestrymen, for he, like his late father-in-law, was on the parish council: 'December 12. I went to London [from Dulwich, where he had a country retreat] and supped at the Cardinalls Hatt wt. Mr Austen Mr Archer and Mr Ordes. 4.0 shillings. Dec 17. Dinner at Cardinalls Hatt wt. Vestry men. 3.0 shillings. Supper ther wt. Mr Austen etc. 2s.6d.' In a world in which a working man was doing well if he made twenty pounds in a year (four hundred shillings), and a skilled artisan, shop-keeper or clergymen only perhaps two or three times that, it will be seen that dinner bills counted in shillings indicate a certain standard of prosperous comfort in both inn and diners. People transacted business now in inns, in a haze of newly popular tobacco; it had become customary to erect high-backed settles like screens at each table to create a degree of privacy. Fourteen years later the Cardinal's Hat was clearly still the good inn where theatre people went; there is a record of them dining John Taylor, the waterman-poet, there at their expense.

Many other people connected with the playhouses lodged on Bankside in the early years of the seventeenth century, though not the Burbages: their home remained on the other side of the river in Shoreditch. Similarly, although much scholarly effort has been expended trying to find the name of Richard Burbage's colleague, William Shakespeare, among such records of Southwark residents of that era as survive, it does not figure. Elusive as ever, he seems to have paid taxes to the Bishop of Winchester in 1600, but these may relate to his part-share in the Globe since, apart from hopeful forgeries, the only faint indications are of addresses for him on the London side. Presumably, like Burbage, he com- muted across the river by boat. There is a tale that he used to frequent the Falcon Inn, which was on an inlet on the boundary between Bankside proper and the Paris Garden, near Paris Garden stairs; certainly, if he was living west of Temple Bar, that would have been a logical landing place for him. Then a short walk along the riverfront, past the Cardinal's Hat, and down past the Bear Garden to the Globe.

What *is* known is that Shakespeare's younger brother Edmund, who followed the successful elder to London but had not much acclaim as an actor himself, died aged twenty- seven in 1607 at his lodging in Hunt's Rents, Maid Lane.

Maid or Maiden Lane was the first track to develop across the meadows immediately south of Bankside and roughly parallel with it. It followed the line of the long, meandering drainage ditch that had been cut in the thirteenth century to channel waters off the land and round into the Thames the other side of Paris Garden. The lane still exists today as Park Street. Straddled by Southwark Bridge Road and by railway viaducts, but now without the iron gantries between warehouses that made it cavernous in its industrial heyday, Park Street is a classic example of an urban contour persisting through time when the world that created it has utterly passed away.

It has been said that the playwright John Fletcher lodged for a while at the Cardinal's Hat. I have not found any reliable authority for this, but John Aubrey, that invaluable seventeenth-century gossip and man-about-town, wrote of Fletcher and his co-author Francis Beaumont: 'They lived together on the Bank-side, not far from the Play-house, both bachelors, lay together, had one Wench in the house between, which they did so admire, the same cloathes and cloake etc. betweene them.' In spite of the implications of this, Beaumont eventually married and fathered two daughters, before dying, less than three years later, in 1614. Fletcher very quickly took up with another stage writer, Philip Massinger, and apparently lived as closely with him as he had with Beaumont till his own death in Southwark in a plague year: 'In the great Plague 1625 a Knight of Norfolk (or Suffolke) invited him to the Countrey. He stayed but to make himselfe a suite of Cloathes, and while it was making, fell sick of the Plague and dyed.' (Aubrey again.) Clothes seem to have been an important item for Fletcher. The image of the dramatist feeling he must have a nice suit to accept a grand invitation adds a further touch to our picture of the stage world, in which actors were regularly the recipients of cast-offs from noble wardrobes. Ostensibly these were for use on stage; in reality, they were often worn as part of a flamboyant lifestyle, or else sold off to Henslowe or another dealer to raise ready cash. Henslowe, incidentally, knew Massinger well, had him as a lodger at one time, and once bailed him out of debtors' prison. He reproached him for extravagant entertaining.

Massinger was buried in St Saviour's church in the same grave as Fletcher. Massinger's wish to join his great and good friend there must have been well known to his associates, for he himself was not by then an inhabitant of the parish and it cost more for 'strangers' to be buried. Their joint dust is in theory still there, though in practice it was probably scooped out, along with that of many others, when the old floor was levelled in the 1830s for the nave's rebuilding and the grave-slabs re-laid. Perhaps that debris, human dust and all, was used as hardcore beneath some terrace of houses in the then-expanding suburban districts of Kennington or Camberwell.[6]

What was Southwark like in the early seventeenth century, in the days before the Commonwealth drove out the Bishop of Winchester from his palace, before the Fire gutted the City opposite, before Ludgate Hill, Holborn, Charing Cross and Westminster began to coalesce into a greater metropolis? London Bridge was still crowded with houses (some of which, near the north end, would not escape the Fire either), and the heads of the executed were still displayed on poles over the gatehouse at the southern end: you can see them on Visscher's panorama. Where Borough High Street ran down from the bridge there was a row of butchers' shops, interspersed with the odd tailor and shoe-maker. Since butchers did their own butchery then, there must often have been cattle or sheep in the yards and enclosures adjoining; the problem of smelly offal cast carelessly into the river, as most rubbish was, became sufficient of a nuisance later in the century for rules to be made about disposing of it only at night and by an outgoing tide. Naturally, all streets and lanes were dirty: in fact the chaplain to the Venetian Ambassador, visiting in 1617, remarked particularly in London on 'a sort of soft and very stinking mud, which abounds at all seasons'. He did add, however, that this served 'as excellent manure, rich and black as thick as ink, and which is conveyed at small cost by the innumerable carts which are bound to clean the streets'. In Southwark, the ubiquitous presence of hogs must have increased the dirt, although these creatures also did some useful scavenging. Hogs being allowed to run wild in the area of Bankside continued to be a matter of contention up to the late eighteenth century.

Not till after the Restoration did London or its suburbs have any form of public street lighting. But the dark lanes of medieval London had seen some progress by Elizabeth's day: each individual householder was now required to hang out a lantern in the winter months, except at the full moon. By the early seventeenth century all foreign visitors remarked how busy London was with modern trade. There were small shops everywhere, and a mass of wheeled vehicles in the streets, from handcarts to great waggons, were replacing the immemorial figures of the pedlar and the packhorse. Southwark participated in the general boom: as well as the butchers in the High Street there were grocers, saddlers, linen-drapers, barber-surgeons, hatters, pastry-cooks, poulterers and many other businesses, including the string of taverns. (John Harvard, who would leave in 1637 for the new world across the Atlantic, after another round of plague had killed most of his family, was the son of a Southwark butcher who also kept the Queen's Head in the High Street. He prospered in America: the university he founded there is his monument.) There was an old established market in the High Street on Monday, Wednesday, Friday and Saturday, till two in the afternoon in winter and three in summer. It sold fruit, vegetables, rabbits, cheeses and the like, brought in by country people, who were frequently in dispute with local people for taking away their custom. The Borough Market, which flourishes today under the booming railway arches that crowd close to St Saviour's, is the direct descendant of the ancient market.

But prosperous and lively as Southwark was, it was by the same token becoming more built up in a piecemeal way, with new alleys and 'rents'. The day of the old, grand houses was passing: even before the bleak time of the Commonwealth, mansions were beginning to be partitioned into tenements. In one of them was established a soapworks which was soon to be one of the biggest in London. Glassworks, too, were appearing. Since the City authorities were not keen on smoky businesses within their own district, Bankside was an obvious location; there was already a tradition of small-scale glass-blowing in the Borough. The Bishop was still in his palace when a glassworks was set up within its precincts, in an ex-brewhouse, the forerunner of others that were to open at several places along Bankside later in the century.

While the theatres played and the inns were full of City folk come over to enjoy the late afternoon sun, as office workers do today, Bankside's industrial destiny still lay in the future. But the future, by the time of Charles I, was just beginning to signal its coming.

Chapter IV

OF WATER, FIRE AND THE GREAT REBUILDING

The river Thames runs through this story as a constant presence, but its role changes over the centuries. After the Tudor period it was no longer a defensible barrier against foreign or home-grown marauders; instead, it became London's open space, a combination of highway and arena. Elaborate pageants were staged on its surface, especially by London Mayors. An early seventeenth-century show, which celebrated the burgeoning trade with the East India Company's newly established ports, featured five artificial floating islands complete with exotic fruit and spice trees. The great world was opening up and the Thames was England's gateway to it.

But essentially the river was the main road running between one end of the City and the other, or between the cities of London and Westminster, or up river further to Richmond, or down river to Deptford and Greenwich and eventually to the sea. The town streets were narrow, either muddy or dusty according to the weather, choked in many places with stalls and cryers of wares, with workmen plying their trades and with clamorous crowds. Coaches were a rarity before the seventeenth century, and when they did begin to replace horseback as a means of transport they were at first boxy, unsprung contraptions that jolted their passengers over the uneven stones. At most times of year the river offered a smoother and quicker ride, and boats rowed by watermen were the standard means of transport. The Venetian chaplain who spent a period in London towards 1617 might, you would think, be used to such craft, yet he like several other foreign visitors seems to have been charmed by the efficency of the whole system:

'. . . the boatmen wait . . . in great crowds, each one eager to be the first to catch one, for all are free to choose the ship they find most attractive and pleasing, while every boatman has the privilege on arrival of placing his ship for best advantage for people to step into.' (In fact other evidence suggests that customers were sometimes greeted with a cacophony of 'I am the next man – take me' or the same phrase in Latin.) 'The wherries are charmingly upholstered and embroidered cushions are laid across the seats, very comfortable to sit on and lean against, and generally speaking the benches only seat two people next to one another; many of them are covered in, particularly in rainy weather or fierce sunshine. They are extremely pleasant to travel in and carry one or a couple of boatmen.'

Wealthy families, especially those living in the Thameside houses along the Strand, would employ their own watermen in livery. Those who made do with the watermen who plied for hire would often have their favoured men among them, with whom they came to regular terms. Samuel Pepys, who lived and worked near Tower Hill, seems to have had such an arrangement. Others used the boats as communal taxis, joining up with strangers going in the same direction. 'Eastward ho!' a waterman would cry, meaning that he was going down river, or 'Westward ho!' when he was bound for Westminster or beyond, and prospective passengers would form groups accordingly. But the boats were also used to ferry people from one shore to the other, as a logical alternative to London's one bridge whose narrow right-of-way was threaded between the houses crowded on top of it. You could take a diagonal route from St Paul's, say, to Lambeth, or from Bankside to the Strand; individual watermen tended to have their own set routes.

Journeys that involved going under one of the nineteen

arches of London Bridge – 'shooting the bridge' – were the ones that required particular skill and judgement, for the current there was compressed between wooden 'starlings' which were built out further and further to protect the stone work. In fact they created a huge problem in their own right, for any unwise move could drive a boat against them. They also choked the river flow, so that at certain turns of tide the water would build up and an artificial drop was created, like that in a lock. Accidents happened, and nervous customers in every generation avoided making that particular trip, preferring to get out, walk round the bridge, and rejoin their boatman on the other side.

On Bankside alone, between the Royal Barge House at the end of Paris Garden and London Bridge under a mile distant, there were fifteen stairs or other docking places, including Mason stairs just to the west of the Cardinal's Hat Inn and Goat stairs a little way to the east. Large numbers of men followed the thriving trade of rowing people about: an Elizabethan survey indicated nearly a thousand of them, and by the end of the century Stow reckoned there were many more. At that date the population of St Saviour's parish was about twelve hundred, of which two hundred and one were stated to be watermen, many of whom lived on Bankside. The one whose name has come down to us, and who has become an emblematic figure for all his kind, apparently lived there: at any rate he was a parishioner of St Saviour's, had friends living near the Hope Theatre and many contacts among the actors. He is said to have plied his trade regularly between Bankside, Whitehall and Old Swan stairs, which was a major boat station just by London Bridge. This was John Taylor, the self-styled 'water poet'.

He was born in Gloucester in 1578, made his way to London like many other people in that time of expansion, became an apprentice waterman, then a freeman of the Watermen's Company. He was forcibly induced to join the Crown ships during the Spanish Wars, but he returned safe and full of travellers' tales. With his production of rhymes, his polemic pamphlets, his noisily proclaimed friendships with important people, his publicised trips around England and to the Continent, and his insistent self-promotion, it is tempting to see him as the forerunner of the archetypal chatty taxi-driver and card – 'Had that Will Shakespeare in the back of my boat the other day . . . Want to know what my good friend Mr Henslowe said to me? . . .' But with his undoubted intelligence, nerve and entrepreneurial flair he did also typify in a more general way a skilled profession that was then at its zenith. As a prominent Waterman (he became an Overseer and spokesman for the Company) he prefigures another of the same Company a hundred years later, who was to become a key figure in the story of 49 Bankside.

The Watermen's Company was established in 1555, in an attempt to regulate and raise the status of what had always been considered rather a rough profession. Watermen, having customers literally at their mercy, had had a reputation for over-familiarity, smart backchat, swearing, spreading scandalous stories, extortionate fare-demands and also for fighting and drunkenness. John Taylor maintained it was frequently members of the public who treated the watermen badly: parties of drunken, upper-class young men, he said, would hire a boat, have themselves ferried, tell the boatman to wait for them and then not return. By the beginning of the seventeenth century the Company had acquired its own coat of arms and Watermen's Hall was built in Upper Thames Street. A proper system of a seven-year apprenticeship was established and a fare-scale was laid down. John Taylor, with his aspirations to literary fame and to a general rise in status, and his championship of the watermen's cause, was highly representative of the new, meritocratic world that was being born in his lifetime, against a background of revolution and change, out of the wreck of a feudal society.

He was a man of radical views in some ways, puritanical about Sin but a great eater, drinker and merrymaker, a fervent egalitarian but also a convinced royalist. He became one of the watermen ceremonially appointed to James I and helped row the Queen's barge to Oxford, although by that time most of the daily rowing of his own boat was done by apprentices. In the early seventeenth century London had for the first time in history a large number of inhabitants who could read. It was for this public that Taylor poured out writing of all kinds: satires on current life, joke books, religious reflections, accounts of his own travels, scripts for water pageants, tirades against the new hackney coaches – which he actually managed to get banned for a generation from taking passengers on short journeys that began and ended within two miles of the river. But his most fervent ambitions, social as well as personal, were invested in his poems, and in plays which were never particularly successful. A showman himself by nature – he and a vintner friend once rowed down the Thames in a boat made of paper, and later made a much-publicised trip down the Rhine and the Elbe – he cultivated the actors of Bankside just as eagerly as he did the great and good of London. John Aubrey, who was familiar with some of the cleverest men of his time, described John Taylor as 'very facetious and diverting company'. Thomas Dekker, the playwright, called him 'the ferryman of heaven', but there may have been a touch of irony in this description.

This life strung out, literally as well as metaphorically, on the moving waters between the two constrasting banks, periodically brought Taylor into trouble. In 1613, when he had just been appointed a King's waterman, the Bankside theatres were going temporarily through a bad time: Burbage's Globe had caught fire and burnt during a performance of *Henry VIII*, though it was soon rebuilt, and the Rose was out of action too. There were evidently fears among the watermen that the theatres would migrate back to the northern shore (as indeed they eventually did, though not till after the Restoration) and that the watermen would thereby lose a significant part of their trade. Espousing their cause, Taylor petitioned the King to issue a prohibition against theatres on the City side. Maybe he thought this would also please the Bankside theatre set, but it did not. The players did not care where they were located provided the show went on, and in any case, under royal patronage, the profession was becoming more respectable: theatre-people could now aspire to be gentlemen, and why not in London proper? This was the point at which a group of them, including Philip Henslowe, took Taylor to supper at the Cardinal's Hat. No doubt, in the course of a convivial evening, he charmed them again and swore that he would do nothing against their wishes. The petition to the King failed anyway: there was no particular reason for the King to agree to it, and probably Taylor had misled his fellow watermen by boasting of his royal appointment and his friendships in high places. But many watermen believed that his actor friends had bribed him not to press his suit, and they were not pleased with him.

Taylor retained his leading role in the Company, however, and a few years later, in the bitterly cold winter of 1620–21, regained favour among his peers by publishing a passionate poem about their sufferings. The Thames froze over above London Bridge, and for weeks the watermen were out of work, most of them with no other resources to keep them going. Taylor reckoned that all-in-all about twenty thousand people – wives, children, apprentices and servants, as well as the men themselves – were affected by this misfortune. Since a mini ice-age set in as the seventeenth-century progressed, with long spells of winter frost becoming more common than in the preceding centuries, this lament was to be repeated and repeated again by other voices. During the following century, too, the Thames froze solid some twenty times. The last of these ferocious winters did not occur till 1813–14, after which the climate became a little milder again. But by that time the watermen had a number of other threats to their ancient livelihood.

The theatre trade on Bankside collapsed with the beginning of the Civil Wars in 1642, and by then Taylor had other, more pressing problems. In the general social unrest the power and prestige of the Watermen's Company had also collapsed; Taylor was threatened by enemies he had carelessly made and was once nearly lynched; his royal salary was at an end and, as a known royalist, his goods were confiscated. His wife died, and he had to flee from London, taking refuge with a brother who was an inn-keeper near Abingdon. Aubrey saw him then and judged him to be 'near fifty', handsomely dressed, with 'a good quick look'. In fact, he was over sixty, too old to row any more for a living. He came back to London later, and in his last years we find him living in near-poverty but married again, to a wife who kept a small ale-house off Longacre in the recently developed district of Covent Garden, where he held court. 'His conversation was incomparable for three or four morning's drafts: but afterwards you were entertained with *crambe bis cocta* [stale old stories]' – Aubrey again. Taylor made one last great journey on foot round England, but died a few months later, in the summer of 1653, before he could see the Stuarts return to the throne. His dust is buried somewhere behind St Martin-in-the-Fields, where the graveyard of the old church lay, and where present-day travellers and aspirants to fame gather with backpacks and their own travellers' tales.

With the Cromwellian closing of the theatres, Bankside's glory days were over. But then London in general passed through a bad time during the Commonwealth, with many of the great houses abandoned and shut up. Valuable collections, such as those in Whitehall Palace or at Arundel House on the Strand, were pillaged or left to deteriorate. The Bishop's palace on Bankside was divided into tenements and the buildings were much damaged. Churches suffered further assaults on their fittings and decorations, as they had done at intervals since the Reformation almost a hundred years before. The altar rails of St Saviour's, which had stood there 'anciently, time out of mind', were thrown down to conform to low Church ritual; the medieval Lady Chapel at the eastern end became a bakehouse, and then a pig-stye. At least that church continued to function: at the height of the

Civil Wars St Paul's cathedral was used by Cromwell's trained bands as a stable for their horses.

Since the parishes provided the structure of day-to-day authority and such social services as existed, dislocation in the Church led to general breakdown. Many of the public water conduits that had been installed over the last few generations became blocked or holed; streets flooded and paving disintegrated. Crime and street disorder also increased. John Evelyn, returning from a circumspect exile in France in 1652, found the inn landlords on the journey from Dover lacking in their old respect and that, as he passed through Southwark on the way into town, small boys pelted the coach with mud and stones – 'You would imagine yourself among a legion of devils', he wrote, 'and in the suburbs of hell.'

But in fact, away from the main road of Borough High Street, and crowded Bermondsey to the east of it, Southwark was still quite a rural, peaceable place: the houses on that side petered out very soon into meadows to the south and Lambeth marsh to the west. There was the odd glasshouse and soap-boiling works established near London Bridge, with more to come later in the century; and a brewery started near the site of the defunct Globe which, a hundred years later, was to become the great works owned by Dr Johnson's friend Henry Thrale. But then the north shore of the river too had its share of new wharves, workshops and smelly manufactures, even as far west as Whitehall, to the disgust of John Evelyn who took the view that these signs of crude economic activity were unworthy in 'the Imperial seat of our incomparable Monarch'. The British Empire in its full resplendence still lay a long way in the future, but it was true that fragile ships setting out from the Thames reached as far as America to the west and India, or even China, to the east. They brought back from these ends of the earth decorative goods which found their way into London houses and new plants which began to be cultivated in London's gardens.

There was one particularly splendid and innovative garden near the river west of Lambeth palace (that of the Tradescant family, gardeners to the royal family), but Bankside itself was not short of gardens. They appear with great clarity on the bird's-eye map made by Wenceslaus Hollar's friend and colleague William Faithorne in 1658, two years before the Restoration. The fish ponds, still visible near the end of the preceding century, have all gone by this date, and of the entertainment industry only one bear garden is shown. (Twenty-five years later that, too, was suppressed.) But each of the run of houses now squashed together along Bankside in a continuous line, in the way of ribbon-development on the edge of town in every era, has its own garden behind. Drawn as decorative parterres, they must have been for a mixture of flowers and vegetables, and beyond each lies its own orchard. There is, as yet, no sign of the commercial wharves that would appear on Bankside in the next century. The garden plots all end in a narrow stream (the ditch first dug in the thirteenth century) over which each household has its own plank bridge. The houses at the west end of Bankside, which stand between the roadway and the river, have no gardens, but from the roadway numerous little bridges cross a wider section of stream to further individual orchards. The two streams curve round to join one another by Barge House stairs. Evidently Bankside was still a very well-watered place, indeed the water levels in all the channels still rose and fell with the river tides.

The only problem with Faithorne's image of this garden suburb is that, in the tradition of London map making, it stops short at the southern edge of the Bankside properties, the rest of the space on the sheet being taken by the large, rectangular key to the churches of London and its sur-rounding districts. In reality, we know that Maid Lane, complete with quite a few houses, was already there on the southern side of the orchards. The two side paths, Gravel Lane and Bandy Leg Walk, led off from it as well, though as yet these would only have been footpaths to St George's Fields. The future layout of Southwark was tentatively taking shape.

When play-going started again after the Restoration, the

plays were of a new sort, and so were the covered, proscenium-arch theatres in which they were performed. Fashion – and sin – had moved back to the north side of the river and to the capital's expanding western quarters: to Drury Lane and Covent Garden, to the Haymarket and Piccadilly and St James's Park, the districts conveniently adjacent to Charles II's dissolute court. But it had been twenty years since the watermen had had the theatre-going crowds to ferry to and from Bankside, and probably the general growth of London at that time was enough to ensure their livelihood. The south bank seems to have settled again into its historic separateness, so near to the centre of London yet distant from it. When Ogilby and Morgan produced the first survey map of London, showing properties in wonderful detail, the south bank was excluded from it. Alas, we will never be able to see the exact layout of the Cardinal's Hat and its outbuildings.

The years after the Restoration are those covered by Samuel Pepys's diary, as well as by Evelyn's far more extensive one: each makes references to crossing the water. Pepys visited the Falcon Inn, and also the Bear, a very old inn beside London Bridge whose landlady, 'a most beautiful woman', drowned herself in the river. Evelyn, seeking inspiration for his own garden down river at Deptford, visited the Lambeth garden that had belonged to the Tradescants, and occasionally went to Lambeth Palace – once walking there over the frozen river. Both he and Pepys stayed dutifully in London throughout the terrible plague year of 1665, the Great Plague that has eclipsed in memory all the century's earlier ones. In September Pepys recorded, looking across the river, that it was 'strange to see, in broad daylight, two or three burials upon the bankside, one at the very heels of another; doubtless all of the plague; and yet 40 or 50 people going along with every one of them'. Pepys found this 'strange' because in London proper, where this time round the Plague had become serious sooner than it had in Southwark, public gatherings for funerals had been discouraged for months. In any case many London burials were now taking place summarily, and by night, in mass pits.

The processions Pepys saw so clearly on Bankside must have been making their way eastwards from the Cardinal's Hat area along towards Bankend and hence to St Saviour's and its churchyard. There was then no other church to the west of Bankside till you came to Lambeth, and no other burial ground for the inhabitants of the parish but the old Cross Bones ground where the remains of the 'single women' supposedly lay – and that was not annexed by St Saviour's as a general overflow burial ground till the 1670s. The popular Southwark idea that there was a plague pit near Bankside seems to have no basis in fact. Deadman's Place, which was later subsumed into the big brewery, is often cited, but this was a Nonconformist burial ground dating from some years after the Plague. The name 'Deadman' is much older than that, and is probably just a corruption of someone's name.

The river itself was seen as a refuge from the Plague, though many of those hoping to escape the pestilence carried it with them. According to Daniel Defoe, writing a generation later of events in his early childhood:

'As the richer sort got in to ships, so the lower ranks got into hoys, smacks, lighters and fishing-boats; and many, especially watermen, lay in their boats; but . . . the infection got in among them and made a fearful havoc; many of the watermen died alone in their wherries as they rid at their roads, as well as above bridge as below, and were not found sometimes till they were not in a condition for anybody to touch or come near them.'

The following summer the river once again figured as a place of escape, but this time the surviving watermen were in luck. As the Great Fire spread in the City on the 2nd and 3rd September, crowds of people bearing their most prized belongings in coaches, carts or in their arms besieged the waterside. Many were prepared to pay almost any price to load their goods to get them away from the flames. Pepys himself paid eight pounds, which was more than his usual month's total housekeeping and servants' wages bill, to have two lighters bear his best furniture and other valuables away to Woolwich. ('Lighters' were the large sail boats that were usually employed to unload, or 'lighten', goods from sea-going ships anchored in mid-river. The lighter-masters were, by the next century, admitted to membership of the Watermen's Company. Eventually, as the ferry-trade began to decline, they would come to dominate the Company.)

The Watermen's first Hall in Upper Thames Street disappeared into the flames with many other City Company Halls, and by the third day the north waterfront itself was well alight, along with Cheapside and St Paul's. Many premises near the river were stuffed with highly combustible goods, such as pitch, hemp and flax, while the wharf sides themselves were stacked with timber and coal – power supplies for the growing industrial and commercial capital. The Fire had already burnt the houses on the City end of London Bridge, and with them the 'water engine' used to raise water from the river for London's general needs, but then the flames were stopped. This time Southwark was lucky, though the district had known destructive fires before and was to lose five hundred houses round the High Street ten years later.

On the day the Great Fire of 1666 took hold, the dry east wind driving the flames westwards made many City-dwellers such as Pepys believe for a while that the City itself would be largely spared. Pepys's first move was to take a ferry to Whitehall to alert the King to what was happening. Then back to the City to locate the increasingly desperate Lord Mayor and hand him the King's authority for pulling down houses to stop the blaze. Later in the day he, his wife and some friends with whom they had dined took to the river again to observe the situation. The air was hot all round them, and full of smoke and sparks, and the true and growing extent of the disaster became apparent – 'a most horrid, malicious bloody flame, not like the fine flame of an ordinary fire'. The heat, and the unending, crackling roar of destruction drove them to take shelter in 'a little alehouse on Bankside'. There they stayed till dark came, and then hurried home, beginning to realise that, so large was the area of devastation, their own home might be at risk. The Bankside ale-house was, he says, opposite 'the three cranes', which was a well-known loading dock situated between St Paul's and London Bridge, so it must have been from another inn rather than from the Cardinal's Hat that Pepys made the observations which still epitomise the Fire for us after nearly three and a half centuries.

The Fire, coming as it did only a few years after the Restoration, seems to constitute one of those frontiers in time which precipitate changes that were coming anyway, but which then arrive all the faster. By the end of the century, London had been transformed more than at any era in its previous history. With upwards of half a million people,[1] it was more than ten times the size of any other British city. It outstripped Paris in population, becoming the largest city in Europe, and for the first time three-quarters of its population lived outside the old City walls. It was becoming a metropolis – a new word then – and by and by the repercussions of this were felt on Bankside also.

Melchisedeck Fritter, the long-time lessee of the Cardinal's Hat, died in 1673, and his widow took over the business. The ground landlords were no longer the Browker family since the property had been sold to a Thomas Hudson seven years earlier. In 1686 the Widow Fritter handed the tenancy of the inn on to a Sarah Humphreys: the inn may have adopted a different name for part of the Fritter tenancy, and now it was renamed in the lease as the Cardinal's Cap, as if the name of the alley alongside had finally won over other versions. Sarah Humphreys left the lease to her son and grandson, but I do not know for how long the inn-keeping business was continued. Hudson died in 1688, leaving 'his messuages on Bankside' to his sister, Mary Greene, and after her to his great-nieces Mary and Sarah Bruce.

About this family, I have not been able to discover anything more. Did Mistress Greene and her nieces, whose parents were evidently out of the picture, live in one of the houses, perhaps in the former Cardinal's Cap itself? Or was it, as before, a piece of property to be let as a source of revenue? The same family seem to have owned it for many years, but with the new century the nature of the house, and indeed of most of the houses on Bankside, was soon to undergo a great change. For in or about 1710 (the date can only be conjectural, based on architectural features, and on a lead drain-head marked '1712' which used to adorn the front of the next-door house) the timbered Cardinal's Hat/Cap was largely, though not entirely, demolished. It was never again to be an inn, for it was replaced by a decent, but not grand, brick-fronted gentleman's abode, in the new style.

Yet at this crucial moment in the existence of the house opposite St Paul's, we know less of what was going on socially on Bankside than at any other era since the Middle Ages. The house did not have to be rebuilt, for the Great Fire never reached the south bank. The Building Acts of 1667 and 1707, which were designed to thwart future fires by stipulating the use of less combustible materials, only applied to new houses, not existing ones. In other outlying parts of London that had escaped the Fire, particularly Holborn, timbered and gabled houses continued to stand, many lasting well into the nineteenth century. So the fact that most of the gabled houses of Bankside were rebuilt, in the approved modern style, in the first quarter of the eighteenth century, can only suggest that this redevelopment seemed worthwhile to their owners – a fair number of owners. Unlike many better-documented areas on the other side of the river, Bankside was not one estate with a wealthy ground landlord making a comprehensive decision. Bankside proprietors, such as Henslowe and Browker, and now apparently the descendants of Mary Greene, did often own more than one house. The three houses a little to the east of the Cardinal's Cap, which had once been Henslowe's and were to become numbers 44, 45 and 46, belonged at this date to a Sir Richard Oldner, knight, and he owned another house along Bankside in which he lived. But this was the pattern: small holdings of freehold plots, two, three or four houses along the waterfront at the most, and then not always in one piece. Clearly, if so many of these were rebuilt at the same period, a number of individuals must each have decided that Bankside was the sort of desirable location on which it was worth laying out money. The banking system as we know it today was just beginning to form: credit was easier to get than it had been when much wealth tended to be kept in solid form in purses; London's population was continuing to rise, the town was growing rapidly westwards. There would surely, it must have been said, be a demand for genteel houses on the south bank also, where the air was purer than on the City side?

A new church, Christ Church, had been built in 1671 in the Paris Garden manor, to serve a new parish split off from St Saviour's. The money for this had been left in the Will of a Southwark worthy in 1631, but the religious uncertainty of the mid-seventeenth century meant that the executors waited prudently till after the Restoration to put the dead man's wishes into practice. Apparently they did not realise that the Paris Garden was still very poorly drained at that date: in fact, over the following decades, the new church and its yard became so waterlogged that it had to be entirely rebuilt in 1741. This perennial water problem may have been one of reasons why, apart from Bankside itself, the increase in houses south of the river was always rather slow – perhaps slower than the church-builders or the citizens of Bankside anticipated. Only three hundred and forty-nine houses are recorded as having been added to St Saviour's parish between the time Charles I came to the throne and the Restoration of Charles II, and then none till the late 1670s. But there must have been a substantial increase in the last three decades of the seventeenth century, with in-filling along Maid Lane, ribbon development down the tracks leading south from it and many more houses near the Borough High Street, for in 1708 the number of houses in St Saviour's parish was said to be 'about 2,500'. They housed a total population of some fourteen thousand, an increase of more than tenfold on Stow's figure of twelve hundred not much more than a hundred years before. Fourteen thousand does sound about right, if the figure of two thousand five hundred houses is to be believed, as that would indicate an average of 5.6 people per house, including children, servants and apprentices. But if the population for the whole of the London area at that time is to be estimated at between five and six hundred thousand, it is clear that Southwark was as yet far from built up. Indeed great tracts of it were open land, with paddocks, market gardens and cloth-drying grounds, and continued that way for much of the eighteenth century.

It was not a backwater, however. Conforming to its traditional role as a refuge for those who could not be accommodated officially within London proper, the suburb of the south bank had for some time been home to a number of respectable Nonconformists who, after James II's Act of Indulgence, could declare themselves as such. A Quaker Meeting House was built near Bankside, and several other dissenting chapels. The best known of these was a place that crops up in incidental references of the era as 'Shallett's meeting house'; it was a pretty wooden building in a newly constructed cul de sac off Gravel Lane which was christened 'Zoar Street' – Sanctuary Street. John Bunyan is always said to have preached there, but as he died within a year of the chapel being put up (1688), this is by no means sure. A charity school was also run from there, and several other free schools were started in the following decades, including a Roman Catholic one – whose existence spurred the low-Church factions to greater efforts. These little schools were intended primarily to inculcate Christian virtues into the offspring of the lower classes, to promote a proper spirit of obedience and to 'suppress the beginning of vice': too much book learning might, after all, have encouraged the children to get above their station. But the schools did induce a basic literacy and numeracy, and must have given many youngsters a first glimpse of other things beyond the street and the vagaries of casual labour. St Saviour's too, thanks to two bequests from wealthy parishioners, started its own free school for small, poor boys (as distinct from the Free Grammar School for older boys which had been in St Saviour's churchyard since the days of Queen Elizabeth) and also made efforts towards providing them with respectable clothes and getting them apprenticeships.

The modern, decent, progressive-minded citizens who busied themselves with such works clearly required modern, cleanly built houses to live in, did they not? Otherwise, in the absence of such a stratum of society on the south bank, the gabled Elizabethan houses would simply have remained, let out into tenements as such houses were in other parts of Southwark, gradually becoming 'rookeries' or slums, to be swept away more summarily by later waves of progressive thought.

The reason that I know that many of the houses along Bankside were rebuilt in the days of Queen Anne, or soon after, is that I have seen them. Not in real life: except for number 49 they have all vanished now, like the river ice of long-past winters. (The pair standing next to 49 across the alley look convincing, but they are little more than a decent simulacrum of what were originally three houses, re-constituted after incendiary bomb damage in the Second World War.) Everywhere else on Bankside late nineteenth-century warehouses gradually replaced the Queen Anne houses, to be replaced again now by still larger blocks of modern flats.

None of the extant early nineteenth-century panoramas of London, of which there are several, manages to show the sweep of Bankside with any clarity. But, when in pursuit of nineteenth-century drainage, I chanced upon a set of Flood Prevention plans of 1881. There was the whole river wall of Bankside, laid out detailed section by section complete with suggested extra defences, and beneath each section was a little elevation drawing of the one or two buildings relevant to those particular few yards. By re-drawing these elevations for myself, carefully measured, and then stringing them together in the right order, I was able to achieve my own Long View of the Bankside we have lost. (See pages 178–9.)

As my laborious vista accumulated, it became apparent from the style of many of the houses still surviving in 1881 that they were of the same period as number 49, or only a decade or so later. There was a building boom in London after Marlborough's wars ended in 1715, which lasted till the mid-1720s: I believe that the bulk of Bankside's initial rebuilding dates from then. As you would expect from the multiple land-holdings, although the houses butted up against one another they did not anywhere form one complete terrace, but hung together in twos and threes, a procession of slightly varying rooflines, cornices and windows. Evidently many minds had had the same idea for improving their property within the same era, and had all gone about it in the same way, with just an *ad hoc* gentleman's agreement about style and proportion. As for the old footpaths running alongside the garden walls and down onto Bankside – Moss Alley, White Hind Alley, Cardinal Cap Alley, Pond Yard – these were simply slotted under masonry arches that ran, in several cases, *through* the ground floors of the new houses. Cardinal Cap Alley now emerged onto Bankside beneath the upper floors of what would become number 50.

Architectural historians have ignored Bankside, training their sights rather on the great estates north of the river and on what has survived rather than what is lost. In popular London mythology the playhouses and bear pits gave way to smoking chimneys and 'slum courts' with no intervening period. But the days of Queen Anne and the early part of the reign of George I were, arguably, Bankside's own time in the sun, its moment of near-elegance. Even the more modest two-storey houses that were going up in the new side streets, and were sometimes still made of timber, were not then the working-class hovels they were later to become, but could be described by a contemporary (John Strype) as 'clean and handsome . . . pretty well built and inhabited'.[2] Across the water Wren's huge new St Paul's, almost the only baroque building in London, glimmered in white splendour. There is some indication that Wren himself lodged on Bankside for a while – not in the yet-to-be-rebuilt 49, where he is mis-leadingly commemorated, but in another house further along by the Falcon Tavern. The story, which was collected from a 'very old man' some eighty years later,[3] is that Wren designed this house himself for a Mr Jones who had started an iron-working business there, and that he rented a room there as a vantage point from which to survey the progress of work on his new cathedral. What *is* a fact is that Jones supplied the ornate railings that were eventually fitted at pavement level round the cathedral. Apparently, in the mid-eighteenth century, a porcelain plaque referring to Wren was made and placed on Jones's house, which survived for another hundred and fifty years.

The iron for St Paul's railings (and for similar ones round Jones's own house) was said to be from the last load of iron to leave an ancient forest smelting works in Sussex, such as the one owned by Henslowe's family a hundred years before. It travelled by boat round the coast and up the Thames, to the site above London Bridge which Jones had decided would be a promising place to establish his works. After that date, the manufacture of iron migrated almost entirely to areas where the available fuel for the forges was not wood but coal. So Wren and the Falcon Iron Works, as it was to become, coincide there on Bankside, on the cusp of a world that was passing and a new one that was soon to come.

Chapter V

GENTEEL HOUSES AND
A GLAMOROUS TRADE

The impetus to rebuild the fabric of London was not only driven by the wish to avert further terrible conflagrations. For the first time, those in charge of the spreading metropolis had a vision of the *kind* of town they wanted the capital to be. This owed much to the Palladian ideals that had been first expressed by Inigo Jones in the days of James and Charles I, and which surfaced after the Great Fire in the form of a grandiose Venetian style design for the Thames's north bank. This never got built – the wharf owners would certainly have objected. Nor were other schemes that were equally visionary and short on practicality, such as the transformation of the dirty Fleet ditch, which poured into the Thames opposite the Paris Garden, into an arcaded ship canal.

But the spirit of these grand projects was now diffused into a general architectural agreement about what was correct. The late seventeenth-century perception among educated people was that there was a universal law of proportion and beauty, of which architecture was only one manifestation. House widths in relation to heights, the placing of windows and their corresponding height and breadth, all now began to be codified. So was the positioning of houses. It had been a peculiarity of London that substantial and even aristocratic mansions were often approached down narrow side lanes, but this was to become a thing of the past. The country-style individualism of London building practices, in which each house was built by rule of thumb according to the fancy and habits of the original owner, and then enlarged and altered in any direction to meet the needs of subsequent ones, was to be controlled. Only four distinct types of house were now officially recognised – a concept of the Building Act of 1667 that was to dominate the building and leasing systems for the next two hundred years. These types were, firstly, mansion houses; secondly, big houses with four storeys, basements and attics; and thirdly more ordinary houses of three storeys, basement or cellar and attic, 'fronting streets and lanes of note and the Thames' – a category which covered huge numbers of the newly built houses, including those along Bankside. In the fourth category were two-storeyed houses for occupants in a more modest way of life, and only these were thought suitable for the by-lanes. Most importantly, none of the houses was to have an upper storey, or added further storeys, jutting out from the lower in the time-honoured way, nor dormer windows projecting from the walls, nor outward-opening casements. Instead, sliding sash windows (a new idea imported from Holland) were set flush with the walls. The one major characteristic shared by all these new constructions, whatever their size, was the flat front, and the scaling down of the pitched roof so that it partially disappeared behind this façade.

'Façade' is, however, the word. These new houses were not really as different from the old ones as at first they seemed. Although the classic terrace house that evolved then appeared to be a brick building, it still contained a great deal of timber both in its structure and in its internal finishing. Partitions between rooms and round the staircase were often still entirely of wood; at intervals even in the brick walls bond timbers were laid, to stabilize the whole structure while the lime-mortar slowly dried and also to provide fixings for panelling, lintels, etc. in the old way. After the 1707 and 1709 Acts exterior wooden eaves and cornices were not officially to be allowed, and the wooden sash windows, with their internal shutters, were supposed to be set back four inches from the outer brick, which meant that the brick walls had in theory to be thicker. But in practice these further stipulations were only implemented gradually, and in any case did not strictly apply to houses outside the confines of the City. Number 49 Bankside, built not long after these Acts, shows even today all the internal signs of having been hand-crafted to fit the site in the medieval way.

For all the talk about classic proportion and harmony, most of the new houses occupied the same sort of space as the medieval or Tudor houses they replaced. Much has been written about the logistics of London estate development, but it seems that the system of long, narrow land-holdings, running back from the street in strips, had fixed itself in the London psyche well before the Georgian speculative builders came along to maximise the financial potential of such plots. So ancient custom lay behind the house-frontages of sixteen, eighteen or twenty feet which now became arbitrarily established (according to the house's social status) as the basic unit of measurement from which all the other 'harmonious proportions' were calculated. But in the case of number 49 the identification with the former building on the site is closer and more intricate than this. For it was built in the actual footprint of the Cardinal's Hat, re-using not only the footings but the two deep Elizabethan cellars, front and back, with their timbered and vaulted roofs and stone-flagged floors, where Fritter and his predecessors stored their barrels. Some of the central chimney stack may have been used as well.

The house as it was built c.1710 stands today with its frontage only slightly modified by a later addition of stucco and new window and door cornices. What appears to be the front door, with a fanlight in the style of the time as if to light a passageway behind, opens onto Bankside. It is set to one side, in a way that was to become general for houses of that class, with one window alongside, two on the first floor and two on the second in the approved 'harmonious' manner. But, when it was built, was this door really the principal entry? For it leads not into the standard hallway/passage, with a room to one side and stairs at the end, of later Georgian houses. Instead, it opens directly into a pleasant panelled room, with a window-seat overlooking the river and a fireplace set diagonally in the far corner. We might almost be in the parlour-bar of Fritter's tavern.

So which way is number 49 really orientated? The front façade is only sixteen foot wide, but the house goes back much further. The nearest thing to a hallway is beyond a doorway at the far end of the front room, in the middle of the house. Here, quite out of sight from the Bankside door and facing sideways to it anyway, the square, dog-leg staircase rises in an open well, with its original newel-posts and oak treads intact. It also descends from the same point into the cellars. The corner-set flue backs up against this staircase, and naturally this pattern continues on the upper floors and also down below. Here is the central nexus of the building around which the rest of the house is deployed. This was a not uncommon pattern in late seventeenth- and very early eighteenth-century town houses, but in most of them an internal side passage leading to this centre from the door at the front gave an appearance of new urban logic to what was, in essence, a traditional, rural-type structure.[1]

With 49, however, these vernacular origins are much clearer. For down Cardinal Cap Alley at the side of the house, roughly at its mid-point, are the remains of another substantial entry, now blocked up, with a gridded light above it. If you could get in here, you would step directly into the central lobby with the staircase facing you and a room opening off on either side. Here in the by-lane, I suggest, was the main door of the inn, allowing people to come and go both from Bankside and from the gardens and lanes behind. And here too, I think, when the house was remodelled and given a brick face-lift, did the old entry survive and for a long time was probably more used than the cosmetic Bankside door which led straight into a room. The entrance in the centre of the house would obviously have been more convenient for deliveries (unlike later Georgian houses, 49 never had a basement area with its own service-stairs) and also more convenient for servants, children and anyone else coming into the house to run directly up those wide, creaking stairs with their hint of a ship's ladder. Some timbering apparent in the wall where the stairs go down to the cellars, and in the main beams of the cellar itself, suggest days far more distant than those of Queen Anne. What we have here in 49, surrounded by wood and airy spaces, with Fritter's cavernous storehouse below, is only the simulacrum of an eighteenth-century terrace house with its front on the street. The benign ghost that co-exists on the same site is that of a much older structure, built sideways on, with its gable-end to Bankside.[2]

Although owning a few houses had long been a popular way of securing an income, especially for respectable widows, the logistics of this meant that the majority of Londoners had always been tenants paying an annual rent. This system in fact continued well into the twentieth century and ran right through society: it should not be taken as indication that the tenants were necessarily of any lower social status than the landlords, nor that the landlords themselves were wealthy. It is clear, however, that the people who lived in 49 Bankside when it was newly rebuilt were not among London's poor. I do not know if the property-owning Bruce sisters lived there themselves, nor whether either of them had acquired a different name through marriage; none of the Poor Rate and Land Rate records for St Saviour's parish have survived from before the year 1748. (Such records are the main source for information on pre-Census populations. The very fact of being liable to pay one or both of these rates indicates a social and financial status above that of ordinary working people.)

We know that the gentlemanly Oldner family lived near to 49. There was also, quite early in the century, an Edmund Shallett living nearby whose father, Arthur, had been a founder of the Baptist chapel and school in Zoar Street: references crop up elsewhere to 'Shallett's chapel'. In the 1740s the Shalletts acquired another house by renting it from

William Oldner, nephew and heir of Sir Richard, and this house was to become 46 Bankside. Another family, who came to own several houses in that part of Bankside besides the one they lived in and remained there for much of the century, were the Astells or Astills, boat-builders. A further substantial inhabitant for a time was a John Cator, who was to be an executor for Henry Thrale, the brewery owner, and whose descendants were to lay out the Cator estate in Greenwich.

These people were worlds away from the fashionably idle society of the newly built quarter of St James's. But it is equally certain that they were far from being what their contemporary Daniel Defoe called 'the mechanick part of mankind . . . the meer labouring people who depend on their hands.' The popular history of our own egalitarian time has perpetrated a misleading two-nations or upstairs-downstairs view of past societies, as if to be rich or poor in eighteenth-century London were the only alternatives. But in reality, more than any Continental city at that time, London was characterised by a large and constantly increasing class of what Defoe called 'the middling sort, who live well.' These were not people with money behind them, but those in some sort of trade or who owned small-scale manufactures – most enterprises were small then, by later standards, usually employing no more than half a dozen people. Although they probably did not get their hands dirty or callused, 'the middling sort' had to work hard and keep their wits about them to maintain the position to which they had risen.

But their wives did not need to labour, either at some money-earning occupation of their own or at the heavy work within their own homes. In fact Continental visitors were surprised at what relatively easy lives such married women had compared with the French or German housewife. London was famous as a town of shops, so that by the eighteenth century the London housewife no longer needed to spin, brew or make her own bread, or candles, as her counterpart had done in previous generations. She would, however, have been likely to undergo numerous child-births (even the illustrious Mrs Thrale, in the big Bankside brewery later in the century, was almost constantly pregnant) and she would have had the children that survived round her feet a good deal. She would have stitched many of their clothes and would have taught them herself, at any rate while they were small. The upper-middle-class Victorian habit of segregating the children at the top of the house with a Nurse in charge lay far in the future, and servants in a house like 49 had too much physical labour to be able to baby-mind effectively as well. Of course the children of 'the middling sort' needed to acquire literacy, and manners and, unlike the offspring of humble people, the boys would not have been expected to join their fathers in the shop or workshop until they were of a suitable age to be formally apprenticed. It is no doubt significant of a general ease of living, as well as of the prudence of the self-made businessman, that the eighteenth-century English had the reputation of being kinder to their children than were their Continental counterparts and of taking more trouble with them.

It is difficult to generalise because 'the middling sort' were such a large, catch-all group, ranging from prosperous craftsmen and master-watermen to well-to-do merchants, but essentially the people who lived in 49 when its handsome panelling was new were not needy. They could afford to keep a servant or two, although these were usually very young girls who might require a good deal of supervision and teaching by example. The employers could read and write and had the spare energy to take an interest in the world at large – the first daily newspaper started in 1702. They attended church or chapel; they had few but relatively expensive clothes of good cloth; they could entertain guests elegantly, if they wished, in their first-floor room with its view of St Paul's. They weren't, perhaps, quite gentlefolk (though the old appellation 'gentleman' for a member of the landed upper classes was being more and more widely applied to anyone who looked and sounded the part) but they might reasonably expect, if business continued to prosper, that their sons or grandsons might be gentlefolk. Meanwhile, it was reckoned that on an income of no more than £50 a year (which was about three to five times that of a labouring man) a small family could live, with care, in genteel comfort – though many 'middling people' had a considerably higher income than that.

Our popular image of eighteenth-century interiors is largely derived from the surviving grand houses of the time, and should be treated with caution. It is nevertheless true that general levels of both comfort and gentility in London were steadily increasing. Just as, in the seventeenth century, pewter had replaced the old wooden trenchers and chairs had replaced the oak benches and stools, so now blue and white 'Oriental' pottery – much of it made along the river in Lambeth – became more widely used, and chairs became more comfortable with new paddings. Small 'Turkey' carpets now covered bare boards. It would seem from this – though I have not seen the point expressly made – that those age-old household nuisances, rats and fleas, had at last been banished from well-run homes, though constant vigilance was no doubt still required to protect the nice new furnishings. In addition to the heavy old cupboards, lacquered cabinets appeared, and cane work from India and small marquetry tables; silver tankards and bowls were more widely distributed, so were mirrors and prints. A clock became a standard feature of a comfortable home, as did tea-pots, tea-caddies and delicate cups for the new expensive habit of 'taking tay'. Candles, earlier carried around in single candlesticks, could now be stuck in fixed wall-sconces, often with a mirror behind them to reflect more light.

But sheer space in a family house was still quite restricted, as compared with later English middle-class norms: living rooms frequently contained beds that folded away for the day into cupboards or were tipped up and disguised as bookcases. In 49, the one or two servants may have slept in the attic, which at that date was a small room tucked away behind the cornice so as not to spoil the house's 'rational proportions'. (The present larger attic is a twentieth-century addition.) But there cannot have been anything of a subterranean 'below-stairs' life in this house in the eighteenth or much of the nineteenth century: its cellars, built long before for storage not for habitation, were penetrated by little air or daylight, and artificial light was not then a feasible option. I am not even sure that, in the eighteenth century, the cellar at the front had the narrow, gridded opening in the pavement above that appears in early twentieth-century photos. (This was covered in again by the 1950s.) It is most likely, given Bankside's vulnerability to flooding up to the late nineteenth century, that the front cellar had no opening to daylight at all and therefore could never have functioned as the classic Georgian or Victorian kitchen.

I believe that the kitchen was where it had probably been in the days of the inn: in the back room on the ground floor which opened onto the yard and garden. The front room, on the opposite side of the central lobby and stairs, may have served as a family dining room – although, within a generation or two, it had probably become a place of male resort, where the master of the house and his associates smoked and talked and where paperwork was done. In any case, it was customary in the eighteenth century for meals to be taken in the best room in the house, usually (as in 49) the first-floor front room, even when this room also served as a bedchamber.

A business or trading household rose early to keep the apprentices or men in the workshop up to the mark. The master and his wife breakfasted on bread rolls and hot drinks: chocolate, coffee or tea. The habit of drinking small ale for breakfast as at other meals, which ran through all the preceding centuries, was dying out among the politer classes. Dinner, the main meal, had traditionally been eaten at midday and continued to be in working-class households, but in middle-class circles it was slipping to two or even later as the main part of the day was used for more pressing matters. Supper was therefore a fairly light meal: bread and cheese and ale, perhaps, or apple pie maybe, with more tea. The sober Dissenting tendency on Bankside probably meant that 'ardent spirits . . . mixed with hot water' appeared less liberally there than elsewhere, though the idea of total abstinence from alcohol had not yet set in. A visiting Frenchman[3] provided the following description of dinner 'among the middling sort', apparently regarding it as more succulent than the usual dinner across the Channel:

'. . . they have ten or twelve sorts of common meats, which infallibly take their turns at their tables, and two dishes are their dinners: a pudding, for instance, and a piece of roast beef; another time they will have a piece of boil'd beef, and then they salt it some days beforehand, and besiege it with five or six heaps of cabbage, carrots, turnips, or some other herbs or roots, well pepper'd and salted, and swimming in butter: a leg of roast or boil'd mutton dish'd up with the same dainties, fowls, pigs, ox tripe, and tongues, rabbits, pidgeons, all well-moisten'd with butter, without larding . . .'

The amount of meat consumed in England, rather than the Continental staple of bread, had long been a source of foreign comment. No wonder large numbers of farmers, small-holders and market gardeners from the country round made their entire living by providing for London tables, bringing their produce several times a week to markets such as the one in Borough High Street.

The back room on the first floor of 49 would have been used for sleeping but perhaps also as an extra sitting room. There were two similar-sized rooms on the floor above. Off each of the two larger upstairs rooms was a small closet. This was not a cupboard nor, yet, a water closet, but the only form of private space in houses where the other rooms had multiple uses. This closet might contain a dressing table or a wash-stand, a wig-stand, a locked cabinet for jewellery or papers, perhaps a writing desk. There would be a chamber-pot kept there, or possibly a more comfortable close-stool (commode), for the only lavatory at 49 at this period, as in all but very grand houses, was a privy somewhere outside at the back. This would have had no water, but went down straight into a cess-pit, individual or shared with another house. Chamber-pots were often used in the main rooms as well as in the closets, called for as needed with a nonchalance we would today find hard to emulate. They were afterwards removed by the servant for emptying in the privy, carried down the same staircase up which the steaming roast dinner had recently been brought. Sluttish servants, according to the satirist Swift, thought nothing of answering the front door pot in hand, and were quite likely to deposit the contents in the street gutter if that saved a trip to the back regions.

There were no drains on Bankside at this date, as we understand drains: only open ditches meant for rain water (though frequently sullied with other matter). Water for washing, cooking and drinking was mainly supplied through pipes from the 'water engine' at Bankend, towards London Bridge, which raised water from the river. It would have been an intermittent, unpressurised supply to the ground floor only, usually running into a lead cistern in the kitchen or yard. Many houses supplemented this with a rain-water cistern also, for in spite of the heaviness of water and the floors up which it had to be carried, foreigners commented on how much water the English used and how clean inside their houses were. No doubt this was all part of a concerted effort to counteract the dirt of London without: the greasy black mud in the mainly unpaved side streets, and the capital's growing problem of soot from the burning of coal in open grates. But coal-dust was a problem indoors too; so were the stains left on walls and ceilings by the burning of the smelly, guttering tallow candles which were the standard form of light after dark. Beeswax candles were expensive luxuries, and domestic oil-lamps, with their superior light, still lay many decades in the future.

The fact is that, for all its improved comfort and fine wood panelling and its air of elegance, in the eighteenth century 49 Bankside must have been, on winter nights, a place of icy draughts through the sash windows and shutters, with only oases of warmth in front of the fireplaces – so much less effective, foreigners complained, than sensible stoves. Yellow candle-light made only feeble pools amid the surrounding darkness, with no lamps even outside but those provided at doorways by individuals, or by the occasional shop-window lit with many candles to advertise its wares. In summer, the sulphurous scent of burning coal might have been less, though it still had to be used for cooking, but through the open windows would have come a medley of other smells: hot pies, raw fish, dead rabbits and live chickens hawked on the street, joints being carried to and from cook-shops, the coarse 'black soap' used for scrubbing, the household privy, the street gutter, the neighbour's stable. In addition, there was the dank, watery scent of the ever-present river, and its muddy shore below the Bankside which was exposed at each low tide and onto which the open ditches poured their contents. Nearer St Saviour's, where the old houses had not been rebuilt, in the ancient heart of what was commonly known as 'the Clink Liberty', St Mary Overie's Dock was contaminated with slaughter-house refuse not far from the point where water was raised by the 'engine' to be piped to households. There was an early workhouse among the lanes, overlooking a burial ground, and, as the century went on, this area round the old Bishop's palace acquired a reputation for poverty. No wonder Bankside itself, however neat its new houses and fine its view, never became truly fashionable.

The English use of coal for domestic heating and cooking, and the prodigal way it was burnt in open grates, was a frequent source of comment among visitors from abroad. By the early eighteenth century coal had become a key commodity for London and was soon to become so for many other towns. Coal was to fuel the industrial revolution which, occurring earlier in Britain than anywhere else, was to carry the British into a position of power and influence unparalleled in the world. It was also to play a major role in the individual history of 49 Bankside.

Up to the mid-sixteenth century London householders, like those everywhere else in the land, had burnt only wood. But the demand for wood was huge, and growing, since it was used to make practically everything, from buckets and tools to houses and the ships that were so important to

England's power and prosperity. Much was also burnt to make charcoal to fuel the gradually developing industries. The little coal that was extracted, mainly from open-cast sites, might be used in some of these, but in general the furnaces and kilns that made iron, tiles, bricks, pottery and glass, the ovens that refined sugar, made soap and saltpetre, dried malt and hops for brewing and baked bread – all were traditionally dependent on supplies of wood. By the time Elizabeth was on the throne it was obvious that the heritage of forests had dwindled alarmingly; prices of wood began to rise, and attention was turned to coal. The 'sea-coal' that had been brought by ship in small amounts from Newcastle to London since the thirteenth century now arrived in much larger quantities. At first used just for industry – it was made obligatory for glassworks in 1615 – it soon moved 'from the forge into the kitchen and hall'.[4] It was soft, brownish coal with a faintly sulphurous smell: wood was considered nicer, so the Palace of Westminster and other grand mansions went on burning logs. It was the mass of ordinary Londoners who took to coal.

By the Civil War, when winter supplies were temporarily disrupted while the royalists held Newcastle and some of the poor were said to have died of cold, coal was recognised to be 'absolutely necessary to the maintenance and support of [London] life'. After the Restoration it was the generally used domestic fuel even in wealthy households. It was also a valuable commodity, subject to City speculation. Unlike their Continental neighbours, the younger sons of great families in post-Restoration England did not hesitate to go into what later generations of the same families would stigmatise as 'trade'. Many landed families in the north of England were delighted to exploit the seams of coal discovered on their land, while others bought into trading and mining ventures. 'Coal-merchant' was then a term for a substantial stake-holder: it had none of the connotations of lower-class grime it was later to acquire when the description was appropriated by minor middle-men. Sir Edmund Berry-Godfrey, the one who was implicated in the 'Popish Plot' of

1678 and was later found murdered on Primrose Hill, dealt
in coal and wood, supplying Whitehall customers. He owned
a house and wharf near Charing Cross, where Northumberland Avenue now runs down to the Embankment. A
hundred years later the great coal firm of Charringtons was
established at the same address.

Taxes on coal brought in important revenues for the
Crown, and extra taxes were imposed for specific ends, such
as rebuilding St Paul's and other churches after the Fire and
– later – the construction of bridges. These additional levies,
plus the transport costs and the numerous middle-men,
raised the cost of coal to London customers to five times the
cost at the pit mouth. But at the same time the government
tried to keep prices down by waging an interminable war on
price-fixing cartels and other forms of corruption, such as
short-measure, or hoarding by suppliers when bad weather
or enemy action interrupted the trade from the coaling ports.
Pepys recorded in 1667, when Rochester was blockaded by
the Dutch and the colliers could not make it up the Thames
to the Pool of London, 'the want already of coals and the
despair of having any'. The usual London price of about
£1.10s. a chaldron (the unsatisfactorily imprecise heaped
measure of between twenty-five and twenty-eight hundredweight that was then used) had gone up to £5.10s. It
returned to base a few months later. Though the shortage
was real, some people certainly made a good thing out of it.
On a national level, the coal-industry was the equivalent of
the petroleum-oil industry of our own day, with Tyneside
and its fortunes as susceptible to outside interference as those
of the Gulf States. Coal was 'Newcastle gold'.

Coal-burning, however, was pollutant. It was to be the
origin, by the nineteenth century, of those famous London
fogs which were to take on a life of their own in the
imaginations of people across the world. The fogs had not
yet appeared in the later part of the seventeenth century, but
the dirt of coal was becoming evident. John Evelyn devoted
a whole short book to the subject (*Fumifugium*, 1661),
declaring passionately:

'The weary Traveller, at many miles distance, sooner smells, than sees the City to which he repairs. This is that pernicious Smoake which sullyes all her Glory, superinducing a sooty Crust or furr upon all that it lights, spoyling the moveables, tarnishing the Plates Gildings, and Furniture, and corroding the very Iron-bars and hardiest stones with those piercing and acrimonious Spirits which accompany its Sulphure . . . It is this horrid Smoake which obscures our Churches, and makes our Palaces look old, which fouls our Clothes, and corrupts the waters, so that the very Rain, and refreshing Dews which fall in the several seasons, precipitate this impure Vapour, which, with its black and tenacious quality, spots and contaminates whatsoever is expos'd to it . . .' He also maintained, possibly with reason, for he was an expert gardener, that the fall-out of soot damaged flower buds and killed bees. The proof of this was that in a recent year, when Newcastle was blockaded and coal consumption in London dropped right down – 'Divers Gardens and Orchards planted even in the very heart of London . . . were observed to bear such plentiful and infinite quantities of Fruits, as they never produced the like either before or since' – a claim that provides a telling glimpse into a metropolis that still had plantations near its centre. Smuts, he said, also got onto clothes laid out to dry and onto the 'Hands, Faces and Linnen of our fair ladies'. Soot was bad for the health too, probably leading to 'Consumptions, Phthisicks, and Indisposition of the Lungs . . . There is under Heaven such a Coughing and Snuffing to be heard, as in the London Churches and Assemblies of People, where the Barking and the Spitting is incessant and most importunate.'

But Evelyn felt that coal-burning home hearths were less to blame than the chimneys of 'Brewers, Diers, Limeburners, Salt, and Sope-boylers'. In this opposition to industries within cities, he was more than two hundred years in advance of his time. He singled out for particular dislike 'a Lime-kiln on the Bankside near the Falcon', which, he said, sent smoke in clouds towards St Paul's, creating a fog 'thick and dark'. Since the south bank lime-kilns were down river in Bermondsey, I suspect that what he may actually have been looking at was the ironworks that were to provide St Paul's railings. A glassworks with a large, cone-shaped brick kiln was also to appear on Bankside near the Falcon Inn, but not for another twenty years.

As well as advocating the planting of more trees every-where to supply England's various needs, Evelyn also believed that locating sweet-smelling plantations up river in Lambeth might 'purify' the London air, driving away the smoke and infection with it – an early example of the pre-occupation with air-borne ills that was long to characterise the British social reformer. And Evelyn's complaints came near the beginning of the rise of King Coal. The 'sooty crust or furr' was, by the following century, getting relentlessly worse. It was still firmly adhering to London surfaces two hundred years after that, and remains engrained today in the memory of Londoners who were alive and aware before the 1960s.

No wonder the Londoners of the eighteenth century took to cleaning their houses with so much water. They could do little about the outside bricks, but they could at least take a pride in keeping their interiors nice – interiors that were furnished now with the very comforts and elegances that England's growing manufacturing wealth was helping to fund. The dirt and the money had a common source.

At one end of the early-capitalist chain that was now taking shape were the merchants operating from the City, who either owned mines themselves or bought and sold whole ship-loads of coal as these made their (sometimes perilous) journey round the East Anglian coast. And at the other end were the street hawkers, who peddled coal to those with only one hearth and no storage space, selling it by the half-bushel – a measure of volume roughly equivalent to four one-gallon petrol cans. But who came in between?

There were of course the masters of the collier-ships from Tyneside, who took their cut. So did the various factors whose job it was to market the coal wholesale once it arrived in the Thames, and the 'coal-meters' who watched over the stuff as it was weighed out. But at this stage, rather than being unloaded straight onto a wharf, where space was at a premium, much of the cargo would be unloaded downstream into a lighter, one of the all-purpose Thames cargo-boats, which could then deliver it to where it was wanted by retailers.[5]

In 1729 a pamphlet row broke out about monopolies in the coal-industry, and a cabal of ship-owners and factors combining to manipulate prices. One of these factors was a Quaker called Benjamin Horne, of a family whom we shall meet again on Bankside. The lynchpin of the association was said to be the owner of a tavern in Billingsgate where all agreements were negotiated: then and for a long time to come, tavern keepers were inextricably bound up with the coal-market and with the hiring of the men who heaved the sacks around. The ship-owners and factors retorted that they were simply protecting themselves against a similar combination of lightermen to whom back-handers had to be given, since 'two Parts in three of all the Coals that are brought to London, are brought by the artful Management of about fifteen Lightermen'. A further pamphlet disagreed with this, since '. . . there are about eight hundred Lytermen who keep Lyters and Barges . . . above three hundred of these make it their business to load and carry coal'.[6]

The result of this airing of grievances was a new Act, allowing anyone who traded in coal to maintain his *own* lighters, barges and wharves, provided always that the crews were accredited watermen. This was a key moment in which the coal traders and the men of the river tacitly recognised that their futures were bound up together. Ostensibly, the benefit was to the coal-traders, who would have their own lightermen under their control, but in the long run the real beneficiaries were the lightermen, for the Act provided the opportunity for them to specialise. It was, after all, hardly desirable to put a load of wheat-flour into a barge previously used for coal. In 1730 a number of lightermen formed their own Society of Owners of Coalcraft. A future member was to become the owner of 49 Bankside.

When the watermen joined forces with the lightermen in 1700 they had, as well as their proud and antique tradition of abusive wit, newly licensed cap badges, and a new scale of fares. A proportion of them were now allowed to work on Sundays. It had also been agreed that no more watermen should be 'pressed' into service on the King's ships, as had happened to John Taylor in youth and to men more recently in the wars with the Dutch. Watermen technically counted as 'skilled labour', earning their living by their own physical exertions, subject like any other working-class journeymen to the vagaries of chance and season. But such was their status, their responsibilities and their potential earnings that they were generally regarded as a special group. Defoe recorded that some of them were 'very substantial fellows [who] maintain their families very well'. Their lifestyle, that is, approximated more to that of 'the middling sort'. So why did they decide to make common cause with the carriers of goods, whom they had always rather despised?

The answer lies in the increasing competition of road traffic and in particular hackney carriages, as London was growing so far beyond its earlier, readily walkable limits. Roads outside the town were getting much better, and regular coach and carrier services were being established on long-distance runs. At least a dozen inns in Southwark itself, as well as many in the City, were now departure and arrival points for these services, which were gradually but surely eroding the old pattern of travelling down river and round the coast to reach other parts of the British Isles. Owners of private coaches, too, wanted to be driven from home all the way to their destinations. But over the whole stretch of river between London Bridge and Putney there was no river-crossing, except by boat. The Falcon Inn on Bankside had chaises and horses for hire once that side of the river was reached by ferry, but that was not the same as setting off in your own turn-out. There was one large, flat-bottomed ferry between Westminster and Lambeth which could take horses and even a coach (its memory survives in Horseferry Road) but it had room for only one coach at a time.

So the most immediate perceived threat to the watermen's livelihood was the prospect of extra bridges across the Thames. As yet London Bridge still stood alone, choked with houses and traffic and dangerous to get through by water, but other bridges were taking shape on drawing boards. The need for one at Westminster had been mooted soon after the Restoration: the idea had been rejected by the City Corporation and the Watermen's Company banding together, but the spread of London into Westminster and St James's meant that it was soon revived. In the 1690s Parliament debated the matter, and it was observed that Paris, which London had now overtaken in both extent and population, had several bridges. It was also ominously noted by one MP that in Paris 'there is no use for watermen at all'.

Westminster Bridge was eventually opened in 1750, Blackfriars Bridge in 1769. During the same period London Bridge was denuded of its houses and widened. It is a measure of the power the watermen still enjoyed that some of the money from coal-taxes that was devoted to bridges went towards compensating them for loss of trade.

For the long slow decline of the trade was under way. Many freemen of the Watermen's Company, who had served out their apprenticeships and were not stupid, began to see that the future on London's river lay less with passenger traffic than with goods. They also saw that the goods business itself could be extended. You needed to develop your own particular line and build up your contacts . . . Then take orders, get three months' credit, and become a buyer and seller in your own right . . . A Woodmongers and Coal-Sellers Company had existed near London Bridge since the fourteenth century, but now the lightermen, combined into one Company with the Watermen, virtually cut the old Sellers Company out and were said to have complete control of the river coal-traffic.

In 1747 another of those prolific eighteenth-century

pamphleteers that were the newspaper columnists of their time wrote: 'Coal-Merchants now begin to multiply apace. If a footman had been . . . a Runner to a Coal-Owner to distribute Bills, and collect straggling Debts, why in a short time he commences Beau, puts on trimmed Cloaths, and sets himself up for a *Coal-Merchant.*'

If an essentially unskilled footman might chance his luck in the then-glamorous trade, how much better placed was a man of the river, with all his special knowledge? One of those who, in the mid-eighteenth century, turned to the coal trade and succeeded admirably, was a young waterman called Edward Sells – the first. His son, grandsons and great-grandsons were to trade on Bankside for the next hundred years. Their name is preserved even today in the discreet but long-lasting immortality of a twentieth-century poem by John Betjeman:

> . . . *Rumble under, thunder over, train and tram*
>   *alternate go,*
> *Shake the floor and smudge the ledger,*
> *Charrington, Sells, Dale and Co.,*
> *Nuts and nuggets in the window, trucks along the lines*
>   *below.*

Chapter VI

OF BONDS, LEASES AND OTHER DIRTY DELIGHTS

At first, Sells was a mere name to me on the nineteenth-century Census returns for Bankside. The earliest usable Census return dates from 1841, and is a less than satisfactory research tool since it does not number houses or necessarily distinguish separate households. But the individual names and ages (these last rounded down to the nearest multiple of five) are pregnant with potential meaning. Indeed, this is a common experience of researchers who study the Census returns: you begin to feel the weight of all those spent, packed-away lives pressing in on you, as if innumerable stilled voices were yearning wordlessly for recognition. Almost any one of the names, you believe, might be rescued from the oblivion of time and brought forward in some recognisable shape and substance if you devoted time itself – enough time – to delving away in further archives, combing parish records and ancient rate books, speculatively ordering up birth and marriage certificates, browsing among probated Wills, running an eye down the meticulously handwritten accounts of long-extinct charities, bingeing on local newspapers full of ancient quarrels . . . But how much time? Many years of a current life, you begin to realise, could be expended on the excavation of a handful of these past lives: ultimately the desire to re-confer humanity and personality on the lost runs the risk of compromising life in the present.

But with the Sells family I was lucky. Almost as soon as I began going through the eighteenth-century rate books for St Saviour's parish – the earliest extant is the record of those living comfortably enough to pay the Poor Rate in 1748 – I realised that the Sells had been present on Bankside long before Censuses were taken. They did not appear in 1748, though Edmund Shallett of the prominent Dissenting family did, and so did the Astell family of barge-builders and oar-makers, whose large timber yard is later recorded as covering part of the land behind Bankside that had once been the Queen's Pike Garden. However, in the record for 1760 we first find Edward Sells, living next door to Shallett in a house recently vacated by John Cator, who had simply moved a few doors along Bankside. I think, from the conjectural evidence of a later drawing of a run of Bankside houses, that Shallett's was probably one of the surviving timbered and gabled constructions of Elizabethan date. Maybe it had once been one of Dekker's 'continuous' ale-houses, like the equally venerable Falcon Inn a little further west. Rateable values were loosely based on the number of people a house might theoretically accommodate, so Shallett's house must have been quite big as it was assessed, in those years, at £12 per annum, resulting in a Poor Rate in 1755 of £3.18s., whereas most of the adjacent houses, including the abode of Cator and then Sells, were assessed at this period for only £2 or £3 per annum, resulting in a rate of about 13s. (Similar houses in newer districts north of the river were valued more highly.)

It would be satisfying if the house next door to Mr Shallett's, where Edward Sells was then living, was the one that later bore the number 49, but I rather think it was several doors further west. It is difficult to be sure since, as the years passed, the quantity of houses documented along Bankside increased, due to apparent in-filling and the construction of side alleys ('rents') of smaller dwellings. But working backwards from about 1780, when numbers were allocated to houses, and using the names of certain long-standing occupiers as fixed points, I believe that in his early years on Bankside young Edward Sells rented a house that later became number 54. It has long since been obliterated, first by a warehouse, then by the original, many-chimneyed power station, and today by the green grass and silver birches that surround the re-invented Power Station/Tate Modern – as if the willows of boggy Paris Garden had been born again.

So what else could I discover about the first Edward Sells, he who came to Bankside in the days when some of the 'Pye Garden' was still an orchard, and fields and hedgerows were only minutes away to the south-west, but when great changes, of which he himself was a harbinger, were already on their way?

As a member of the Honourable Company of Watermen and Lightermen he is still traceable through that Company's records, preserved in London's Guildhall. He first appears there in 1738 when he was bound apprentice. Apprenticeship, which was for seven years, normally happened at the age of fourteen or fifteen, which argues a birth date of 1723 or '24. The family lived in one of the Westminster parishes: the father was called Thomas, but there is no record of him being in the trade himself, so this apprenticeship of the son may have marked the first step for the family on the social ladder up out of the labouring classes. The conditions in which he served his apprenticeship, however, were hardly very uplifting, for his master, Samuel Price, lighterman and – yes – coal-merchant, traded near Dowgate Dock on the north bank of the Thames where the polluted Walbrook flowed through a conduit into the river. This dock, approximately opposite the point on the Surrey side at which Bankside gave way to Clink Street, where Southwark Bridge now stands, was a narrow entry for barges. It was then still the principal location for the coal-trade wharves, and was also one of the places where the night-soil men, who carted the contents of London's countless privies, were allowed to discharge their loads into the long-suffering river. The theory was that the sluggish outfall of the Walbrook, in combination with the twice-daily ebb of the tide, would

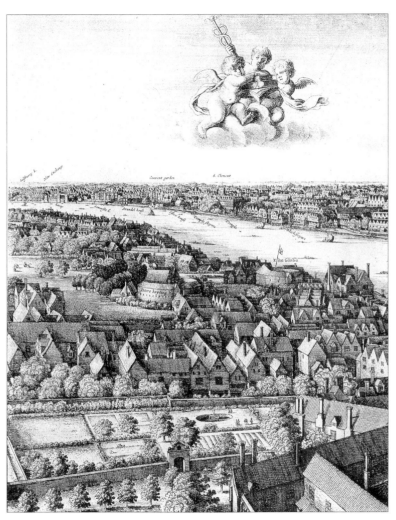

A segment of Wenceslaus Hollar's *Long View of London*, c.1640, showing Bankside with the Bishop's Palace gardens. Note the Globe theatre and the bear-baiting ring (though in fact these two have been labelled the wrong way round).

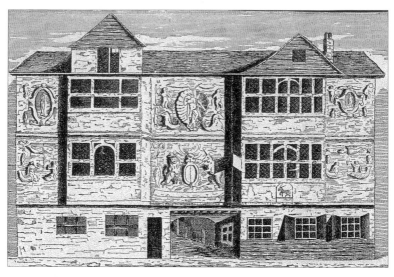

The Tudor 'Fish House' that originally formed the entrance to the Great Pyke Gardens by Mason stairs. It was not pulled down until near the end of the eighteenth century.

The Falcon Tavern, also Tudor though partially reconstructed in the late seventeenth century, drawn in 1805 when it was soon to be demolished.

1827: the run of houses on Bankside where several generations of the Sells family lived and worked. Number 49, projecting a little beyond the entrance to Cardinal Cap Alley, is instantly recognisable. While the artist (John Chessell Buckler) may have used some licence in the varying heights of the houses as they tail away to the left, his passion for detail lead him to reproduce faithfully the names 'Sells', which is just discernable in the original on the gabled house that was by then number 54, and was probably the original house leased by the first Edward Sells.

The View from Bankside, said to be c.1820 but possibly rather earlier. See the Doggetts race crew of watermen with two barges of spectators looming over them. The crew are all in red, and the man working on the quay wears a red cap.

Testimony of Edwards Sells's first venture into the coal trade, 1755.
The 'P' for Perronet seems already to have appeared in the family name.

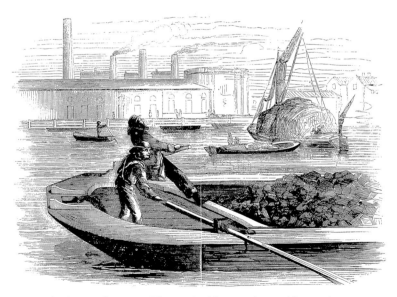

A nineteenth-century Thames Coal-boat, as depicted by Mayhew.

St Saviour's Church (earlier St Mary Overy's, today Southwark Cathedral)
still had old wooden houses crowding round it in 1827.

St Saviour's National School, built on part of the Cross Bones graveyard, 1792.

The earliest gas holders on Bankside, 1826, with the actual house in which Sir Christopher Wren is believed to have rented office-space standing alongside. This house disappeared soon after the beginning of the twentieth century.

carry everything away, eventually out to sea. Such notions of the river's hygienic power were to persist for another hundred and twenty years, eventually culminating in the crisis of the Great Stink of 1858 and the long-overdue introduction of a main drainage system.

Edward Sells duly became a freeman of the Watermen's Company in 1745, when he was twenty-two or twenty-three, and moved to the much cleaner, still-rural surroundings of St Mary's parish in Lambeth, near the horse ferry. There were no coal-wharves there then; possibly he worked as a lighterman for the timber wharves a little way downstream, for it was still customary for everyone except the very affluent and grand to live as close as possible to their place of work. In 1752 his father died, and two years later we find him taking a lease of the first of his Bankside houses. The other party to the agreement was a William Killingworth, who made blocks for the rigging of sailing ships from an address near the Tower of London: he was presumably the ground owner of the house, as he does not appear as a previous occupant paying rates. However, it is another six years before Sells himself appears as liable to pay the Poor Rate in 1760 – years during which one must suppose that the lighterman was saving to buy first one barge and then another, and by this means gradually making his way into the modest comfort of 'the middling sort'.

His move to Bankside was a shrewd one, for it was during those middle years of the century that the coal-wharves had begun to shift there: the Rocque map of 1746 marks several. Both Edmund Shallett and another prominent neighbour, Edmund Smith, had interests in the coal business. They were apparently part-owners of a mine, but I do not know if they traded in coal themselves. They were business associates of Thomas Horne, of the Sussex Quaker family who had set themselves up as coal-merchants a generation before and had prospered greatly. Thomas began trading on Bankside in 1762, and two years later bought one of the houses near number 49 that had earlier belonged to the Oldner family, and then to Ralph Thrale the brewer. Ten years later he,

Shallett and Smith, together with a baronet and a lady from Greenwich, were sued for compensation because their miners in Northumberland had broken through a coal face to an adjacent mine and taken its coal – a not uncommon occurrence in those days when mines were an unsurveyed labyrinth. They paid out the then very considerable sum of £600, which indicates the substantial world these people inhabited.

Edward Sells's concern with the coal-trade was, as yet, at a more literally hands-on level, but he had in fact embarked, as soon as he had settled on Bankside, on what was to become the family business, handed down through the generations. I know this since, by a fluke, a piece of testimony to it survived into the mid-twentieth century. In 1755 he and a Matthew Arnold, who seems to have been another lighterman, put their confident signatures to the market sale note for an entire shipload of coals, which the ship-master was selling them for £30.10s., at 30s.6d. the chaldron. I rather think this must have been Sells's first real venture into the marketing business. Why, otherwise, should this solitary bit of paperwork, without lasting practical importance, have been preserved in the family as a token of his life's endeavour long after he himself was gone?

In October 1763, when he was about forty and twin children of his were baptised in St Saviour's, he was still giving his occupation as 'lighterman', rather than 'coal-merchant' as he styled himself in later life. The babies must have been conceived in the depth of a cold spell that had occurred the previous winter, when all river-traffic was at a standstill. Edward Sells's wife was called Martha. I do not know when they were married, but logic would suggest that the twins were their first children, since the boy and girl were christened Edward and Martha after both their parents.

Forty was then rather an advanced age for an ordinary man to become a father for the first time. I cannot help wondering if there had been an earlier wife who died in childbirth, an earlier small Edward who did not survive: one of those irrecoverable domestic griefs that our ancestors had stoically to contain? (Even Mrs Thrale, living by then in some state in the big house attached to the brewery at Bankend where Dr Johnson was soon to be a frequent vistor, lost child after child.) I came across the twins' christening in the St Saviour's baptism records for the 1760s and '70s. These are not quite complete and in places illegible, so I may have missed other Sells births, or indeed Sells burial entries with the poignantly commonplace inscription 'Inf' alongside that indicates a child. But had such events been numerous in the Sells's household I would have found some: a few other Bankside names crop up in those tattered papers quite regularly. What I do know is that the twins lived, for it was this second Edward who was to follow in his father's footsteps and consolidate the family fortunes.

The market sale note, from a few years before the twins' birth, I have seen reproduced in a privately printed book on the origins of the coal-trade that was published in 1931.[1] Extracts from the lease that Edward Sells took on his first house on Bankside (see below) are to be found quoted in another privately commissioned company history that came my way, that of the Charringtons, written c.1950. It was clear to me from these two books that, when they were being researched, a substantial archive concerning many inter-woven coal-dealing families existed in the bosom of the huge firm of Charringtons, who had eventually absorbed them all. In 1952 Charringtons employed two thousand five hundred people, and the book's author could express confident thanks to 'those who preserved the records through the years, for the interest and perhaps the edification of their descendants today. May my successor, writing in the year 2000, be equally fortunate.'

Alas. When I, as a 'successor', went looking for this same archive, believing that such a prestigious firm would surely have ensured its future reputation, whatever decline in the coal-trade may have supervened, I found precisely – nothing. The firm no longer exists, and it was not one of the many former enterprises with a head-office in the City which bestowed its papers on the Guildhall archive collection. I followed the trail as far as I was able, but it began to be clear that at some point in the 1970s, as Charringtons was finally swallowed up by an international consortium of oil interests, everything – eighteenth-century house deeds, bills of sale, letter books, ledgers, early photographs and goodness knows what other evidence of a great commercial empire in an epic era of trade – must simply have been dumped into a skip.

All this history was probably disposed of into a landfill site near the Thames mouth, the very place past which so many coal-boats had once come. With it had disappeared the last remaining physical evidence of the first Sells on Bankside.

So I cannot quote in full the description from the lease of Edward Sells's original home there, but only those parts of it I have seen reproduced. It was apparently described as a 'wharf' (a river frontage with berthing rights), shed, back yard and house at Mason stairs', which would indicate a house a few doors up river from number 49. It had been formerly occupied by another lighterman. Sells signed up for fourteen years at an annual rent of £10, payable quarterly; though in fact it would seem from the rates record that he then renewed the lease for another seven years after that. What appears to be the same house, by then numbered 54, crops up in a Land Valuation record in the early 1800s, fifty years later, as 'a house, rooms and shed next the River', by then valued at £22 a year. Clearly, with its rights over the quay, and with one of the many river water-stairs opposite, it was just the place for a man carrying on a river trade.

A brief extract from the fixtures and fittings mentioned in the 1754 lease gives some idea of the level of simple comfort the Sells enjoyed, including a water supply. It was evidently a two-storey house, probably plus attic. The upper floor seems to be described first:

'*In the one pair of stairs back-room*, a Closet, one shelf, one row of pins [i.e. clothes hooks], two Windows and two Bars, one Chimney board and Wainscot up to the Ceiling.' (So, a house with a good deal of wood panelling in it, like 49.)

. . . '*In the back Parlor* a Beaufet ['buffet' = dresser] with five shelves for Pewter . . . *in the Wash-house forward* One leaden Cistern, A Leaden Pump and Sink lined with Lead . . . *In the backyard* the pavement with Newcastle stone, a door to the Necessary house in the shed over the Wharf.'[2]

The geography is not quite clear: the 'backyard' must have been at the side rather than right behind the house, if it gave access directly to the quay, but there can be no mistaking the nature of the 'Necessary house in the shed over the Wharf'. Evidently, a number of the Bankside houses at this date, instead of the usual privy over a cess-pit somewhere at the back, made use of latrines straight over the river: convenience, indeed, if by then of a rather old-fashioned sort. The Holland's Leaguer house, the one-time brothel a little upstream near Paris Garden stairs, which was finally pulled down in the 1760s when Blackfriars Bridge was built, is said to have had its own latrines over the river in the previous century, augmented by a system for pumping water up to turn them into water closets – a revolutionary luxury in Stuart times.

In the mid-eighteenth-century the water closet was still a rare object mainly confined to the London houses of the very wealthy, but ideas about the best way of disposing of human waste were gradually changing. This shift is discernible in the reports of Town Hall sessions on problems arising in the local sewers; these were not intended to be sewers in our sense of the word but were, rather, open ditches to act as storm drains. On Bankside, they ran down at intervals into the Thames through sluices with ancient names. There were four of these between London Bridge and Paris Garden stairs (one, Boars Head Sluice, emerged under Moss Alley, just up river from number 49). There was continual trouble about their blocking and requiring to be cleared, usually by the proprietors of the adjoining properties who owned that section of the quay. Elsewhere in Southwark the parish 'scavengers' or 'rakers' were supposed to clear out and dredge the wayside ditches that were the remnants of the medieval land-drainage system, but it is clear that since time immemorial local householders had been erecting latrines over them. What is significant is that complaints about these 'boghouses' in St Saviour's parish become numerous only around the middle of the eighteenth century, as if it was only then that public opinion began to find such practices unacceptable.

The earliest complaint I have found was in 1743. Thomas Stonor was told to stop up the 'Six Brick Drains of his Boghouses at the Back of his several Tenants in the Bear Gardens, Maid Lane' – but after about 1760 such complaints become a feature of every session. Constructing actual brick drains was clearly taking far too much of a liberty: most of the boghouses appear to have been more flimsy structures in people's vegetable gardens where these abutted conveniently onto ditches, as in Bandy Leg Walk and Gravel Lane. There were also complaints about animal manure, reminding one how rural Southwark still was at this date: 'We amorse Thomas Tiller of the parish of St Saviour's in Southwark . . . for suffering his hog soil to run into the common sewer on the back of Mr Astill's premises on the Bankside' (1761). That was to cost Mr Tiller the not inconsiderable sum of £5, or £10 if the ditch were not scoured within a reasonable time. Taking one's neighbours to the justices in the Town Hall on such matters was probably a last resort.

In May 1775 a watermen's regatta was held on the Thames with flags and bands – perhaps a riposte to the new bridges. A couple of months before, Edward Sells and his growing family had moved five doors eastwards. This house is now easy to pinpoint in the records because, for the first time, Cardinal Cap Alley is listed alongside separately from Bankside: some small houses had been built down it. The Sells's new home, which we will now refer to as 49, was bigger than the old one, less of a workplace and more of a comfortable family abode. The head of the house may have used the ground-floor front room, with the door that opened conveniently straight onto the quay, as an office where work-visitors could call without disturbing the rest of the household, but any shed or store would have been at the back of the yard with direct access via the alley.

Evidence from his Will near the end of the century suggests that he leased the house at first from a neighbour, and then bought the freehold two years later. He was clearly prospering, and no doubt employing others on the river, as his income now put him into the category of those liable not only for the Poor Rate but also for the Land Tax.

Later evidence indicates that, as the years went by, numbers 54, 55 and 56 were also bought by the Sells family, and that eventually they owned numbers 50, 51 and 52 as well. (For whatever reason, they never seem to have owned 53, an old house, I think, and later a shop.) Sometimes in subsequent generations different members of the family would use one or more of these properties as their home, sometimes also as their office, or exclusively as an office for a while. At periods this or that house would appear to be tenanted by one or another family closely associated with the Sells's business, and then revert to occupation again by a Sells son, grandson or nephew. One can thus pursue through the rates books, London Directories (after 1790) and Censuses (after 1840) a cat's cradle of interlocking relationships and house-occupancy, including also properties in the hands of other families such as the Hornes and the Joneses, who entered into various partnerships with the Sells. There were other neighbours too who made items essential for the coal-barge business, such as oars, masts and sails. The web of connections along this part of Bankside between trades, owners, occupiers, employers and employees seems to have been both socially egalitarian and extremely complex.

We, however, shall stay as far as possible with number 49 at Cardinal Cap Wharf.

The same year that his father bought 49, Edward Sells II, he who had been baptised with his sister in 1763, entered the waterman's trade in his turn at the age of fourteen. As was usual in such families, he was bound apprentice to his own father. The year before, a Thomas Arnold of St Saviour's parish had also been apprenticed: my guess is that he was the son or nephew of the Matthew Arnold who had clubbed together with Sells to buy the first ship-load of coal. These boys and their fellows must have had a rewarding childhood, growing up with boats on their doorstep, learning to row skiffs as soon as they had the strength, aware of the skilled and excitingly hazardous nature of river work long before they were allowed to participate in it in any formal way.

But Bankside, and Southwark generally, in the years when the second Edward Sells was doing his apprenticeship, was not quite the same place where his father had set up twenty-odd years before. At long last London Bridge was losing its supremacy as the only river crossing. With the building of two bridges up river between 1750 and 1770, one linking Westminster to Lambeth and the other going from Blackfriars to the old Paris Garden stretch, the whole geography of the Surrey shore was altered. A transformation that was before slow and piecemeal was now accelerated: it would culminate in Southwark at last becoming urbanised.

But did this change indicate greater 'civilisation', as our ancestors would have put it, or a social decline? This question tends to lead to generalisations about the course of London life during the eighteenth century, and these are notoriously unreliable. Two conflicting views seem to have been handed down to us, depending on the viewpoints of different witnesses at the time but also on the perspectives of those looking back from the vantage point of later generations.

On the one hand, there is the substantial figure of Hogarth: his pictures, whether showing a dissolute moneyed class devoid of any social conscience, or a brutalised and poverty-stricken underclass perpetually drunk on gin at a ha'penny a glass, have tended to loom large in our mental picture. There is also the poignant image of the retired sea-captain Thomas Coram, establishing his foundling hospital in the 1740s because he was so shocked by discarded babies he saw lying on waste ground or even in the streets. There were complaints at the time that London was growing too fast, drawing in from all over England young men and girls, prey to all kinds of moral temptations: these uprooted people, it was said, crowded into unhealthy and inadequate lodgings 'often separated from Vice only by a deal or lathe and plaster partition'.[3] The working classes had become 'insubordinate'; the town was dangerous, and the main routes leading to and from it, what with highwaymen and footpads, were even worse . . . Southwark Fair, on St George's Fields, was just the sort of rowdy gathering that should be suppressed . . .

But the reality was that Southwark Fair, like the Borough Market which was also thought objectionable, had been a feature of Southwark since the Middle Ages. It was also a fact that people had been seeking their fortunes in London for centuries, and that its inexorably growing population had always owed more to this immigration than to a high birth rate. Though London did double its population between 1710 and 1820, and remained the largest city in the world, its actual growth rate was far less than that of some northern cities, which developed over the same period from tiny market towns into industrial centres never before seen, and imposed an entirely new way of life on the masses who poured into them from country districts. There had been people in London living in squalid conditions, vulnerable to vice, since the days of the Flemish women on Bankside and doubtless long before: abandoned babies were nothing new, nor were drunkenness and violence, nor were the deaths from starvation in hard winters. The fact that these social ills now began to be commented on as something that might and should be remedied was in itself a sign of changing ideas, and of an increasing number of people with essentially altruistic views about the way society should be run. The Gin Acts of 1751 and '53, imposing taxes and limiting sales, were an early attempt by the governing classes to regulate public behaviour by means other than harsh punishment. They were the beginning of a whole raft of rules and provisions that the following century would bring. Successive generations brought new consciousness to bear on old problems, and formed the habit of congratulating themselves on society's progress compared with the situation in 'the bad old days' – whenever these were currently deemed to have been. This tendency to patronise and pity our ancestors has continued to the present day.

There is, however, another possible view of eighteenth-century London. This is of a city in which wages were high in comparison with those in major foreign cities and life generally less primitive, with a great many things to buy. To many visiting foreigners London seemed an orderly, pleasant place, where, it was commented, people were mild-tempered, beggars did not cringe, and working men did not go in fear of their masters. After the mid-century, when gin-consumption had been successfully reduced, a number of home-grown complaints actually centred on the new working-class appetite for tea and sugar ('luxurious tastes'), the amount of meat eaten by this supposedly 'degraded' class, and the fact that fine wheaten bread had now, in London and its surrounding area, largely replaced the traditional rye. The new cheap calico, as an alternative to the traditional woollen and linen cloths, now made it possible for all but the poorest women to dress in a more 'cleanly' way: this too came in for criticism on the grounds that 'you can't tell the maid from the mistress'.

The birth rate picked up after the mid-century; more children survived their first few years, and among people of all ages death rates, which had always been high in London, began to go down. Plague, which had been a regular visitant on the Bankside of Henslowe and Taylor's day, was by the eighteenth century a thing of the past. Now other traditional diseases, such as scurvy, dysentery and malarial fevers, declined also. Free lying-in hospitals and dispensaries were founded. Doctors, including a prominent Southwark medical man named Lettsom, began to have some notion of hygiene and of the importance of Good Air – an English preoccupation which was to become something of an obsession as the air generally available in London became increasingly polluted. Strolls on the new river bridges were recommended as a preventative against typhus. As for crime and violence, the reforming magistrate Sir John Fielding felt that he and his new system had had some impact on this by the mid-1770s, when he wrote that 'the rabble [were] . . . very much mended . . . within the last fifty years', while still considering them 'very insolent and abusive'.

That was, however, before the Gordon Riots of 1780, which was the last major outbreak of apparently senseless violence in London. The crowd broke open the Southwark prisons, including the Clink, and set on fire the King's Bench prison. They came near to firing the Thrale brewery on Bankside too, under the impression that Henry Thrale was 'a Papist' because he believed in religious tolerance; they were foiled only by the manager cleverly 'buying them off with meat and porter' while he called in the troops. Elsewhere in town they marched on the house of the Lord Chief Justice and burnt his library. Then Fielding's concerned comment was that 'the mob' had become a kind of fourth estate 'threatening to shake the balance of our constitution'. Prophetic words, when we consider that the French Revolution was to overwhelm France a decade later. But what is significant is that revolution did *not* occur in England, and that in retrospect the Gordon Riots appear to have been a final spasm of ancient popular violence and paranoia which, by the end of the century, was becoming a thing of the past.

Collective street life, in the form of old fêtes and fairs, was diminishing, and London's social fabric was beginning to show many of the characteristics it would have in the century to come. The mix was complicated, because, at this time, and into the nineteenth century, well-to-do households such as the Thrales would still often live cheek by jowl with the poor ones who occupied the side alleys. Each class pursued its own preoccupations, sometimes with a robust disregard for others' problems, yet shared inevitably the same environment – the same floods on Bankside, the same smells of boiling hops and tan-yards and drains, the same cries of street sellers and tolling bells of churches.

*

The major change in the course of the later Georgian period that particularly affected Bankside, followed by Southwark in general and the neighbouring and newly accessible district of Lambeth, was the arrival of many more industrial premises. The importance of industry in London from roughly the mid-eighteenth to the mid-twentieth century has been understated by many commentators, who have written as if trade, in the form of shipping and wharves, were the whole of the story. Indeed, one writing in 1925, a time when the Surrey side of the river seems to have fallen so far socially that those on the north bank hardly recognised its existence, actually described the Industrial Revolution as 'a storm that passed over London and broke elsewhere'.[4] It is true that the capital was not physically transformed by large factories in the way that some other parts of Britain were: it did not ever harbour much heavy industry. But Clerkenwell and Shoreditch, like Bermondsey, Southwark and Lambeth, all districts which had been right on the edge of London in 1700, saw over the following hundred years a great growth and proliferation in their traditional industries. Many of these required workshops rather than 'dark satanic mills'. Many were quite small firms that were containable in one-time residential buildings, old chapels, stables, ale-houses or granaries. But clustered together with others of the same kind they came to form a substantial industrial presence.

The traditional trade of Bermondsey had been leather tanning. Tanning smells awful, even without the vats of dog-excrement that were used to steep the skins, so this had for some time already made Bermondsey less than wholly desirable for living. Associated with tanning was wool-fulling, for the production of felted material for heavy coats and hats – many of the drying grounds still shown on early eighteenth-century maps of Southwark were for this purpose. Now hat making, another related trade, began to be important on the west side of London Bridge also. The Rocque map of 1746 shows 'the Skin Market' covering an area behind Cardinal Cap Alley that was originally one end of the Queen's Pike Garden. I think this was probably related to the hat business, as many of these were made out of rabbit skins, suitably plucked and brushed with mercury to keep the wet out.

Printing was another traditional trade in Southwark which now, with many more books and papers being produced, also expanded, adding its characteristic clack and thump to the background noises of the streets. Then of course there was the glass industry. Becoming more and more important at the western end of Bankside, the Falcon Glass Works co-existed for decades with the Tudor public house from which it had taken its name, but finally swallowed up the old house in the first decade of the nineteenth century. With the bridge at Blackfriars there was no call any more for the ferry and the chaises for hire. To the ironworks near the same place which had been there since Wren's day were added other firms, to make the new machines for yet more firms, mills and presses near by. The use of steam to power machines, even in small works, was coming in now. By the late eighteenth century the Rennie family, who were to be responsible for Southwark Bridge, Waterloo Bridge and eventually for the rebuilding of London Bridge, had set up their general engineering works in Holland Street, near where Holland's Leaguer had stood.

But the major time-honoured trade along this stretch of the river, which had settled there because it needed a plentiful supply of water on hand, was brewing. In earlier centuries each inn had done its own brewing – that was what the term 'ale-house' implied – but by the late seventeenth century the activity tended to be concentrated into fewer and larger wholesale enterprises. As London had spread so little to the south, the Kentish hop fields remained readily accessible, and hop-dealing too became a major Southwark business. (An elegant Victorian Hop Exchange stands to this day in Southwark Street, put to other uses.) By the mid-eighteenth century, west of London Bridge, there was a brewery off Gravel Lane and another further west on the site of the one-time Royal Barge House, but much the largest was the Thrale brewery nearer to London Bridge, at Bankend.

Ralph Thrale, MP for Southwark, had clerked in the brewery for many years for his uncle; eventually he acquired the place himself as a flourishing concern and built it up much further. His son Henry inherited the business in 1758. He is a good example of a well-educated man of the period, undeniably a gentleman, who thought it quite in order to live within the precincts of the family manufactory. It was not till well into the nineteenth century that captains of industry habitually sought out countrified retreats, at a decent distance from the prosaic source of their wealth, where they assumed the lifestyle of landed gentry. Henry Thrale's wife, Hester, actually *was* from this class, her mother being the widow of a Scottish landowner. She did not particularly like living on Bankside, preferring the house and large garden that Henry owed in Streatham, an hour's drive away by coach over country roads. However, her contacts and her spirited intelligence led her into friendship in London with Dr Johnson and his circle, which included Joshua Reynolds, David Garrick, Edmund Burke and Fanny Burney.

She seems to have comforted herself with the idea that the stench of the tan-yards, not far from their house in Deadman's Place, protected against infection. (This was presumably an alternative theory to the Good Air one that would later be promulgated by Dr Lettsom.) As many of her children, including their only son who was to have inherited the business, disappeared at an early age into St Saviour's churchyard (their extinguished names are there to this day in the burial registers), this theory must have worn thin, but Hester Thrale was indomitable. She managed to steer her erratic husband through several near-disasters, including bursting casks, a failed experiment with brewing a liquor to protect ships' bottoms from worms, and the winter when 'Mr Thrale over-brewed himself . . . and made an artificial scarcity of money in the family which has extremely lowered his spirits. Mr Johnson endeavoured last night, and so did I, to make him promise that he would nevermore brew a larger quantity of beer in one winter than 80,000 barrels, but my Master, mad with the noble ambition of emulating

Whitbread and Calvert, two fellows he despises – could scarcely be prevailed upon to promise even *this*, that he will not brew more than four score thousand barrels a year for five years to come.'

Large-scale trading indeed – though not as large as it was to become on that site in the following century. A steam-engine was installed by Thrale in 1770 to raise the water for his works that had previously been raised by a horse-powered treadmill. This was replaced again twenty years later by a more elaborate steam-piston engine, made by the great James Watt and his partner Boulton, but by then Mr Thrale and his mad ambition were dead and gone. Very corpulent, he collapsed with apoplexy in 1780. Mrs Thrale set to work in the counting house herself to sort the business out, helped by Thrale's executors: these included a cousin, an illegitimate son, John Cator of Bankside who was now an MP – and Dr Johnson. A contemporary description has the great man himself, 'bustling about, with an ink horn and pen in his buttonhole, like an exciseman'. Evidently the romance of the new commercialism had captivated even him, for when asked by a prospective buyer for his estimate of the real value of the brewery, he famously answered: '"Sir, we are not here to sell a parcel of boilers and vats but the potentiality of growing rich beyond the dreams of avarice."' Mrs Thrale commented in her journal:

'Johnson . . . desires above all other good the accumulation of new ideas [and] is but too happy with his present employment . . . difficult to win him from the dirty delight of seeing his name in a new character flaming away at the bottom of bonds and leases.'

I daresay that much of the same delight was felt by others, who, in that propitious era, were beginning to build big fortunes by trading in basic commodities – others such as the brewery Charringtons, their cousins the coal-merchant Charringtons, the Horne family and indeed the Sells.

Mrs Thrale, who wanted only to dispose of the business profitably, was delighted when she received through the offices of John Perkins, the brewery manager who had seen off the Gordon Rioters, an offer from 'a knot of rich Quakers'. They paid £135,000. The first Thrale had got it early in the century for £30,000, so even though Mrs Thrale suspected that Perkins was in cahoots with the Quakers (the Barclay family) to ensure his own future, she was satisfied with the deal. She was now free to retreat into 'peace and a stable fortune, restoration to my original rank in life' – in which she married an Italian music master and lived to eighty far from Bankside. The brewery, briefly renamed the Anchor Brewery, became Barclay Perkins by the 1790s, though local people long went on calling it 'Thrale's'. For the whole of the next century it was one of the sights of London and was visited by generations of respectful foreigners, often ladies, who have left fervent descriptions of its vats, boilers, grain chutes, huge output, sweating muscular employees and scores of equally muscular dray-horses.

Although, with the rise of the Victorian temperance movement, the amount of beer drunk by the working classes would come to be seen as an evil in its own right, in the late eighteenth century this counted as a good old English habit, much preferable to gin-drinking. It could even be seen as central to England's increasing influence throughout the world and to the founding of her empire. A Southwark worthy – Concannen – wrote in 1795:

'*Thrale's intire* is well-known as a delicious beverage, from the frozen regions of Russia to the burning sands of Bengal and Sumatra . . . It refreshes the brave soldiers who are fighting the battles of their country in Germany [what were to become the Napoleonic Wars had begun for Britain in 1793], and animates with new ardour and activity the colonists of *Sierra Leone* and Botany Bay.'

As the brewery expanded further, it came to dominate a whole stretch of Bankside, swallowing in the process burial ground, almshouses, remains of Tudor houses and the sites of the old theatres. (Mrs Thrale thought she had seen the last of the Globe demolished to allow more light into their house. In fact, these 'ruins of Palmyra', as the family christened them, seem more likely, from their position, to have been those of the last Bear Garden, which may have gone on with furtive bear- and dog-fighting activities almost to the time when Mrs Thrale arrived on the scene in 1762.)

The brewery was still flourishing in the first half of the twentieth century, but shrank into a bottling plant in the 1960s. It shut at last c.1980. Today, flats and offices cover the site. But the Anchor pub, discreetly rebuilt but not much changed in appearance since the seventeenth century, still sits on the river at Bankend and once again attracts crowds of drinkers on fine summer evenings.

On such evenings two hundred and fifty years ago where did the Bankside bourgeoisie go? Apart from taking evening walks on the bridges to ward off typhoid fever, what did they do for entertainment, the Sells, the Cators, the Shalletts, the Astells, John Perkins and all the others who were turning the Surrey shore to good account? Today, we are so accustomed to the post-William Morris concept of places being degraded by 'the spreading of the hideous town' that it takes a conscious adjustment to realise that dingy urbanisation was not uniformly spread – and that that was not, in any case, quite how the eighteenth century saw the matter. In the middle decades of the century at any rate, the influence of new commerce was perceived as bringing with it a desirable civilisation and gentrification to the rural backlands of Southwark.

St George's Fields, a large and puddly common heath immediately south-west of the Borough, had long been a popular place for early morning duck-shooting, duels, assignations and also for large assemblies of people. The rowdy late-summer Fair there that Hogarth had painted was suppressed in 1756. Mineral springs, that enthusiastic pre-occupation of the period, were 'discovered' among the pools. The old Dog and Duck tavern[5] turned itself into a Spa, complete with breakfast room, bowling green, a tea-garden and a Long Room with music and dancing. Even Mrs Thrale was not above recommending the waters for health. The fact that so many people were prepared to believe in the special properties of waters from the spas, which were now dotted plentifully round the fringes of the great city, is probably an indication of just how polluted many other London water supplies were, including that produced by the Thrales's own engine from the river.

A few years later another place of resort, Finch's Grotto, opened near by in the grounds of a former country house. Apparently aiming at a slightly more exclusive clientele than the Dog and Duck, it boasted *more* supposed medical springs, garden walks, evening concerts and other delights including 'A Lodge of Free-Masons and a Club composed of the most respectable persons in the vicinity'. Excerpts from Mr Finch's handbills for his Grotto over the years tell their own tale of how the St George's Fields area was developing. In the 1760s the 'coach road' was said to be by Blackman's Street (an old name for the Borough High Street), while 'Such Gentlemen and Ladies as chuse to come by water, will please to observe that Mason stairs' [very near 49 Bankside, with a way through to the Gravel Lane] 'are nearest to the Gardens.' But by the '70s, when Blackfriars Bridge and 'Great Surrey Street' leading from it (today's Blackfriars Bridge Road) were established, cutting across the old lanes, the publicity could make reference to the coach routes being 'from Westminster and Blackfriars Bridges'. This meant that these bridges, though widely separated on the shore-line by the curve of the river, now had new south-bank turnpike roads linking them and also picking up the old main road from Southwark. The central point where these roads met was on St George's Fields: an obelisk marked the spot at the time, and now does once again today (St George's Circus). Thus a whole new district, suitably drained, would become ripe for the building of new streets of houses.

This fairly soon began to happen for, forty years after the last building boom had petered out at the end of the 1720s, another one was under way. Finch's Grotto did not even last a generation, dying with its owner in 1777. Perhaps the nearby opening of a white lead manufactory, among other works, did not encourage any new proprietor. The site has ended up today just on the western side of Southwark Bridge Road, at the bend in the road immediately south of the junction with the much older Great Guildford Street – the one-time Bandy Leg Walk. It was bought by the St Saviour's Vestry to build a new workhouse, 'spacious and convenient', to accommodate four hundred people, at a much-disputed cost of £5,000.

Other, more prestigious new constructions in the 'classical' style soon arrived in Great Surrey Street. An octagonal chapel was built there for the popular Nonconformist preacher Rowland Hill. In 1788 a rather similar building appeared, the Rotunda, built to house natural history specimens, then very fashionable objects as the world opened ever wider. Some of these specimens had allegedly been brought back from Australia by Captain Cook. Eighteen years later the deteriorating remnants were auctioned off and the Rotunda, renamed the Surrey Institute, was used for lectures on the sciences. Later again, less improvingly, it became a place for concerts and general entertainments.[6]

But the real drama of change going on under the eyes of those who lived on Bankside in the late eighteenth century was connected with the central business of living, and the grandest building in Great Surrey Street was a temple to steam. It was the type of industrial architecture that was now creating a new world in the north of England, but it was a novelty in London and much admired by some as a sign of Progress. This was the Albion Flour Mills, designed by Samuel Wyatt and equipped by Rennie with the latest in steam-powered rotary machinery. It could grind far more wheat, night and day, than the wind- and water-powered mills that were still in general use: millers all round London and the south-east were alarmed, seeing the future and not liking it. However, the mill was in business only four or five years before a fire destroyed it in 1791. It was widely rumoured that arson was involved, though Wyatt and Rennie themselves thought that badly lubricated machinery was to blame. At any rate, local millers rejoiced, and are said to have been seen dancing on Blackfriars Bridge in the light of the flames.

It does not seem to say much for Progress that the Mills' blackened, roofless walls stood for eighteen years before they were pulled down. Albion Terrace was erected on the front of the site, using some of the façade, with Rennie's workshops at the back. During part of the time the Mills stood ruinous, William Blake was living not far away in what was still – just – known as Lambeth Marsh. There, in 'lovely Lambeth' that 'mourned Jerusalem', his visionary view of the world around him began to cohere. He passed by the shell of the Mills every time he walked into the City, and one may believe that it was this sight, rather than any general acquaintance with England's new manufacturing towns, that was the inspiration for his 'dark satanic mills'.[7]

By the end of the century, the growing perception that Progress came at a price was being voiced by a number of Southwark inhabitants, notably by Concannen and Morgan, the authors of *The History and Antiquities of the Parish of St Saviour's, Southwark*. Their comments on Potts Vinegar Manufactory show this ambivalence. Vinegar, which uses the waste matter from brewing, had long been made in the Borough, but in 1790 two families already in the trade combined to open a much bigger works near the south-west end of the Anchor Brewery: 'The alterations made by these gentlemen can hardly come under the denomination of an improvement only, a total change having taken place by entire new erections and apparatus for the purposes of manufacture, which is now deemed to be the most extensive and convenient of the kind in England.'

They also noted that near St Saviour's Church, where the Bishop's palace had once had a riverside view, were now a range of buildings right on the waterfront: Fell's Flower Wharf, Keen and Smither's Coal Wharf, Lingard and Sadler's Mustard Manufactory, Calvert's Corn Wharf, and several more including a dyeworks. The Mustard works in fact had built a gantry over narrow Clink Street to the remains of the old palace, which had been built into the walls of their warehouse. Some twenty years later a fire destroyed the warehouse, exposing the surviving late-medieval and Tudor stonework to the gaze of local people, who were just beginning to develop a greater interest in relics of the past. Without this providential fire, all vestiges of the palace would probably have been swept away in further rebuilding. As to Bankside itself, Concannen gives up on detail, but his message is clear:

'This spot presents us with so great a variation from the ancient situation which history relates it to have been in, that we are almost at a loss how to introduce the subject . . .' He then launches into the praise for the brewery and for 'Thrale's intire' quoted earlier.

He is, however, at his most eloquent on the subject of street paving, that issue of the time which provided for endless arguments in Vestry meetings about cost, need and rate-payers' money. Some efforts had been made by Parliament to get Southwark properly paved and lighted in the 1760s, but the Paving Act that specifically related to the Clink Liberty (the parish of St Saviour's) did not come in till 1786. It is not clear how well implemented it was:

'Before the passing of this act of Parliament the Clink liberty merited all that opprobrium with which even those who were acquainted with it beheld it. It was supplied with something like light, watched by subscription; the variety and ill state of the pavement and the inconvenience it was to passengers is almost inconceivable; it is now improving, and though the progress is far from rapid, it is yet considerable and the benefit resulting to Society is evident . . .' While some of the new lamps (which would have been oil-lamps) were 'numerous, and tolerably brilliant', others were 'dismal and dirty'. There are obscure but meaning-laden references to 'duty' and 'the business of everyone attended to by no one' and the passage ends with the pious hope that 'future writers [will] record improvements'.

Whose duty was it to see that these matters were attended to? It was that of specially appointed commissioners, 'gentlemen being inhabitants of, or householders within the said Manor', and their names are given. Among the obvious prominent citizens such as Robert Barclay, John Perkins, James Harris (a hat maker, who was to become the local MP), Thomas Prickett of the Falcon Iron Foundry, Samuel Rush (who was one of the proprietors of the large vinegar works) and Thomas Horne of the wealthy coaling family, I recognise several other Bankside citizens including a hop-factor. Also there is Edward Sells.

This is the first time a Sells appears as a member of the Southwark establishment. The name, a few years on, becomes a familiar one in the records of local affairs. In reality this Edward Sells, the first on Bankside, had died in 1791 or '92: Concannen's record, of a few years later, does mention in an apologetic footnote 'several of these are now dead', which makes one think that at that point the paving committee was going through one of its less efficient phases. But by the end of the decade his son, the boy who had been born in 1763 and apprenticed in 1777, the year the new workhouse was built, was to become a moving spirit in the district.

Chapter VII

THE WORLD OF EDWARD SELLS II

Edward Sells II became a Freeman of the Watermen's Company in 1785 at the age of twenty-two. He joined his father in the coal-business: Edward Sells I was then in his early sixties and would be dead seven years later. The trade was flourishing as the domestic and the industrial demands of the capital grew and grew. In 1705 a few hundred coaling ships, many of them small, had been enough to service London's needs. In 1805, London received 4,856 cargoes of coal, containing about 1,350,000 tons. Fifteen years later there were to be 5,884 cargoes, accounting for nearly 1,700,000 tons, rising to over two million in 1830 and two-and-a-half million by 1840.[1]

Much of the increase after 1805 arrived in town not from round the coasts and up the Thames from the east, but from the west, via the new canal system. Canals had begun to be built in the north of England from the 1760s, expressly to shift coal from mining areas into Manchester and other growing industrial centres. Gradually these short, locally owned waterways were extended, linking up with one another and with the Humber, Mersey and Severn rivers. The Oxford Canal, which was completed in 1790, brought the whole network nearer to the south of England. Over the next ten years what became the Grand Union Canal was constructed: branching off the Oxford Canal, it finally made an efficient link between the coal-producing north and west of England and the Thames at London. The new

Paddington Basin and Regent's Canal link round the north side of London carried some of the increased coal-trade, but much of it joined the river at the Grand Union junction at Brentford and came down river. So, whether it arrived by canal barge from upstream, or by lighter via the Pool of London in the traditional way, great quantities of this black wealth continued to pass through the wharves of Bankside.

Edward Sells II married within a year or two of attaining man's estate, as a Waterman and a coal-merchant. His eldest child, Edward Perronet Sells, was born in 1788. His wife was one year older than him and was called Sophia Gardiner Briggs. She apparently came on her mother's side of Huguenot or possibly Swiss Protestant stock, which is said to be how the elegant Perronet was inserted into the traditional family name and continued in the family down the generations. Caution, however, is recommended, for here we are in the unreliable area of website genealogy. A posting by an Australian Sells, who from internal evidence is a direct descendant of the Sells of Bankside, nevertheless ignores the long coal-trading history of the family and the even longer connection with the Thames. He states that Sophia Briggs was the grand-daughter of Henry Briggs, chaplain to George II, great-grand-daughter of one of King William's physicians, and descended from aristocracy on her mother's side.

Admittedly the Sells enterprise had done well, in the thirty-odd years since the lighterman had set up in a small way with his first shipment that cost £30.10s. But what I know of Edward Sells II's subsequent life suggests that, whatever his prosperity, he went on regarding himself as a hands-on riverman. He had no scholarly education beyond the age of fourteen, when his apprenticeship began. I think it most unlikely that soon after emerging from this apprenticeship, and still in his early twenties, he would have been in a position to marry a girl of relatively upper-class origins.

The names Briggs and Perronet clearly were connected in some way, since a John Perronet Briggs was born in 1792 in

Walworth, which was then a fast-developing suburban area immediately to the south of Southwark.[2] He was four years younger than Edward Perronet Sells; his father worked for the Post Office, sent him to school in Epping (which was on a coach route from Southwark) and encouraged his artistic talent. He eventually became a successful Victorian painter of portraits and historical scenes, and a member of the Royal Academy. Possibly it is with him that a close family link might exist?

There is, however, a further scrap of evidence which, like a clock striking thirteen, tends to cast doubt on the whole idea that the Perronet name came in via an advantageous marriage in the 1780s. Edward Sells I's market sale note of 1755 was made out by someone other than the two signatories, someone with a decorative hand. Among the little flourishes added is a clear letter 'P' tucked into the upper part of the Greek E for Edward. So it is possible that the Perronet addition to the name long pre-dated the third Edward Sells, though he was to be the first one to use it habitually – no doubt to differentiate himself locally from his father, and also to add a touch of class. Perronet is not an uncommon Huguenot name. An eighteenth-century Edward Perronet, son of an Anglican clergyman, became a fiery Dissenting minister and an associate of the Wesleys – he wrote the rousing hymn *All hail the power of Jesu's name, Let angels prostrate fall* – but I doubt if he was a Sells connection. As to whether Sophia Briggs's maternal grandmother was really descended from a family who owned a castle in Switzerland, as the website mentioned above also claims, I have no idea. As the nineteenth century progressed, many thriving, upwardly mobile Victorian families must have cherished romanticised versions of their mainly modest origins.

After Edward Perronet in 1788, other children followed: Sophia, named after her mother, in 1790, Vincent in '94 and John in '96. I know that all these, plus at least one other, survived to a good age, and there may have been more whom I have not located. The time when babies and young children of all classes died very readily was passing; the nineteenth century was to see larger families than ever before, or since. From the mid-eighteenth century a number of progressive doctors had been advocating what we would still regard today as sensible principles for the rearing of babies. The ideas of Jean-Jacques Rousseau on the wisdom of Nature and the nobility of simple instincts would hardly have gained a wide currency had not the feeling of the times in any case been moving in that direction.

'. . . The Mother who has only a few rags to cover her Child loosely, and little more than her own Breast to feed it, sees it healthy and very soon able to shift for itself; while the puny Insect, the Heir and Hope of a rich Family, lies languishing under a Load of Finery, that overpowers his Limbs, abhorring and rejecting the Dainties he is cramm'd with, till he dies a Victim to . . . mistaken Care and Tenderness . . .'

The doctor writing this, who was probably Richard Meade, honorary physician to Coram's Founding Hospital,[3] advocated 'laying aside all those Swathes, Bandages, Stays and Contrivances, that are most ridiculously used to close and keep the Head in its Place, and support the Body . . . Shoes and Stockings are very needless Incumbrances, besides that they keep the legs wet and nasty, if they are not chang'd every hour . . . Some imagine that clean Linnen and fresh Cloathes draw and rob [babies] of their nourishing juices . . . I think they cannot be changed too often, and would have them clean every day . . . Children [should] be kept clean and sweet, tumbled and toss'd about a good deal, and carried out every day in all Weathers.'

Breast feeding had not been much in vogue among the comfortably off classes for a long time, but this same doctor was in favour of breast milk alone for the first three months, preferably from the child's own mother, then a gradual introduction of 'light broth made from beef juice, and bread pap 'without sugar or spice'. '– I earnestly recommend it to every Father to have his child nursed under his own Eye . . . Nor suffer it to be made one of the Mysteries . . . from which the Men are to be excluded.' Rather charmingly, he also referred to a baby as a delightful 'rattle' – that is, plaything – for a father.

This doctor and his wife had successfully reared their own children. Edward Sells II was evidently another successful parent and he himself cannot have been brought up to grand ideas. I like to imagine him sitting after work opposite his wife Sophia in the airy first-floor parlour of 49 Bankside, appreciatively watching her feed a procession of healthy babies, each clad in clean flannel and cotton: little Edward, little Sophia, Vincent, John and perhaps several more.

In the year of John's birth Jenner's discovery of how to vaccinate against smallpox was publicised. It is probable that the Sells availed themselves of this, since Southwark at that time had a well-known medical practitioner who was a fervent advocate of vaccination. This was Dr Lettsom, he who had also recommended walks on London's bridges to combat 'foul airs'.[4] Anglican, but strongly influenced in boyhood by Quaker principles, he had married money and used his good fortune over the years to found philanthropic enterprises – soup kitchens, a dispensary, a lying-in hospital, schools for the blind and the deaf (the latter an entirely new venture) and even a Sea-Bathing Infirmary at Margate for 'the scrofulous poor'. (The future Prince Regent and his circle were colonising Brighton and making sea-bathing fashionable for the first time, and Margate had long been accessible from London down the river Thames.) In 1779 Lettsom had moved to a handsome house standing in its own park on Grove Hill, Camberwell, two to three miles from the river. Pigot's *New Commercial Directory* for 1823–24, a few years after his death, described the area in glowing terms:

'The Grove, which is one of the principal ornaments of the neighbourhood, is a delightfully embowered walk, nearly half a mile in length, having a gradual ascent from Peckham Road. The view from the summit is extensive, rural and picturesque ... The air around here is genial and invigorating: Dr Lettsom, the celebrated physician and botanist, used to designate this place and its immediate neighbourhood as the Montpelier of England.'

The area round the Grove was then being developed, though sparsely and with high-class houses. Through subsequent decades it retained its status as a good address, and it was to there that Edward Sells II eventually retired in gentlemanly comfort before his death in 1841. But while Pigot was lauding the rurality of Camberwell, its lower-lying meadows were already sprinkled with 'stock jobbers' villas'. By and by whole streets of close-packed houses were to follow, eventually driving the stock-jobbers themselves, with their dreams of country living, to more distant fields. Bankside with its orchards and drying grounds was, for hundreds of years, a semi-built suburb. But Camberwell, so remote till the new bridges began to span the Thames, then became accessible by a network of new, inter-connecting roads and subject to the pressures of the exploding metropolis. The new omnibuses ran back and forth to the City. By the later part of the nineteenth century the whole district was built up, an embodiment of the phrase 'urban sprawl', becoming more crowded and insalubrious as rows of smaller houses were squeezed in between the existing streets.

Such a transformation of a landscape, from open country to dense-packed town well within the span of one lifetime, calls into question the very meaning of the word 'place', and with it personal identity. In 1800 London, though huge by the world standard of the time, had fewer than one million inhabitants. By the mid-century the figure stood at over two million and was rising in proportion: by the end of the century it would be over six-and-a-half million. The idea of change and progress as a Good Thing, or at any rate a necessary one, was rooted in the Victorian mind, but a note of bemused regret for a lost world becomes frequent in writings towards the century's end:

'The expansion of London during the Nineteenth Century is in itself a fact unparalleled in the history of cities . . . I have before me a map of the year 1834, only sixty-four years ago . . . It is difficult, now that the whole country south of London has been covered with villas, roads, streets, and shops, to understand how wonderful for loveliness it was until the builder seized upon it. When the ground rose out of the great Lambeth and Bermondsey Marsh . . . it opened out into one wild heath after another . . . as far south as Banstead Downs . . . Villages were scattered about, each with its venerable church and its peaceful churchyard; along the high roads to Dover, Southampton and Portsmouth bumped and rolled, all day and all night, the stage coaches and the waggons; the wayside inns were crowded with those who halted to drink, those who halted to dine, and those who halted to sleep . . . All this beauty is gone; we have destroyed it: all this beauty has gone forever; it cannot be replaced.'[5]

Let us reel time rapidly back again, before 1834, before 1800, back to the young manhood of the second Edward Sells.

Even if loveliness had already been driven from the immediate vicinity of Bankside by the late eighteenth century, memories of former days were preserved with the phrase 'in the Bishop's Park', which was still used to describe plots of land immediately south of Bankside which were being gradually filled with houses. The last of the oak and apple trees that had stood in the Park and its orchards must have been cut down in these years. The local worthies were still preoccupied with errant hogs and dung-filled ditches. They also had a new, though equally earthy concern: grave-robbing.

Southwark was sown with small cemeteries. Many of these, such as the one near Deadman's Place by the Anchor Brewery, were attached to Nonconformist chapels and meeting houses and, as such, were not consecrated ground and had no particular status. The increasing pressure on space in the district meant that most of them were to disappear beneath builders' yards, workshops or rows of small tenements over the next century; one must suppose those that were interred there had also disappeared from human memory and that their remains were no longer anyone's business. Their lives of chapel-going virtue and internecine battles over the True Interpretation of the Scriptures remain profoundly forgotten today, so much so that when bodies are discovered in the course of building works, the local press breaks out in stories about pits from the Great Plague. In fact, when such discoveries are plotted on old maps, it becomes apparent that what have been unearthed are simply the massed bones of a congregation of Quakers, Methodists, Particular Baptists or whatever, just where you would expect them to be, for these little yards beside chapels were intensively used.

There were also pauper graveyards attached to workhouses, which tended to be sold off summarily when the workhouse was removed to a new site – presumably any surviving relatives of the paupers were not thought likely to complain. This happened in 1808, when St Saviour's 'spacious and convenient' workhouse that had been built in the grounds of Finch's Grotto barely thirty years before was sold to Mr Harris the hat maker for use as a works – part of that graveyard survives as a triangle of greenery on the west side of the bend in Southwark Bridge Road. Similarly, the ancient ground attached to Cure's College almshouses not far from Borough High Street was eventually swept away by a railway viaduct.

However, the parish of St Saviour's, represented by the Vestry, did concern itself with its own graveyards in current use: these were St Saviour's churchyard and the medieval Cross Bones ground which had, since 1673, been used as an overflow ground for the more humble of its parishioners. I suspect that a good many of the older remains had earlier been disinterred and perhaps stacked in a makeshift bone-house, and that this was the origin of the picturesque name. By the late eighteenth century this ground, which had once been isolated in the fields, found itself on the corner of Red Cross Street and Queen Street – which, after about 1780, was extended and became Union Street, to mark the Poor Law Union of St Saviour's parish with St George's to the south of it.

In December 1788 the Vestry was concerned about

security of burials. The increasing needs of medical schools for dead bodies, for the burgeoning science of anatomy, was leading to the era of the 'Resurrection men'. These were rumoured to come with picks and shovels at dead of night, and what with both St Thomas's and Guy's Hospitals only a few minutes away . . . The Vestry proposed offering a reward of five guineas for information leading to the conviction of 'Person or Persons who shall hereafter Dig up, take and Carry away any Corps interred in any or either of the Burying Grounds of this parish'. They offered a similar reward for information regarding burglaries, but one may assume that the whole body-snatching phenomenon, which lasted for two or three decades and which we now regard with an incredulous disgust tainted by humour, was seen as a crime of particular horror. Had post-mortems been generally acceptable, surgeons would not have had to resort to criminal sources: as it was, the dissection of the body and the dispersal of its parts was believed to inhibit the true resurrection on the Day of Judgement. Evidently the reward offered did not bring enough results, for in 1790 the Parish Commissioner of Estates[6] – effectively, the holder of the purse-strings – 'took a View of the Cross Bones Burying Ground in Red Cross Street, and [found] the Walls on the West and South sides thereof very insufficient for preventing Persons from Stealing the Bodies interr'd there'. Better walls were to be built, topped by broken glass.

Two years later, in 1792, the Boys' Free School, which had been founded in two houses in the Borough about a hundred years before, moved to premises specially built for it on part of the Cross Bones ground. The cover of the pamphlet published to celebrate the opening of this depicts a rather elegant little building with arched windows like a piece of early industrial architecture. A closed carriage with a crest on it stands near by and a well-clad lady and a young girl seem about to get into it: presumably they are two of the charity school's valued patrons. What can be seen of the remaining graveyard over the (rebuilt) wall suggests that it was by then heavily overgrown.

A decade later, when the parish's lease of the workhouse site was soon to expire, one of the many possibilities discussed in Vestry meetings was the use of the rest of this graveyard to build a new workhouse. However, the general feeling was against this: 'The Committee conceive it essentially necessary that the Cross Bones Burial Ground should not be converted to any other purpose . . . the parish is bound to use any other endeavour to retain a spot so sacred to the remains of the departed.' Anglican departed were clearly more highly regarded than the Dissenting sort. But in spite of these parish endeavours it was reported the following year (1803) that the Cross Bones ground had again been the target of grave-robbers, and that 'Mr Cooper the Sexton has suffered the keys, at times, to go out of his Hands.' A door was to be blocked up and a new sexton appointed – Mr Cooper had, in any case, recently died. One wonders if *his* grave remained undisturbed.

By a quirk of chance, or by the persistence of folk memory when so much other passionately lived history has sunk into oblivion, the dispute over the use of the Cross Bones yard has been revived at intervals ever since. The ground was shut for burial, along with most of Southwark's remaining small grave-yards, in the early 1850s, when Parliament was attempting to shift all London burials to more salubrious, out-of-town sites such as Highgate, Nunhead and Kensal Green. Thirty years later, Reginald Brabazon (later Earl of Meath), the Chairman of the Metropolitan Public Garden, Playground and Boulevard Association, wrote to *The Times* objecting to a parish plan to sell the ground off for the building of Model Workmen's Dwellings, such as were then going up in many parts of Southwark. At that time the Boys' School, to which had been added in the 1820s a similar building for girls, was still in place on the Union Street frontage. 'The wardens [from the parish of St Saviour's Newcomen charity] are quite prepared to let or sell this ground for this or any other purpose, so as to enable them to obtain funds for the payment of the stipend of the rector of this parish; and the

Home Secretary, on the 30th of October 1882, granted a licence to assist this design.' This would be illegal, he went on to say, because the ground had almost certainly been consecrated.

Evidently the might of Brabazon together with his Association saw off St Saviour's wardens for, in the early twentieth century, another newspaper report[7] raised the alarm about a fresh scheme for the same site. The school had by now been moved to a new building across the street, and the old ground had apparently been used as a pitch for stalls, Punch and Judy shows and the like. Any remaining gravestones must by then have disappeared, for when an attempt to dig a foundation trench revealed bones, these apparently came as a surprise. But now that they had been discovered again the popular consciousness proved tenacious. By then, vestiges of medieval archways, Elizabethan inns and the debtors' prisons that Dickens had known had almost all been swept away. Huge tenement blocks and soaring warehouses had replaced much domestic-scale architecture, and 'Old Southwark' had become the stuff of myth. People needed to feel they were still in touch with it.

Once again nothing solid was built; the place simply became a works' storage yard. Another entire lifetime passed. Manufacturing businesses left the Borough. The millennium arrived. Shortly afterwards, London Underground, which had recently completed a new tube line through Southwark's ancient earth, tried to build an office block on the Cross Bones ground. Once again the attempt was obstructed – 'I think it's immoral to develop a graveyard for profit,' the campaign leader told the local newspaper.[8] She went on, with questionable accuracy as to detail but making a basic, irrefutable point: 'As well as being a burial site for paupers and prostitutes, it was also the resting place for the community of St Saviour's. There are lots of ordinary people buried here. People who just did normal jobs and helped build up the Borough.'

The paupers and prostitutes were clearly irresistible, since that is what we currently want history to be about. A torchlit vigil was held. The Deputy Mayor, a man of West Indian origin, weighed in: 'These [people] deserve to be treated with a bit of respect. They probably got little enough in their lifetime.' There, at the moment of writing, the matter for the moment rests.

At the beginning of the nineteenth century, when the Cross Bones ground had escaped becoming the site for a new workhouse, expensive proposals and counter-proposals as to the best way of disposing of the poor continued for years, sometimes acrimoniously. Finally an old wooden building 'such as many of the poor live in' was rented at Newington Butts, where the Elephant and Castle meeting of the ways was taking shape. Child paupers were to be farmed out to individual women living in the countryside round London. Among those at the heart of this debate, I came across the name of Edward Sells, an 'ordinary man doing a normal job' and helping to build up the Borough.

Browsing my way through the Vestry minutes for the last decade of the eighteenth century – luckily one of the volumes that the London Metropolitan archive does not regard as too dilapidated to be looked at – my aim had not been specific. I wanted to get a general feel for the times and for the successive preoccupations of Southwark citizens. I had no particular reason to expect to find Edward Sells II – but there, suddenly, he was. Or rather, a 'William Sells' appears, just once, but in the next list of local inhabitants 'blessed with a competence' (i.e. with a respectable income) the name becomes 'Edward Sells' and William is never heard of again. He *could* have been an otherwise unrecorded brother or cousin – William crops up as a name in subsequent Sells generations. But a more likely explanation is that the Vestry Clerk simply wrote 'William' by mistake on the first appearance of a man he would soon come to know well.

It was a charitable impulse that first drew Edward Sells into Vestry circles, which was to say local governmental circles. The reason that comfortably-off local inhabitants were being canvassed was that the winter that marked the turn of the century was excessively cold. Once again the Thames froze solid above old London Bridge, as it had done a number of times since the days of John Taylor a hundred and eighty years before: another of the famous Frost Fairs was held on the icy expanse. But the Fairs, which were such a cheerful diversion to the many middle-class Londoners whose businesses did not depend on the river, brought no joy to the numerous watermen, lightermen, waterfront traders and dock-side porters, whose trades were at a standstill. Still worse off were the really poor, who just scraped by at the best of times and to whom any winter rise in the price of necessities was disastrous. The narrow alleys of old Southwark sheltered many of these.

On 3rd December 1799, and again on the 5th, general meetings were held in the Vestry of St Saviour's church – actually in the one-time St John's chapel. I don't imagine there was a fireplace to allow the assembled company to warm themselves. This was long before the days of central-heating boilers installed in crypts and iron pipes behind wrought-iron grids, and St Saviour's, like all other churches in winter, was bitterly cold – and apparently damp too, from its age and its situation at river level. Two years later the Vestry was 'considering the propriety of attempting to Warm the Church . . . by stoves', but when it was found that the stoves would cost about £800 to install it was unanimously decided that 'any attempt to warm this Church . . . is impracticable', and there the matter rested for very many years. Still, a generation later, there were complaints by the master of the parish Free School that parents were reluctant to send their children to the unheated church on winter Sundays, especially to the two services in one day that were then regarded as appropriate, and that 'good attendance cannot be expected in such a cold and comfortless place'.

Presumably, when sallying forth through the hard-packed snow to a Vestry meeting, prudent men put on, over their already heavy coats, waistcoats and breeches, those caped and many-collared great-coats that were also used for travelling on the outside of coaches. They cannot have been under any Scrooge-like illusions as to the problems experienced by those with no good broadcloth coats and no warm supper waiting for them at home. Their own working lives, taking them out and about the warehouses and wharves of Southwark must have made them well acquainted with the lives of their poorer neighbours, a number of whom they would have employed at times as labour.

So, as Christmas 1799 approached, the meetings were held 'to take into Consideration the Most effectual means of affording relief to the Poor in the Parish during the Continuance of the Very high Price of <u>Bread</u>, <u>Flour</u> and <u>Fuel</u> . . . An earnest attempt to appeal to the benevolent and well-disposed.' That autumn's harvest had also been bad, for bread was said to be nearly double the price it had been the year before. A drive for donations was launched; plans were laid for a soup kitchen selling 'good Meat Soup at one penny per quart', and for the purchase of potatoes to be sold to the poor at a reduced price. Also, 'it would much increase the comforts of the poor if from the proposed Subscriptions, or by means of a Loan from any Inhabitants, a supply of good coals could be procured on the best terms, to be retailed at wholesale price under the direction of the Committee.'

Although this charity was being organised under the auspices of the Anglican Church, of which all those dwelling in the area were technically parishioners, the Committee for the First Clink Division was headed by Robert Barclay, who was a Quaker. Dignified by the addition of 'Esq.' to his name (most of St Saviour's worthies at that time are simply 'Mr'), Barclay the brewery owner was clearly the most prominent citizen on Bankside. The list included several other recognisable Bankside names, including Anthony Horne who was another Quaker, and also Edward Sells who was present at the meeting.

One is aware that both Horne and Sells, as coal-merchants, stood to benefit from the fact that ships bringing fresh coal to London could not make it up or down the frozen Thames. Stocks held in their warehouses and barges were therefore potentially very valuable, since retail prices could be raised and raised as the shortage continued. One hopes that Horne and Sells's presence on the Committee means that they felt a higher social obligation than the profit motive. It may indeed have been through their good offices that the cut-price coal reached the shivering poor that year. At the same time, the basic assumption of the meeting was clearly that, for their own good, the poor must pay *something* for their soup, potatoes and coal. It was also piously hoped, by some of those present, that handouts of soup would do them good in a less immediate way – by teaching them how to support life 'at less expense and in a better manner than their ignorance of useful cookery enables them to do at present'. There speaks the voice of thrift: the organisers of this charity were not the rich, ignorant themselves of soup-making. There was also anxiety that, while helping 'the Industrious Poor', they must take care not to encourage the unindustrious, undesirable sort – a preoccupation that was to become familiar in Victorian Poor Law circles.

The amount of money raised over the next two months was remarkable, for a parish with very few really wealthy people and many needy. Potatoes were got cheap, at £5.10s. a ton, from a Borough market dealer. By mid-February forty-three tons of them had been distributed and fifty more tons were planned for March and April – over £500 worth. Distribution of rice (brought, thanks to imperial trade, from the other side of the world, and doubtless grown by people almost as poor as the eventual recipients) was on a similar scale. This was in an era in which £30 a year – or about twelve shillings a week – was cited as an acceptable minimum figure on which a working man with a wife and several children might live respectably; many families habitually got by on much less. For such a large fund to have been collected there must have been a vein of considerable energy and decency running through the minor bourgeoisie of Bankside. They probably had useful contacts too in the City, the river's wealthier opposite shore.

The hard winter passed; warm days at last returned, with

eggs and early vegetables once more for sale in the Borough market (hotly defended by the Vestry against a competing market which had been set up in St George's Fields). In the streets watercresses were hawked, and caged song-birds and bunches of country flowers, bringing a whiff of the pastures of Camberwell and Peckham Rye to the now-enclosed lanes of Bankside. But Edward Sells did not relinquish local activity. He had evidently acquired a taste for it, and it is clear too that the Vestry were pleased with their latest recruit. By the middle of 1800 he had been elected a churchwarden.

After that, for over thirty years, his name crops up regularly, in minutes, on committees, as warden of this or treasurer of that. During the same period he held office at various times in the Watermen's new and elegant little Hall near the Monument. He also became a well-known figure in the Coal Exchange in Lower Thames Street, through which, after 1807, all dealing had to be done. He consolidated and expanded the family business by entering into a partnership with a long-established Bankside neighbour: *Johnstone's London Commercial Guide and Street Directory* for 1817 lists the business as Jones & Sells, coal-merchants. At that time the office was in number 56 Bankside. Sells and his wife were living in 55, while 49 was temporarily let to another coal-merchant, Thomas Fuce, who had a wharf further up, near Falcon stairs. (By the mid-1820s number 49 was back in Sells family occupancy.) At 47 the Hornes had their business, while the Sells's neighbours at 54 were two brothers called Holditch, who traded in coal as well as cider, and were later to work for the Sells enterprise. Altogether, the Directory for that year lists twenty-five separate coal-merchants on Bankside, which was clearly the centre of the London trade.

Yet it would be a mistake to imagine Bankside piled with coal. The middle-class inhabitants who resided there and continued to do so fifteen and twenty years later, including several of the St Saviour's clergy, would hardly have lived surrounded by mounds of nutty slack. Some owner-occupiers did have attached to their property what a land valuation of the period described as 'warehouse and yard': Thomas Horne did at 47, as did his father Anthony at 44. There was another Horne wharf up by the Falcon. What with these, and the laden lighters moored off the Bankside, the whole place probably did smell of coal, that tarry, not unpleasant pungency that has now gone from our cities. But other 'brass plate' coal-merchants, including the Sells, seem to have had their discharging depots elsewhere, since most Bankside addresses were not in themselves storehouses but were used as places for the paperwork of negotiations with shipmasters, customers and the lowlier carters who actually delivered the stuff.

A view[9] of about 1820, from the windows of a house on Bankside opposite St Paul's, shows what is probably the quay in front of Wyatt's stone-yard a few doors down river from number 49. There are sail-boats meandering in the background, ferries tied up, an ancient-looking wooden pulley on the quay, a few blocks of stone, and some iron rollers. Two men are fiddling with chains on the pulley, another is measuring something. Two barges will soon arrive, each with a crowd of well-dressed people on them, and alongside them is a racing boat manned by a team of red-clad oarsmen. Can this be Doggett's race, an annual competition for young watermen which had been inaugurated a hundred years before? The measuring man also wears a red cap, and his red jacket is lying near by. A small child – probably, from his hair, a boy, although he wears a dress and a pinafore – is busy with his own play as he kneels beside a block of stone. Although the river is animated, the atmosphere seems almost to belong to a sylvan, pre-industrial world rather than to one in which already the first steamship had made its appearance on London's river. Looking at it, one can believe that, on a fine Sunday morning when the Bankside workshops were idle, London did then still appear, as it had to Wordsworth twenty years before, 'Open unto the fields and to the sky – All bright and glittering in the smokeless air.'

*

Vestry minutes make odd reading: subjects arise in them, become obsessive for a season or two and then give way to others. High-minded and sometimes genuinely far-sighted perceptions are expressed alongside others of relentless pettiness ('This will put up the rates . . .'). Often it is only when a sudden row explodes that it becomes apparent that what has not been stated in previous minutes is as significant as what has been. There are periodic scandals over the years: this collector of Church rates has died while omitting to hand over the money first; at another time money has been misused to buy port for the Vicar; someone else has published 'very Slanderous and False representations reflecting on the conduct of your Commissioner of Parish Estates' – but the overall picture is that things did in the end get done.

Edward Sells seems to have played a key role for several years in the on-going fuss about the workhouse, whose lease was soon to expire. Should a new one be built? Should an old house be re-used and, if so, where? Could some money from the Newcomen bequest for binding apprentices be used for the workhouse? (Answer from legal advice, No.) Should the existing building be purchased from the trustees of the Winchester Park estate, and if so for how much? . . . No, no, the trustees were asking too much. It would be better to try to renew the lease. But the suggested rent was also considered too much: the Park estate was being 'unreasonable' . . . The problem was the one encountered by local authorities in every era, including the present one: a district with a large number of poor people has many calls upon its funds and relatively few monied rate-payers to meet them, whereas a wealthy district, which could easily afford a high rate, doesn't need one.

A specially appointed sub-committee of four, including Edward Sells, found that, by renting, 'It is . . . demonstrable that in 72 years the Parish would have paid the Lessors the Amount the Freehold would have cost.' Apparently it was not envisaged, in 1805, that the new century would bring such changes to the physical fabric of London and to social structures that long-term predictions about what would be good value were meaningless. This, too, is a problem of every era.

However, by the next meeting the Committee had evidently reflected further, for they had decided that the rent demanded by the Park estate could be accepted after all – 'This brought on a debate of considerable length when the Vestry found it necessary to adjourn to a more extensive and roomy part of the Church, when the matter was reason'd and fully argued, till the Question was loudly called for and again read by the Clerk and a show of Hands was made.'[10] The verdict was not clear, so they resorted to the Parliamentary system of Yeahs and Nays filing through different doors; however, it was still claimed that 'several persons gave their votes without clearly understanding'. A subsequent vote went against the proposition, and the various options were looked at all over again.

Two years later Sells was an auditor, with the others, of the parish accounts. He was also one of four people responsible for a more fundamental report on the workhouse issue. This stated that the workhouse, essentially, was costing too much. The Master, Mr Hey, to whom the running of the place was sub-contracted, was allowed 'a considerable sum' in tea and sugar for the inmates, while claiming 'rags and grease that are the property of the parish'. It was also pointed out that, since Mr Hey was running his own manufacturing business (nature unspecified) in the workhouse, he had an interest in hanging onto healthy, able-bodied inmates. '. . . Your Committee are of the opinion that if any great reduction of the rates is ever to be effected it must be from an increase in the virtues of the poor.'

It is not clear whether this comment was over-optimistic or, rather, ironic. It was, however, followed up by the radical suggestion that the workhouse should be broken up, with the old and the young separated out from the 'profligate and vicious', and that more out-relief for the deserving poor would be a better system. (This humane perception seems to have prevailed till it was overturned by governmental edict in the Poor Law Act of 1834, when St Saviour's formed a

Union with Christchurch parish and shared their workhouse off Upper Ground. Later again, a huge Union House shared with St George's parish was built.)

The young children were to be boarded out in small groups in Norwood and Mile End, and Sells became one of the four new voluntary Guardians responsible for their well-being. It is evident from subsequent reports over the years that the quartet took their duties seriously and made regular trips by chaise to see their charges. Indeed, in 1809 they had written expressly of the need for parish officials to ensure they visited 'at least eight times in the year . . . We would appeal to their feelings as parents, whether they would think this too often to visit their own children under similar circumstances.'

Edward Sells had brought up a number of children, of which the eldest were now grown: it was that same year that Edward Perronet, aged twenty-one, became a Freeman of the Watermen's Company as his father and grandfather had before him. I do not know where he, John, Vincent and others received their schooling, but the Sells family were of the class who, while not of course aspiring to the classical education on offer at schools such as Winchester or Rugby, often sent their boys to board at the small academies that were by then sprinkled round London's rural fringes. As for younger children, Edward Sells had lived at close quarters with his own in a modest-sized house and obviously knew what he was talking about. The following year, he and his fellows reported of one foster household:

'All the nurse children want shoes and linnen which the Nurse says has been promised for some time by the officers – the woman is very deaf . . . She is assisted in her care of the children by a hearty young woman who was brought up in the Parish house and is apprenticed to her . . . she is able, and the children are clean.' There followed a catalogue of things required, including shifts, shirts, pin cloths [baby's napkins], bonnets and bed-linen. But it was concluded that the situation in Norwood was generally good, and that the parish was to be congratulated on the state of 'these helpless children of indigence'. The one household at Mile End, however – Mile End was then at the stage of ribbon-development out from London – was much less satisfactory; the children were 'very confin'd' in a small house and it was doubtful whether the nurse should go on being employed.

Ten years later most of Southwark's boarded-out poor children were being taught to read and write by their nurses, and one nurse was specially commended for having her children 'looking more like tradesmen's children than paupers'. Since it had been noticed on a previous visit that the children 'were accustomed to ramble about the Common', it had been agreed that to keep them occupied the bigger ones should be sent to a local school at the cost of one penny each per week. This had worked well, in that several had now learned their catechism and one had 'whole chapters of the Bible by heart'. (The Bible was the main reading matter provided at these early National Schools, like the one in the Cross Bones yard in Southwark.) The only inconvenience of the penny-a-week school in Norwood was that the children had caught ringworm from other children from poor families who were not so carefully looked after as the boarded-out children.

By this time Edward Perronet Sells, then aged thirty-two and a husband and father himself, had been appointed as overseer to the poor in the Clink division. Edward Sells senior's duties had shifted towards the proposed repair and/ or rebuilding of the dilapidated, part-medieval church, an issue that was to occupy parishioners for several decades.

The wrangles about the state of St Saviour's church were redolent of growing Victorian antiquarianism on the one hand and Victorian progressiveness and utilitarianism on the other. In 1817 Edward Sells was in favour of restoration, for he was on the Church Repairs Committee when it emitted the sanguine proposal that 'we will begin at the Tower and proceed regularly from year to year, until the whole is completed, the Vestry voting such sum of money annually as in their judgement shall appear proper.' But, needless to say, matters did not proceed as smoothly as that; every repair seemed to reveal that a different part of the church also needed attention, and after a great deal of money had been spent restoring the old Lady Chapel (with its whiff of Popery) the parishioners began to get restless and then vociferous.

By the 1830s, when London Bridge was being rebuilt, with its approach road much higher and running much closer to the church than the old way to the bridge, there was a question as to whether the church should not be substantially rebuilt at the same time. Some of the suggestions for this in the local paper were less realistic than others – 'A Church if built on arches might be brought to the level of the road, and we should thus not only improve the comfort and appearance of the building, but possess the additional accommodation of Vaults, and save the Parish the expense of a new Burying ground which will otherwise soon be wanted.' (This was the Useful Railway Arch theory of architecture – the first railway line was even then making its inexorable way into Southwark, and there were unrealistic hopes of charming little houses to be inserted into each arch of the viaduct).

A pamphlet war ensued, instigated by two Southwark citizens who realised, too late, that they should have attended parish meetings themselves. Opinions varied from St Saviour's having been 'spared from ruin by the more enlightened and civilised portion of the parishioners' to – 'Any Parish church which requires the enormous sum of £22,000 for *remaining repairs only* ought to be taken down. We can have a new building for £15,000 . . .' There were elaborately mocking gibes about 'refined gentlemen' belonging to 'the Gothic interest' perpetually running out of money for 'St Saviour's temple'. From this period (November 1831) there has survived[11] a letter in particularly beautiful copperplate from one such refined gentleman; it is signed, in the same hand, 'Edward Perronet Sells, Hon. Sec.' and headed from Bankside, Southwark. It appears to be a pro-forma begging letter: '. . . Trusting you will feel an interest in so desirable a work as the restoration of the ancient Altar Screen . . . Committee formed for that purpose . . .' Along with it has been saved a list of subscribers who had already sent or promised money, including Mr Pott (he of the big vinegar manufactory), Messrs Barclay and Perkins, and also the Sells – including an otherwise mysterious Edward Sells Esq. of Walthamstow. E. Sells Esq. of Bankside was donating five guineas. Messrs E. P. and V. Sells were giving the same sum each, expressed as ten guineas between them.

Yet a long report in a local paper of five years later, in 1836, suggests that Edward Sells senior had by this time changed his mind. He was seventy-three that year, and this was probably his last local appearance before retiring to Camberwell. By this time the argument about the state of the church had degenerated into a quarrel about church rates, which had resulted in the Vestry failing to fix a rate at all. Money was owed to the Bishop – at that time the parish was still, for historical reasons, in the diocese of Winchester. There were fears that, if a ruling was sought from a higher authority such as Parliament, Southwark would end up by losing its fervently contested status as an independent borough and would be merged into London – something that did inevitably happen under the Metropolitan Board of Works a generation later.

It was at a contentious meeting on the question that Mr Sells senior got to his feet. By this time he no longer held any Vestry office but 'claimed his privilege as an inhabitant to deliver his sentiments' and wished 'as an old parishioner' to save everyone from the political consequences of their own folly. His long speech is the only one quoted extensively in a newspaper report, and one sees that he was by then a local 'character' who commanded respect:

'He had taken much pains to save the parishioners from high charges, he had been the first to reduce the rates from one shilling to ninepence, and had paid off a debt of £1000 – (Cheers). They could not do *without* a rate . . . Mr Sells was afraid the Bishop would come among them if they did not pay.' He affirmed that they should not expect members of

Dissenting churches to pay rates that went towards the physical fabric of St Saviour's. (This had long been a bone of contention.) They should not demand money from the poor either – 'He had now stepped forward with the hope of exciting the charitable portion of the church party to save the poorer inhabitants from the charge – (Hear, hear) – When he looked at the pile of building in which they were assembled, he could not help saying it was a heap of rubbish – (great confusion) – and not a noble structure as they were told it was, which was to stand for ages – (Shame, shame) – nothwithstanding the vast sum which had been expended upon it.' Here he revealed that the church repairs committee had issued 'bonds' with the common seal attached that had nothing to back them – 'he felt that they were not binding upon the parishioners and the seal was not worth a dump – (Hear, hear) – He was not a man that acted with injustice, for he was always cautious of getting into debt when he knew he had not the means of paying (Cheers)'.

There followed a little joke about him being prepared, if the Bishop demanded it, to stand in the church in a white sheet for four hours himself, as a penalty for failing to set a rate (Loud laughter). 'He was friendly to the voluntary system, and when he looked round the neighbourhood and saw the noble institutions, all of which were raised and supported by that system, he defied any man to stand up and say it did not and would not work well.' [He was here referring to the parochial schools, and to places such as the Surrey Dispensary and the Surrey Refuge for the Destitute, for which subscription recitals of music had been given in the church.] 'It was the Dissenters who first set this example, and for shame the church party was compelled to follow their steps – (Hear, hear, and laughter) – There was no divine right to compell them to support such a church establishment where bishops were seen rolling in rich equipages with half a dozen powdered lackeys in tawdry liveries at their backs. (Hear, hear) – He should now conclude by opposing the rate which went to uphold such an unchristian establishment.'

A lifetime's experience is evidently rolled up in this peroration. One recognises the tone, as unmistakable then as it was to be in the Labour movement of the following century, charitable but abrasively rational. Evidently, by this time, the faction that wanted to preserve all the old fabric of St Saviour's had been cast in the classic right-wing role of those who cared more for 'old stones' than for the plight of the hungry. One wonders what Edward Perronet Sells, who life's trajectory suggests a rather different personality and set of priorities, thought of his father's speech.

A new committee was formed, to look after 'purely parochial . . . *not* political matters'. The Sells sons were on it. The issue of the rates was eventually brought expensively before the court of the Queen's Bench, who fixed a rate. In 1838 another proposal for a new church was launched, this time to cost £8000. By the following year the plan had been reduced to the rebuilding of the nave only and, in spite of complaints that there was not enough room in the church as it was, this scheme at last went ahead and is the central portion of the church we see today.

At the same time a new church, St Peter's, was built and opened on Bankside on a piece of land donated by Mr Pott, the vinegar manufacturer. At the opening ceremony 'numerous ladies and gentlemen were entertained to an elegant repast' in a marquee, while charity school children who had sung songs were 'regaled with buns and other good things in the ground of Messrs Pott'. Evidently the *perceived* need for more room for congregations was great, as the population of Southwark grew and grew, though whether large numbers of the new urban working classes ever attended church is another matter.

The Bishop laid the foundation stone for St Saviour's new nave. The dust of Massinger, Fletcher, Shakespeare's younger brother, prominent neighbours of the first Edward Sells and countless others was shovelled away with the old flooring to become hard core under the new buildings that were re-drawing the map of south London.

Three years later the Bishop intervened in parish matters

to stop funds for charities being raised by performances in the church. He did not even want the children from the parochial schools singing 'sacred music' there to raise money for their schools. Objections to 'his Lordship's interference' were forthcoming from E. P. Sells, among others, but Edward Sells could not any longer voice his firmly held views since he had died in 1841, in retirement at Camberwell Grove.

His voice speaks out to us in one other preserved document dating from some twenty years before. That was when the question of rebuilding the many-arched London Bridge was at last being seriously discussed, and as a prominent member of the Watermen's Company, Edward Sells was called to give evidence at the enquiry: 'I am a coal-merchant on Bankside,' he said, 'and have been acquainted with the navigation of the river Thames above bridge for upwards of forty years . . . From the nature of London Bridge the inconveniences are very great indeed; because there are only two arches, the centre arch and one besides that. [He is referring to the two arches slightly wider than the rest, which were constructed when the bridge was modified in the middle of the eighteenth century]. It is impossible at particular times of tide to pass through with any safety whatever; I myself have lost many hundred pounds, not through the negligence of my lightermen, but from the state of the Bridge . . .' In fact more than money was lost. In the year of Edward Sells's birth there had been a collison at the Bridge in which ten people drowned, and there were other fatalities through the years. He himself once had a narrow escape: '. . . I have been on board myself at the time accidents happened. I was on board a lighter about twelve or fourteen years ago [i.e. about 1806], she went into one of the small locks [arches] owing to not being able to make any other on account of the pressure of craft, and was sunk, and the whole of the coals lost, and the barge injured to a very considerable amount, almost so much as not to be worth repairing. I should suppose the loss not to be less than £200 in the lighter and cargo . . . I could state many other accidents which have happened to my own craft, but I was not actually on board; they were to the amount of many hundred pounds.'

So we leave Edward Sells II in his role as life-long man of the river. In that he employed others but still worked on occasions alongside them, he was very much a figure of his own entrepreneurial times. Although, by the time he was old, when trousers had come in for general wear, and coats were waisted and skirted affairs on the way to becoming the Victorian frock-coat, I rather imagine that Edward Sells stayed all his life with the breeches, cutaway and neckcloth that had been the standard dress for active men of his generation. It was not till the third Sells, he of the beautiful handwriting, that the artisan mould was broken. As part of this evolution, Edward Perronet Sells was eventually to distance himself, and his own sons, from their Bankside origins.

Chapter VIII

ALL MODERN CONVENIENCES

Edward Perronet Sells, born just before the French Revolution, grew to manhood while Britain was at war with Napoleon. The unregulated, unpoliced, oil- and moon-lit London of Georgian days was his heritage, with fields and hedgerows within easy reach. He married in his twenties, a young woman with another Huguenot name, which suggests a network of inherited relationships. His own eldest son first saw the light in the propitious year of the battle of Waterloo.

He was to have eight or possibly nine more children, mostly boys, all of whom thrived. In the fullness of time several of these younger sons were despatched into the Victorian respectability of Holy Orders. (One assumes that their grandfather's remarks, made not many years before, on the unchristian wealth of Anglican bishops, were carefully ignored.) Two of these young clergymen eventually went to minister to souls, and incidentally to acquire large tracts of land, in Australia, when it was ceasing to be a penal settlement and becoming a desirable colonial destination, thanks to the new steamships.

Edward Perronet knew Southwark when it was a hub of the coaching business, its high street lined with inns. He was in middle life when the first railway line appeared, and lived to see this expand to a vast, countrywide network. The trains' new speed seemed both to cause and symbolise the past's unprecedented rapid retreat. The coach-routes, and all the paraphernalia that had attached to them, vanished like ghosts of a remote era. The villages round London were transformed not just into suburbs but into dense urban districts, unrecognisable from Edward Perronet's youth.

He retired from the family business in 1852, the year after he and his fellow coal-merchants had exhibited a huge block of Welsh anthracite at the Great Exhibition, that celebration of Britain's breath-taking industrial and commercial dominance. He set up house in the comfort of suburban Bristol, where he probably had business connections through the Welsh coal-trade. He lived on for more than twenty years, dying in 1873 in a world now revolutionised by clean water, piped gas, antiseptics, anaesthesia, cheap public transport, the telegraph . . . No generation, before or since, has known such changes in physical habitat.

In 1815, when Edward Perronet Sells II was born, Rennie's long-planned Strand Bridge was well under construction. It ran ruler-straight from the side of Somerset House, across the river at the bend and through the plantations of Lambeth to St George's Circus. In honour of the victory over Napoleon Bonaparte it was renamed 'Waterloo Bridge' when it was opened two years later, thus inadvertently bestowing the name of an obscure village near Brussels on the future site of an international railway station and on an entire, rather drab quarter of London.

Another bridge, a cast-iron one further up river by the hamlet of Vauxhall, had been inaugurated the previous year: it too was designed to open up to building further countryside south of the river. The other iron bridge, however, Southwark Bridge, which dates from the same period, was intended rather to cut a carriage-route through the tortuous lanes behind Bankside. It took in a part of Bandy Leg Walk and created an artificial divide in a close-knit district. It was not popular in prospect: the river is particularly narrow at that point and those on the wharves, such as the Sells, felt that it would be an unnecessary obstruction to river traffic above the Pool. Nor, apparently, was it popular with either wheeled traffic or pedestrians, perhaps because it was a toll bridge. In Dickens's *Little Dorrit* (published in 1857, but set some thirty years earlier, in the time when the Marshalsea off Borough High Street was still a debtors' prison) it is described as being 'as quiet after the roaring streets as though it had been in open country'. Little Dorrit goes there to be alone, away from the crowds in the prison where her father is confined, and it is here that her lovelorn admirer, the gaoler's son, comes to find her: 'She was absorbed in thought, and he wondered what she might be thinking about. There were piles of City roofs and chimneys, more free from smoke than on weekdays; and there were the distant masts and steeples . . .'

Masts and steeples are abundantly on view in the several panoramas dating from the early nineteenth century, which was the great era of such lifelike fabrications. While the old Long Views had been just that, a view from a supposed fixed point like a bird's-eye map, these later visions were inspired by the new possibility of balloon ascents. Regularly exhibited in a specially constructed building in Leicester Square, they were designed to be seen in the round, as celebrations of the unprecedented scope of London which was now opening out on all sides. Robert Blacker, the inventor of the genre – and of the term 'panorama' – created a wonderfully complete 360-degree sweep drawn from the roof of the Albion Mills by Blackfriars Bridge shortly before they burnt down. But, more scientist than artist, he restricted himself so authentic- ally to what he could exactly see that the leadings and chimneys of the Mills loom disproportionately large in every sense. Other practitioners seem to have perceived that, just as with the old maps, some visual sleight-of-hand was needed to achieve an all-round clarity of recognisable street patterns and landmarks, and each artist tended to copy swathes of the town from earlier ones. Nevertheless such constructions give a wonderful impression of London's con- centrated busy-ness, complete with tiny individual figures engrossed in walking, riding, running, playing, fighting, loading boats.

Unfortunately none of the panoramas gives a clear, face-on view of Bankside. Thomas Girtin's 1801 version might, if we had the finished product, for he was the son of a brush maker in Bandy Leg Walk and his vantage point was ostensibly the roof of one of the Bankside glass manufacturers. However, all that survives is a tempting collection of water-colours and unfinished sketches. We see a Bankside shot-manufacturer's tower, a gust of black smoke from a neighbouring chimney, boats moored, the Albion Mills standing roofless and skeletal: otherwise, there is just an impression of low, uneven roofs, in marked contrast to the high, classical, urban architecture that had by that time risen on the opposite shore.

The 'Rhinebeck' panorama[1] of 1810 creates an extraordinarily complete, microcosmic London, but here again Bankside does not much figure except for a distinctive glass-kiln belching smoke. There is also a problem of authenticity. The ships in the Pool of London, which is the central focus of this work, receive extremely detailed and skilled treatment, as do a few warehouses near the Tower. But elsewhere the buildings, including the water frontages of Bermondsey and Southwark, have clearly all been filled in by journeyman hands and show a regularity and symmetry they did not really have.

Moving on a generation to Smith's 'Balloon View' of the early 1840s, one finds something of the same drawing-by-rote in the repetitive blocks of streets, all with their identical roofs – though it could be argued that this sober homogeneity really did characterise the Georgian and Regency London that had grown up, before Victorian grandiosity began to rebuild parts of it. But here at least we get a look at a sliver of Bankside fairly close to, from the rear, as in the seventeenth-century views. Time has moved on here from the Rhinebeck vista. London Bridge has been rebuilt and St Saviour's has been remodelled. On the east side of the Bridge the railway line has appeared, snaking in on a long viaduct from Greenwich: it is the harbinger of many more to come. Southwark and Waterloo Bridges are now in place, with their attached roads, scissoring up the old south-bank geography. On Bankside itself the ruins of the Bishop's palace are quite extensive at this date. Exposed by a fire in 1814, they have not yet been re-submerged in nineteenth-century warehouses. The shore still has its moored boats, but there is apparently much more industry than before. This impression is confirmed by one of a series of articles[2] in *The Penny Magazine*, a popular periodical of the time, which appeared the year before the Smith panorama:

'Those dwellers and visitors to the "Great Metropolis" who cross Southwark Bridge from the City to the Borough can scarcely fail to have observed the array of tall chimneys which meets the eye on either side of its southern extremity; each one serving as a kind of beacon or guide-post to some larger manufacturing establishment beneath – here a brewery, there a saw-mill, farther on a hat factory, a distillery, a vinegar factory, and numerous others. Indeed, Southwark is as distinguishable at a distance for its numerous tall chimneys and the clouds of smoke emitted by them, as London is for its thickly-congregated church spires' – and the rest of the article is devoted to describing the Barclay Perkins brewery, in the reverential tones often used by Victorian observers in evoking some particularly enormous and highly organised temple to capitalism and consumption. But the message is clear: the ancient town of Southwark had by now become the recognised industrial quarter of the supposedly more high-minded and august London on the opposite bank with its innumerable places of worship.

This was the culmination of a process on Bankside which had been coming for many decades. In terms of more recent evolution, the most significant difference between the panorama of 1810 and that of the 1840s is to be found on the river. In the earlier view, the Pool is crowded with essentially the same sort of pot-bellied sailing vessels that we see in illustrations of Napoleonic battles. By the 1840s, however, all the ships, regardless of size, are slimmer, sleeker, more like the clippers that raced cargoes home on the India route. And there are also many, many more of them, moored in mid-stream several deep and crowding the new wet docks that have appeared. Trade has clearly been increasing exponentially, and the time when all foreign and dutiable goods had to pass through the congested 'legal quays' below London Bridge on the north bank is now a past era. However, the most significant thing about these vessels, if one looks at them carefully, is the number that now have tall black smoke stacks, sometimes in combination with sail, sometimes on their own.

Steam power had come, and was gaining over sail year by year. The first steam-powered paddle boat, which had been built on the Clyde and journeyed round the coast of Britain, came up from Gravesend to Wapping in January 1815. Three years later a regular time-table between London and the estuary mouth had been established, something which had never been possible with sailing ships, which were always subject to winds and tides. The journey, however, was slow, at over five hours, and the unwieldy boats were often delayed by broken paddles. Laughed at by watermen and conventional skippers, these steamers were at first regarded as a bit of fun rather than a serious challenge to river ways. By 1822 only two hundred and twenty-seven steam voyages had been accomplished up or down the Thames in six months.

Thirty years later, half that number took place every day. Steamships were arriving constantly from distant places and the face of the river had been transformed. Henry Mayhew, the great mid-Victorian social commentator, wrote: 'The Thames is no longer the "silent highway", since its silence is continually broken by the clatter of steam-boats. This change has materially affected the position and diminished the number of the London watermen.'

At first, work for the watermen continued, since the steamers, like the sailing ships they were replacing, anchored in mid-Channel, and the ferries were still needed to take passengers and their baggage on and off. However, the wash created by the paddles caused trouble: people were afraid; there were many accidents, and also disastrous collisions between steam and sail. By the early 1840s – the very same time that the expansion of the railways was causing a rapid collapse in the coach trade – the steamers were becoming more efficient and manoeuvrable, and riverside piers were built. More and more of these appeared, as competing companies each tried to establish their own monopoly and poach other people's customers. Mayhew noted: 'Since the prevalence of steam packets as a means of locomotion along the Thames, the "stairs" . . . above bridge, are for the most part almost nominal stations for watermen. [These would have included the Bankside stairs that had for so long been location-markers under their ancient names – Goat stairs, Mason stairs and so on]. At London Bridge stairs (Middlesex side) there now lie but three boats, while before the steam era, or rather before the removal of old London Bridge, ten times that number of boats were to be "hailed" there.'

Although the watermen were reluctant to admit it, in fact the development of steam had been one of several pressing reasons for removing the old bridge with its narrow arches. By the same token, it would have been impossible to cope with all the trade in goods that the steamers generated without this surplus being taken by the new wet docks, from St Katharine's by the Tower down as far as the Isle of Dogs. Although the river of the mid-century was perceived as extraordinarily crowded, it was actually rather less chaotically full than it had been in the days when 'all the trade of the country was laying out in the river', as the Clerk to the Watermen's Company remarked.

As for the watermen, their business much diminished, their skills in 'shooting' the old bridge obsolete, they turned, over the space of a generation, from being the jolly, well-placed river-masters of tradition into figures of pity. Many were now only partially employed, taking occasional steam-passengers with luggage to the other bank of the river, and Mayhew noted 'though they are civil and honest . . . they are very poor'. They could not afford to repair their ageing boats, and Parliament said that they needed stronger boats anyway against the steamboat washes. Some took to hanging around the new toll bridges up river, accosting pedestrians and offering to ferry them across for the same price as the money they would otherwise put in the turnstile – a mere penny or two. In the records of St Saviour's parish, where so many watermen had always lived, destitute ones, or their widows, crop up frequently as examples of 'absolute, wretched poverty', reduced from a comfortable income to picking up discarded bread crusts in the gutters. In the very long term John Taylor, with his poetic diatribes against other forms of travel, had been right.

Astute, too, had been the first Edward Sells, by shifting a hundred years earlier into a specialised form of lighterage. The lighterage business was unaffected by the changes, since 'dumb' lighters were anyway dependent on the tides to be moved – and thus on the skill of the lightermen – and ultimately it made little difference if the moving force were sail or steam. Traffic that was taken away from the lightermen by the new docks and railways was well compensated for by the overall increase in trade. As for coal-merchants, since their goods were the essential fuel that was powering all these changes, they had nothing to fear.

This was in spite of the fact that the price of coal fell during the 1820s; and after 1831, when the government finally managed to dismantle the complex and archaic monopoly system of dues, taxes and protected employments that had gathered round the trade, it fell much more. The Sells's Bankside neighbour William Horne, brother to Thomas, gave evidence on this to a government commission. As a scrupulous Quaker, he was in favour of abolishing the whole system under which prices were estimated according to volume by tiers of underpaid and therefore bribeable officials. The 'chaldron' measure was at last to be seen off into history and the sale of coal by weight came in. Horne declared, however, that 'he was doing less business and had higher expenses than formerly', and intimated that the fortunes that had been made by some eighteenth-century coal-merchants were now a thing of the past, which was probably true. He seemed to be suggesting that it was mainly loyalty to the family tradition that kept him in the trade. All the same, he had 'about 12 laden lighters at his wharf on Bankside' at any one time, and said that his net annual profit was about £4000, which was a very large income for that date: it is clear that the business was still a solidly prosperous one. The new railways and steamships, which altered the old pattern of delivery to London by sea from Tyneside, were themselves customers, and they also opened up trade in new directions. Horne exported a good deal of coal abroad, even as far as India, and this business in time came to the Charringtons, with whom Jones & Sells were later to join forces.

There was another new customer too, right on Bankside and by and by in many other places as well. Till the beginning of the nineteenth century the streets of the capital were lit by parish oil-lamps, which produced only pools of light in the general dimness and required regular trimming and cleaning by underpaid 'greasy fellows'. In 1807, however, Pall Mall was given coal-fuelled gas-lamps. These were regarded as such a success that plans were made in 1812 to light Westminster Bridge with gas too – in spite of scoffing from one MP, who refused to believe that you could have a light anywhere without a wick in it. Other people, however, had understood that an essential advantage of gas-lighting was that it could be piped from a distance, and thus centrally organised both physically and commercially. The charter to supply Westminster Bridge was given to the newly formed Gas Light & Coke Company, which built itself a works on Bankside not two hundred yards upstream from where the Sells, the Hornes and several other coal-merchants had their offices.

It was probably because the plentiful coal supplies to make the gas were so near at hand that Bankside was chosen for this innovative venture. Indeed, you could argue that the decision of the first Edward Sells to enter the coal-business there in 1755, even before the Hornes's arrival, had vertiginously long-term effects on the whole character of the area. For, near the end of the nineteenth century, the same logic of proximity meant that one of the first of the new works to generate electricity was built alongside the gas works, which it eventually took over. Then, in the mid-twentieth century, since electricity was already being manufactured on Bankside, when a larger Power Station was needed it was put on the existing site right opposite St Paul's – a place which would never otherwise have been chosen. And this is why, at the end of the twentieth century, a huge and distinctive brick building was there to make an iconic focus for the regeneration of a Bankside from which industrial identity had by then fled.

Thus do patches of London's ground, which are nothing in themselves but gravel and clay and river mud, and the ground-down dust of brick and stone and bones, wood and wormwood and things thrown away, acquire through ancient incidental reasons a kind of generic programming that persists through time.

The first Bankside gas-holders in their round cast-iron casings were relatively small, rising no higher than a genteel three-storey brick house which certainly pre-dated them, as pictured in a water-colour of the period. The business flourished, and was re-christened the Phoenix Gas Company: members of the Barclay and Perkins families were on the board of directors. In 1829, though still retaining its local name, it became part of the South Metropolitan Gas Light and Coke Company. By that time over three hundred miles of London streets were lit by gas. North of the river, the Imperial Gas Light and Coke Company held sway, and gas-holders were developing the elephantine dimensions still familiar to us from the now-disused edifices behind St Pancras Station. Shops took up gas-lighting with enthusiasm: their windows were said to light up the whole street, scaring away thieves and pickpockets but encouraging citizens into late hours and therefore, according to some, into unrespectable behaviour.

After about 1840 gas began to make its way into private

homes, for lighting: first it penetrated the ground floor and only later the bedrooms. Gas cooking-stoves and gas fires, though invented early, were not to become common for another fifty years. Gas-light was received at first with reservations – what a pity one could no longer wear worn silks and taffetas at evening parties, as had been the custom in the forgiving glow of candles! – but by and by came universal acceptance of the convenience of gas by the middle classes, who were in a position to run up bills and pay them at set intervals. Candle-ends remained the choice of the poor. In the more squalid lanes off Bankside, there were still some houses lit only by candle-light in the early twentieth century.

And, of course, it tended to be the poor who suffered from the inconveniences of gas works from which they themselves did not benefit, either directly or financially. In the mid-1860s, by which time gas works were smoking away all over London, an impassioned article[3] on their nuisance appeared in *The Times*:

'Wherever a gas factory . . . is situated within the metropolis, there is established a centre whence radiates a whole neighbourhood of squalor, poverty and disease. No improvement can ever reach that infected neighbourhood – no new streets, no improved dwellings, not even a garden is possible within a circle of at least a quarter of a mile in diameter, and not so much as a geranium can flourish in a window sill.'

That may have been an exaggerated view: there has never been any evidence linking gas works to infection, let alone to total blight. But it was certainly true that the faint but persistent smell discouraged middle-class occupation. A terrible explosion, in 1865, at a gas works up the river in Battersea reinforced the message. In any case, no doubt for a whole range of reasons, by then the Sells dynasty had finally quit their Bankside home.

In the days before the clack of steamship paddles and the sound of their hooters became a constant background to river life, and Bankside was still a good address, how was number 49 faring?

According to the rates books, in the first two decades of the nineteenth century the Sells family were variously living and conducting business at the other Bankside houses they owned. 49 was let for some years to the fellow coal-merchant Thomas Fuce. But by 1824 Vincent Sells is listed in *Pigot's Directory* as living there, and he is still there in 1830. His rates were then £2.10s. per half-year, a little more than those of the Reverend William Mann, the principal chaplain of St Saviour's, who was a near neighbour at 44, and more than was paid by two other St Saviour's clerics, the Reverends Harrison and Benson, who occupied numbers 45 and 46. (Number 49 still had its yard and long garden behind, stretching seventy feet down the length of Cardinal Cap Alley; these other houses did not.) In the Alley, the Sells had rather less select neighbours, for by that time a number of tiny houses had been built at the Skin Market end of the Alley. The Sells owned six of these.

Vincent Sells was the brother of Edward Perronet Sells, younger than him by six years. Edward Perronet and his growing family were then living in 56, Edward Sells the father in 55. Vincent himself appears never to have married. He must have been approaching thirty when he moved into 49, and this, I think, is when the house got the face-lift that is still evident today. It was the early 1820s, and in the boom in property that had followed the end of the Napoleonic Wars it was worth spending money on a Bankside home. There are also indications, in Vincent Sells's Will of twenty years later, that he valued the gentlemanly appurtenances of life.

So, if the original windows that were flush with the façade had not already been replaced by then, they were now, though the design still included interior box-shutters. On the outside, decorative surrounds were added, and the whole of the early Georgian brickwork was covered in a layer of stucco. Inside, especially on the first floor, some new, rather delicate mouldings were added round the doors, and the fine front room was given an elegant new Regency fireplace. Physical signs of other decoration of the period have vanished, but my guess is that much of the wooden panelling was painted over at this time, and other walls were papered with ribbon stripes or 'Grecian' motifs. It is possible also that this was when a narrow, gridded opening, with a window below it, was made in the paving in front of the house. This would have allowed a modest amount of light and air into the cavernous front cellar, and would have given the genteel appearance of a house possessing servants' quarters, though whether it was really feasible to use the front cellar for kitchen purposes before the introduction of domestic gaslight I do not know. Possibly, at the same time, a semi-submerged window onto the yard and the garden beyond it was made in the back cellar.

(The back wall of the house, including the windows on the ground and first floor, and the levels of paving beyond, was modified in the 1930s and again later in the century, so one can only speculate on the original contours.)

It would also almost certainly have been in the 1820s that the first water closet was installed in number 49. One may imagine old Edward Sells, in his nearby house, scoffing that the yard privy that had been good enough for him, his father and all the generations before was surely good enough for his sons, but the fact was that all over London an early version of the flush toilet was now being introduced in middle-class homes. In the year of Waterloo, the connection of cess-pools and house drains to the old sewer ditches, which ran down to other watercourses and finally into the river, was finally allowed. It was the very thing the Commissioners for Sewers had been trying to prevent since Tudor times, yet somehow no one seems to have foreseen what the result would be. Perhaps the awakening of public health consciousness, which produced reports about 'airless courts', and pauper children in 'confin'd rooms', and strange 'miasmas' seen hanging above graveyards, was too firmly attached to the airborne theory of infection to speculate sufficiently on the danger carried in polluted water.

Drinking water continued to be extracted from the Thames and piped straight to customers. By the late 1820s doubts were being voiced about the wisdom of this. Cartoons about the evils lurking in the river appeared in *Punch*; the banker and Radical MP Sir Francis Burdett raised the matter in the House of Commons. A Royal Commission appointed the following year concluded that water ought to be got 'from other sources' – yet at least one engineer who gave evidence was of the opinion that 'the Thames was as pure as spring water'. There seems to have been a persistent idea in the medical profession that just as the air blowing along the tidal river was supposedly full of 'ozone' and might prevent disease, so the water itself somehow purified whatever went into it. This essentially magic notion persisted in the face of accumulating evidence to the contrary. In 1800 the Thames had still been the fishing river it was in medieval days. There were then said to be four hundred working fishermen between Putney Bridge in the west and Greenwich in the east. Plaice and salmon could be caught off Billingsgate, right in the Pool of London. Twenty-five years later, catches had very much declined, but the fishermen themselves blamed such specific ills as 'the refuse of hospitals, slaughter-houses, colour, lead and soap works and manufacturies'. While all these did undoubtedly add to the river's dirtiness, they cannot have had anything like the overall impact of the newly waterborne household sewage. In 1831 came the first epidemic identified as cholera.

Yet more and more water closets were installed in the years that followed. Of course, to the owners and users of these conveniences, the first generation ever to enjoy the comfort of a relatively odourless indoor lavatory, the system seemed wonderfully hygienic. After hundreds of years of periodic visits from men with shovels and stinking night-soil carts, the waste just disappeared: then, as now, out of sight was out of mind. It was not till 1840 that Thomas Cubitt, from the family responsible for building much of late Georgian and early Victorian London, expressed the problem forthrightly, and not till another epidemic eight years later that the wisdom of his words was really accepted:

'Fifty years ago nearly all London had every house cleansed into a large cesspool . . . Now, sewers having been very much improved, scarcely any person thinks of making a cesspool, but it is carried off at once into the river. The Thames is now made a great cess-pool instead of each person having one of his own.'

On Bankside, of course, the houses were ideally placed for using the Thames as their cess-pool. In the previous century, as the evidence of the first Edward Sells's lease suggests, some occupiers had always benefited from 'necessary houses' built out over the river. Number 49 was in any case very near the Moss Alley sluice (anciently called the Boar's Head sluice), one of the outlets of the thirteenth-century ditch-system: the house where Edward Perronet was living was almost directly above it. No very extensive building works would have been required for either of the brothers to find a corner indoors and plumb in a cone-shaped 'Hopper' bowl. This was provided with a trap at the bottom and a tap which, when it was opened, produced a trickling spiral of water that (in theory) cleaned the bowl. At the same time, each house probably acquired a drained sink and a wash basin.

Such amenities tended not to make their way to the upper floors till later in the century, when pressurised water arrived. However, this also seems to have been the period when the closets on the upper floors of number 49 were extended over the top of Cardinal Cap Alley, backed up against the section of number 50 that was already built over the front six foot of the Alley. This would suggest that Vincent Sells organised himself the luxury of a first-floor lavatory, into whose cistern water could have been pumped up by hand.

Some idea of what a prosperous Bankside coal-merchant's house was like at this time, in its basic fixtures and fittings, may be got from the Deeds of three nearby houses, numbers 44, 45 and 46, since by a happy chance these documents have in part survived. These houses occupied the plot of land which had, at the turn of the sixteenth and seventeenth centuries, belonged to Henslowe, and in the early eighteenth century to Sir William Oldner. Around the mid-century, the holding was split up and what was to be number 46 was sold to Edmund Shallett, he of Nonconformist renown, while Henry Thrale the brewer seems to have owned 44 and 45. In 1764 all three houses came together again in a purchase by the Horne family, and were owned by them for over ninety years. The ground floor of 46 was half taken up by a cart-entry, which led into a yard shared with 45 and to big sheds at the back. By the 1830s number 44 was let to the Reverend William Mann, his wife and his six children, but it is clear from the details of a subsequent lease from the 1840s that this house, which was a more handsome width than the other two, had previously been equipped by one of the Hornes for comfortable modern living. It is therefore reasonable to suppose that the same standards would have applied in Vincent Sells's revamped home, at number 49.

A salient feature of number 44 is the amount of strong and no doubt rather elegant brasswork that had been added: brass holders for stair-treads, brass doorknobs and finger plates, shutter fixings, bell pulls, brackets for mahogany flap-down tables in the closets, brass candle-holders in the first-floor 'Music Room'. In what is listed as the Dining Parlour there was 'a composition figure on a pedestal, with brass sconce and glass shade' – presumably a lamp. The production of brass, though of ancient origins, had greatly increased in the early nineteenth century. Much of the newly accessible, decorative 'Benares ware' – bowls, trays, boxes and so forth – that graced middle-class homes, bringing to them a resonance of the Indian Empire, was really made in Birmingham. Other brass artefacts were actually exported to India: a fine 1860s iron and brass turnstile, bearing the trade-plate of a foundry in Bear Lane, Southwark, still functions at the entrance to a museum in Bombay.

However, what these London foundries mainly thrived on was the production of workaday small objects for which there was now a mass demand: the pipes, nuts, bolts and joints on which depended the new steamships, railway engines and mechanised workshops, the new gas industry – and also the accessories for the new plumbing. Number 44 could boast two lead-lined sinks, each with a 'valve sink hole' and 'brass cock' (tap), one of them in a closet set aside for china. Presumably this was for convenience in dealing with the perpetual drift of grime and discolouring fog that was by then London's famous blight – 'Fog down the river, where it rolls defiled among the tiers of shipping, and the waterside pollutions of a great (and dirty) city . . . Smoke lowering down from chimney-pots, making a soft black drizzle with flakes of soot in it as big as full-grown snowflakes . . .'[4] Also on the ground floor, in a Dressing Room that seems to have been conveniently located between the Drawing Room and the Dining Parlour, was 'a large oval brass washstand with solid marble basin and plug, brass cock . . . A corner Mahogany cupboard with water closet.' This was the only one in the house. The long era of chamber-pots kept in the sideboard for gentlemen to relieve themselves at table was evidently giving way to a greater decorum. Whether Mr Mann's wife and his three adult daughters, not to mention the younger children, used this water closet as a general rule, or whether the habit of ladies retreating to china vessels in the privacy of their bedrooms was still engrained in polite circles, only the extremely old, recollecting their own grand-parents, may now be able to tell us.

The kitchen of 44, which I think was in a back-addition down a few steps, and was now closed off by the classic green baize door, had its own old-style tap and cistern, with a 'filter stone' in it – which was no doubt rather necessary. There was 'an excellent stout kitchen range', then a fairly new improve-ment on the old kitchen fire with iron hooks above it. There was also an iron heating stove in one of the upper rooms. The Hornes had evidently turned an eye to Europe. By way of a reminder of the essential underpinning of all this middle-class comfort, the downstairs Dressing Room was further equipped with 'an excellent iron safe', and there was a 'plate cupboard' (silver cupboard) in one of the upstairs back rooms 'fitted up . . . in the most complete and secure manna lined with iron and studded all over the front with iron screws, three excellently well-finished patent locks, a large iron bolt to go into the floor.' No doubt one of the nearby Southwark iron foundries had supplied these needs.

There were also, included in the fittings, a number of window blinds, evidently designed to shut out the industrial views Bankside now enjoyed. Behind these, reinforced after dusk by heavy, lined curtains, the inhabitants could live in a protected cocoon. As a French visitor of the period remarked, English houses were by then 'like chimneys turned inside out' – covered in soot on the outside, but warm, clean and comfortable within.

Both the industries of Bankside and the comfort these earned for their proprietors continued to increase the amount of filth flowing into the Thames. In the 1840s the problem was exacerbated by a prohibition on any new cess-pits and further attempts to get existing ones linked to sewers. This was when the working-class houses in the Skin Market, which was now reduced to a narrow lane off Cardinal Cap Alley, were linked up to the Moss Alley drain and hence to the Boar's Head sluice. There was also the public health reformer Edwin Chadwick's disastrous attempt to 'cleanse' the sewers by flushing them through, which simply drove more filth out into the river. Discussion of a sensible drainage plan was further impeded by an old-fashioned fixed idea that waste was valuable manure and must somehow continue to produce wealth, as it had when the night-soil men sold cartloads to farmers of Kent and Middlesex. Not until another serious cholera epidemic in 1848–9 was the problem really faced. *The Builder* finally declared of Thames water in 1851:

'Our tea is infused in it; our viandes cooked; our toddy mixed; our milk watered with it; our beer brewed in it, and every liquid element commingles with the filthy exuvicae of the foul and every more foully increasing tide: we lave in it; the body linen of the multitude is steeped therein, and when wrung out the desiccated essences of poison envelope the breathing pores of the wearers.'

While this condemnation may have been a little far-reaching (the specific nature of the cholera bacillus was then unknown), you do begin to wonder how the Sells managed, collectively, to rear such large, healthy families. Perhaps, like their neighbours Horne and Mann, they installed a cistern filter: perhaps Edward Perronet Sells's children were of stout constitution and developed an early toleration of impurities, bolstered by a good diet. For the burial registers of St Saviour's parish show the marked difference that had now appeared in the mortality rates of different social classes. In the registers for 1831, the year of the first cholera epidemic, a trickle of people of all ages, including many babies and young children, died in Bear Lane, Moss Alley, White Hart Lane and two in Cardinal Cap Alley itself, whereas none of the names of the more prosperous families, including the Sells, figure in the record.[5]

It is, however, a fact that the departure from Bankside of Vincent Sells, the bachelor uncle, appears to have taken place in 1831 or very soon after. Evidently, even though 49 had been nicely done up and modernised, something induced him to move out. The house was then let to George Holditch, who I believe acted as confidential clerk to Jones & Sells. Vincent remained in the firm, in partnership with his brother Edward Perronet, and he continued to show interest and support for the long-drawn-out cause of St Saviour's restoration, but when he inherited 49 outright, on his father's death in Camberwell ten years later, he did not move back in.

He had not gone far, only to the newly built, rather grand Trinity Square, one of the developments that were filling up the fields south of St George's church going towards the still-countrified cross-roads at Newington – transformed today as the Elephant and Castle. I know this because Trinity Square is the address that appears on Vincent's death certificate. Although he was only forty-eight, he survived his father by less than a year, succumbing in April 1842 to what was recorded as 'pneumonia', a term then widely used to cover any chest complaint including the dreaded, unmentionable tuberculosis. So probably it was not the cholera scare that had driven him from Bankside ten years before but a chronic weakness in the lungs: I can well imagine the doctors of the time telling him he would be better off away from the river fogs in a nice, new district. Oddly, when his Will was proved, he was stated to have died on Bankside, but there is presumably a confusion here with his business address. His collection of 'plate' and 'all my books' he left to his brother Edward Perronet. Number 49 he left jointly to his nephew, Edward Perronet II, and to 'my friend George Ware' for them to hold in Trust. The beneficiary of the Trust was to be his unmarried sister, Sophia Elizabeth, four years older than him, who was to get the rent from it.

As for the health-risks of Bankside, these were real, as later years were to prove. The figures eventually produced by John Snow, who was Chadwick's associate and a far more astute observer, finally spelt out how crucial to health the water supply was. In the cholera epidemic of 1849 the death rates in Lambeth and Southwark were similar. But in the 1854 outbreak Lambeth deaths were very much fewer. In the intervening years Southwark had gone on being supplied by the infamous Southwark & Vauxhall Waterworks, to which the Sells sold coal and about which George Cruikshank had already been drawing scary cartoons over twenty years before. Lambeth, however, had now begun to get water from Thames Ditton, above the Teddington Lock, far from the murky tides down river.

However, during the 1830s and '40s, Vincent's brother, Edward Perronet, continued robustly to live on Bankside with his own large family. In the Census for 1841, when they were at number 54 with the counting house (and no doubt extra living space too) next door in 55, the household included nine children, ranging in ages from mid-twenties to three, plus two female servants. And by 1851 number 49 was once more back in Sells occupation, for the eldest son, Edward Perronet II (Vincent's nephew) was now in his mid-thirties and living there with his wife, a small son and daughter, and the usual complement of two servants. It is to be hoped that he duly paid his aunt Sophia her rent.

Southwark, following the rest of London, finally received a modern drainage system in the late 1860s, under the auspices of the Metropolitan Board of Works (founded 1855). This was also the point at which the Borough had to relinquish the last of its old claims to being a separate town and became administratively one with the capital.[6] But as a footnote to this whole saga of sewage and water, there is a question in my mind that I have not been able to resolve. Information on exactly how the drainage was sorted out on Bankside is not easy to come by. So far, neither the copious Metropolitan Board of Works archives, nor the scant and little-recorded ones in the possession of Southwark Council, have provided much material on this. The accounts of the great works of Joseph Bazalgette all tend to concentrate on his most celebrated and revolutionary plan, that for London north of the river. This involved new cross-town interceptor sewers at several levels, the lowest of which ran right along the Thames, much of it under the new and specially built Embankment, to carry all the waste eastwards in the direction of the sea. This changed for ever the aspect of the north bank of the river above Blackfriars Bridge, sweeping away old wharves and water-stairs on that side and confirming the districts west of Charing Cross as the *beaux quartiers*. The Embankment was, incidentally, funded in part from a new tax on coal arriving in London, as many other grand public building works had been before. Fortunately the Prime Minister Gladstone's appalling proposal, that the Embankment Gardens should be covered in tall, government-owned blocks which could be let at expensive rents to enable the government to do without income tax, was not taken up.

It was recognised that the lower-lying south bank was going to be harder to drain, geographically, and I suspect it was also felt that south London did not matter as much. Since Southwark and Bermondsey were now the major district of wharves and industry, no great riverfront works could be undertaken on that side without upsetting the whole organisation of London's trade. Only a small stretch of embankment was ever built there, the Albert Embankment in Lambeth, west of the Archbishop's Palace: it provided, incidentally, a new site for St Thomas's Hospital, which had been displaced by the railway. After some Parliamentary dispute, the eventual plan for south London was like that for the north, on a modified and (one would think) less satisfactory pattern, making use of some existing old watercourses. A high-level sewer ran eastwards from Clapham to Deptford Creek, with a line in from Dulwich (the old Effra stream). A low-level sewer, which already existed in part as the Earl Sewer, ran from Putney High Street to Deptford, where a pumping station was installed to take the waste further on its way. But since this low-level sewer was well inland from the Thames, it is hard to see how it dealt with the problem of the riverside areas of Southwark and Bermondsey, which had established drains straight into the Thames. Can some attempt have been made to reverse the flow in the old conduits, such as the one that discharged at Boar's Head sluice, so as to have them discharge southwards into the interceptor sewer? Such an idea was not unknown: it was used when drainage was laid in Chicago and the old sewers needed to be diverted from the lake. But if anything like this came to pass on Bankside, the record itself seems to have drained away into some archival pit from which I have not managed to retrieve it.

Before the drainage works were completed, or the Albert Embankment opened, the Sells had left Bankside.

In 1852 Edward Perronet Sells was sixty-four. Through the 1840s he had been the rate-payer on three Bankside properties, numbers 54, 55 and 56, and also on 'a wharf, warehouse and stabling', but by the Census of 1851 these had been let to other people working in the coal-trade. His eldest son, Edward Perronet II, then aged thirty-six, was established in the business and living in number 49 with his wife, servants and his own two small children. Most of the other eight or nine offspring were launched on life in various ways; even the youngest, Arthur, was now fourteen. Like his own father, the first Edward Perronet Sells had concerned himself with Vestry business, taking his turn as church-warden or commissioner for this or that parish charity, and in 1852 he signalled his final departure into a comfortable retirement in Bristol by resigning as Treasurer of St Saviour's National Schools. These then still occupied part of the plot of the old Cross Bones graveyard, which was not finally closed for burial till the following year. Edward Perronet had held the post of Treasurer 'honourably and beneficially to the School for 25 years'. The school committee presented him with a testimonial to say so, mentioning his 'devotion to the cause of education in general' and his 'uniform kindness'. In return the committee offered gratitude and 'their earnest Prayer for his health and happiness', a prayer that evidently bore fruit as he lived to the age of eighty-five. The testimonial, which is the size of a modern poster, contains nine different kinds of typeface, elaborated further with decora-tive flourishes, as if it were a sample-sheet for apprentice printers, and must have brought joy to the heart of a man whose own handwriting was so exquisite. Clearly he prized it, for it remains in the family to this day.

The head of Jones & Sells was now Edward Perronet II. A photograph exists of this gentleman, looking large and cheerful with a spade-shaped mid-Victorian beard, but it is not the kind of face one associates with the acumen and determination of the old lightermen Sells. In 1856 the family firm amalgamated with another to form Wright, Sells, Dale and Surtees, but three years later Mr Wright died and there was a further amalgamation with Charringtons. This firm had been prominent in opening up the trade in soft Welsh coal from the Rhondda; they were now on their way to becoming the dominant coal-merchants of the time. The amalgamation eventually created Charrington, Sells, Dale & Co., which traded under that name for the next sixty years, had its own railway waggons, and was immortalised by John Betjeman.

. . . Charrington, Sells, Dale and Co.,
Nuts and nuggets in the window, trucks along the lines
   below.

The firms with which the Sells had joined forces already possessed wharves suitable for unloading coal up river at Wandsworth, and also down river in Stepney and Shadwell in locations convenient for the Regent's Canal or for railway haulage. Although 49 Bankside was still listed as the business address of Charrington, Sells, Dale & Surtees in 1860, there must have been less and less reason for that as a location. In the early '60s the family occupying it may have been in the Sells's employ, since the eldest son and chief earner is listed as Wharf Clerk, but the Sells family's long association with the river was nearing its end. In 1865 an entire block, comprising numbers 49, 50, 51 and 52 Bankside, and the wharf-space and berthage rights that went with them, was let to Moss Isaacs, iron-merchant. More prosaically, this meant a dealer in scrap-metal, a lucrative trade but hardly a prestigious one. One must assume that Sophia, who was living in York Road, Montpelier, Bristol, with her brother, went on enjoying the income from 49, before being transported into the high Victorian grandeur of Arnos Vale Cemetery there in 1869.

Even without the amalgamations, there would have been a number of other reasons at that point for the family to move out of Bankside. London, as it grew larger, grew ever dirtier too. The time when it was still acceptable for the moneyed classes to live close by the works that produced their wealth – and much of the dirt – was rapidly passing: henceforth, industrialists would wish to live as gentry in the countryside round London and travel to and fro by train. One result of this was that the trains themselves were increasingly present in Southwark, and this did nothing to enhance life for those living near by. There was also the Bankside gas works, which was busy extending its terrain. In 1862 a fire at Price's oil stores nearby, which nearly reached the gas-holders, can have done nothing to reassure the occupants of houses in the area. The riverside, with so many warehouses now stuffed with combustible goods, seemed very vulnerable. The year before, there had been a major waterfront fire on the Bermondsey side, which consumed twenty warehouses full of jute, oil and wax and food stuffs, sending rivers of burning fat out among the lighters on the Thames.

But the exact timing of the Sells's retreat from Bankside, followed by its sale of the property there some years later, may have been influenced by another, more specific factor. The proposal for another bridge over the Thames right opposite St Paul's, which had been revived in the year of the Great Exhibition, was being put forward again with some fervour ten years later and plans were actually drawn up. It did not happen then – but, had it done so, the Sells might have had every reason to hope that the bridge or its approaches would sweep through the Bankside properties they owned, if not numbers 49–52, then numbers 54, 55 and 56 and the various back-lane tenements. This might have made them a nice profit in compensation for loss of wharfage rights, more in fact than ageing early-Georgian houses might realistically earn in rent. Perhaps, therefore, they held onto all this property to see what would happen, and only decided on a definitive sale when the bridge-plan was once again shelved. The sale of numbers 49–52 to the sitting tenant, Moss Isaacs, finally took place in 1873, and, though I have no direct evidence concerning numbers 54, 55 and 56, I suspect they were sold at the same time, since that was also the year of the first Edward Perronet's death and they had evidently been his personal property. Within a few years these three houses were gone, and a large new Crown Wharf building rose in their place.

The contract of sale by which 49 Bankside and its wharf-rights were finally disposed of to Moss Isaacs has come to rest in the house today. It is handwritten on parchment, decorated with seals. Clipped to it is a more modest document, a note written on beige paper headed from '49 Bankside, St Saviour's'. It is undated, but must presumably relate to the time of the sale. The Holditches seem to have been back living in the house, where their family had lodged intermittently over the decades. It rather looks as if they were the Sells's representatives on the site, helping to finalise negotiations:

Dear Mrs Sells,

I called at Mr Ellory's lodging and gave him your parcel and sent you by Hind's hand the twenty sovereigns and the receipts I had from him for the title papers and Sir Christofer's letter. The carved animals he said were not to be spoke of in the receipt. George has covered up the holes in the ceiling with four bits of wood so it don't show now and if Mr John looks in he won't see it. He should be glad you made that good use of the old things instead of his grumbles. Believe me I am glad of the ten sovs.

Your truly thankful
Jes Holditch

One longs to know more about the transaction referred to, and why the note, so informal and opaque, was treated as a document to be preserved. Mrs Sells I assume to be Elizabeth, the wife of Edward Perronet II, who had lived in the house herself and must have known about the carved animals. Where, in 49, were they? Could they possibly have decorated the cellar ceiling-beams, some of which may have been in the house before the 1710 rebuilding? If so, these things 'not to be spoke of in the receipt' were relics of the Elizabethan inn, and the mysterious Mr Ellory or Sir Christofer had presumably realised their antiquarian value. George is, I think, George Alfred Holditch, son of Jessica who wrote the letter and of George the ex-cider merchant: a decade later young George was once more living in part of 49, as a rent collector. John is a name which crops up in later generations of Sells, but this Mr John appears to be the brother of the now-dead Sophia and therefore uncle of Edward Perronet II. ('Mr John' was the usual polite way in which those slightly lower down the social scale distinguished a younger brother from the senior one. It did not imply youth, and indeed John Sells, born in 1796, would now be in his late seventies.) According to the contract of sale, Sophia had left him her interest in the house, of which he was now the vendor. As he too normally lived in Bristol, it was probably safe to assume that he would not be scrutinising the cellar ceiling minutely. Jes Holditch's words seem to suggest the slightly disgruntled family member, ever distrustful of what his siblings or nephews might do, living off some of the proceeds of the family's accumulated property and anxious to get the best price for it. He seems to have taken no active part in the coal-trade.

He did, however, have something to grumble about. A few years earlier the partnership between his nephew and Charringtons, which had been in existence since 1859, went through what seems to have been a very sticky patch. I know no more about this than what I have read in *The Story of the Charringtons*. According to this source, the capital with which the partnership was set up was to be provided jointly, £6000 from the brothers John and Thomas Charrington and £8000 from E. P. Sells & Company. Eight thousand would be the equivalent of several hundred thousand pounds today: the agreed sum presumably reflects the fact that the Charringtons were bringing more to the merger in the form of wharf and railway-yard space. However, the figure turned out to be largely illusory. Thomas Charrington wrote later: 'In the year 1866 – after repeated efforts by John Charrington to get a proper examination of the accounts, a balance sheet was drawn up, and it was ascertained that EP Sells & Company's capital was £345.19s.7d, less than nothing at all, their nominal capital having consisted of one large debt, which proved to be bad, and there is no doubt that their estimate of profits prior to the partnership was utterly fallacious . . . The state of matters (above) . . . caused the retirement of Mr Dale from any part of the management of the business of the firm, Mr Surtees having retired by compulsion previously . . . Hardly any portion of EP Sells &

Company's connection exists now, the Southwark and Vauxhall and Grand Junction Water Companies (which formed the most important part of it) having been lost . . .'

The message seems clear. Even if Messrs. Dale and Surtees were considered to have been the chief villains (or incompetents) of the affair, Edward P. Sells II, with his genial large beard, did not have the business acumen and grip of his forebears. Perhaps matters were made worse by the Overend Gurney bank failure of the same year (1866), with its train of bankruptcies and knock-on effect on general prosperity.

However, John Charrington was in any case permanently at loggerheads with his exacting brother Thomas: he was prepared to renew the partnership with Sells. By and by an Edward Perronet III, who as a little boy had lived in number 49, was making his way into the business, and he evidently proved more able than his father. He was with Charringtons as the family became a household name, even as their distant relations the brewers were. The coal Charringtons naturally supplied the brewing Charringtons with fuel, writing them business letters which began 'Dear Sir' but ended 'Your affectionate cousin'. They came to supply several other breweries, the new electricity company on Bankside, the London Hydraulic Power Company at the same location, several hospitals, the London School Board and Wandsworth Prison. The Sells family maintained a presence within Charringtons into the mid-twentieth century, the last in the business being Sir David Perronet Sells, son of Edward Perronet Sells IV and a stalwart of the Conservative party.

Their present-day direct descendants have careers in banking and the law. Without their help, and the surviving pieces of evidence which they have been able to pass to me, the old lightermen-coal-merchants would have been far more obscurely buried for me in the coal-dust and rubble of the lost Bankside. As for the coal-trade, in which seven generations of Sells prospered so usefully to themselves and to the country, that too is over: the thousands of coal-offices that still perched on the edge of railway yards forty years ago have gone without anyone really noticing it. Only the iron coal-hole covers to hidden cellars remain, all over London and other cities, diminishing in numbers as pavements are relaid but still a presence: tight-shut apertures to a buried past. In the whole of London today there is scarcely a single coal-merchant.

Chapter IX

IN WHICH INVISIBILITY SETTLES ON
BANKSIDE

The railway lines that carried the Sells away from Bankside, to Camberwell, and then Bristol, and eventually to other socially salubrious addresses in developing west London and in the home counties, were by the 1860s becoming a much more intrusive presence.

In the 1830s London's very first line had made its way in from Greenwich to the foot of London Bridge (subsequently extending itself in the other direction to Dover and the steam packets for the Continent), but this affected only the eastern side of the old Borough of Southwark. In the same decade a railway terminus for the London–Southampton line was opened at Nine Elms, in Battersea. Ten years later a long viaduct, like the one straddling Bermondsey, was constructed across Lambeth Marsh to extend the Nine Elms line to Waterloo station, newly built at the foot of the bridge from which it took its name. But early plans to carry the line further, over the river to the City, were for the moment shelved. The railways from south-eastern England remained, logically, south of the river. The London, Brighton and South Coast Railway – the world's earliest long-distance commuter line, and origin of all those day-trips to the seaside immortalised in Victorian songs – ended at Vauxhall.

But the magnetic pull of London north of the river eventually overcame geographical sense. In 1860 the Brighton line dared make its way, over the first railway bridge to cross the river within London, to a new station called Victoria: other companies were not slow to follow this cavalier example. Hungerford Railway Bridge, between Waterloo and a new station at Charing Cross, was completed in 1864. It took its name from old Hungerford market and stairs (the location, as it happened, of the blacking factory where Dickens had worked as a boy) but it formed part and parcel of the Embankment transformation which swept all these old places away. At just the same time the original Blackfriars Railway Bridge was constructed to take a branch of the London, Chatham & Dover Railway over the river to join up with the new Metropolitan Railway. The station was for some time at the south end of the bridge, on the site previously occupied by part of Rennie's works in what had once been the grounds of Holland's Leaguer. Another bridge belonging to a subsidiary of the same company was also built in the 1860s to a new City station in Cannon Street.

The road bridges that had spanned the river earlier in the century had been objects of pride and careful planning; now the railway companies threw bridges over the water wherever it suited them. One south-bank resident wrote to *The Times* about the Blackfriars rail bridge, in what must be one of the earliest complaints about advertising: 'The entire invention of the designer seems to have exhausted itself in exaggerating to an enormous size a weak form of iron nut, and in conveying the information on it, in large letters, that it belongs to the London, Chatham & Dover Railway Company.'[1] To Dickens, the file of bridges across the increasingly soot-blackened townscape were more sinister objects. In his last novel,[2] unfinished when he died in 1870, he spoke of them as spanning the dark waters of the Thames 'as death spans life'. But then, for Dickens, the inexorable power of steam and that of mortality itself were always conflated.

The real blight that the new rail links bestowed on Southwark was not the bridges themselves but the viaducts built to connect them with the London, Chatham & Dover's grandly rebuilt station at London Bridge. Soon Charing

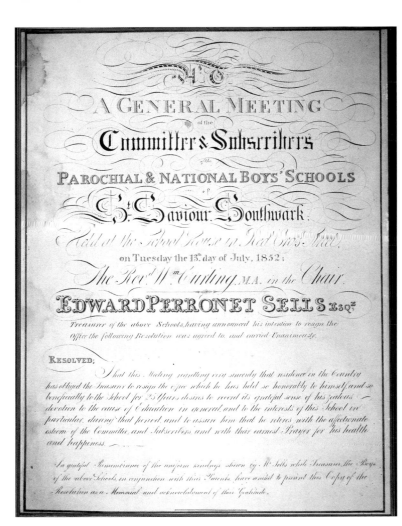

A GENERAL MEETING

of the

Committee & Subscribers

of the

PAROCHIAL & NATIONAL BOYS' SCHOOLS

of

St Saviour Southwark;

Held at the School House in Red Cross Place,

on Tuesday the 13th day of July, 1852;

The Revd Wm Curling, M.A. in the Chair.

EDWARD PERRONET SELLS Esqr

Treasurer of the above Schools, having announced his intention to resign the Office the following Resolution was agreed to, and carried Unanimously.

RESOLVED;

That this Meeting regretting very sincerely that residence in the Country has obliged the Treasurer to resign the office which he has held so honorably to himself and so beneficially to the School for 25 Years, desires to record its grateful sense of his zealous devotion to the cause of Education in general and to the interests of this School in particular, during that period, and to assure him that he retires with the affectionate esteem of the Committee and Subscribers, and with their earnest Prayer for his health and happiness.

In grateful Remembrance of the uniform kindness shewn by Mr Sells while Treasurer, the Boys of the above Schools, in conjunction with their Parents, have united to present this Copy of the Resolution as a Memorial and acknowledgment of their Gratitude.

The testimonial presented to Edward Perronet Sells I in 1852, on his retirement as Treasurer of St Saviour's National Schools.

(*Left*) Edward Perronet Sells II, 1815–1896.

(*Right*) Edward Perronet Sells III, 1845–1915.

A view of barges on the Thames from Bankside, 1901 – busy days, as described in *Living London*.

Bankside 1927, still at the height of its activity. By Grace Golden,

1911: the quay in front of number 49 Bankside, with power station chimney behind. The original has 'Site of the proposed St Paul's bridge' scrawled in pencil on the back.

2004: the same stretch of Bankside, complete with rebuilt chimney
(now part of the Tate Modern).

The rising young film star Anna Lee, at home in number 49. The house in its brief 'art deco' mode (1936).

Anna in film star mode. St Paul's can be seen from the window.

Bankside, looking towards Southwark Bridge. May 7th 1946. 2.25p.m.
Semi-ruinous after the London blitz.

1946: Bankside across the river. Over the next few years the many-chimneyed power station was to be replaced by Sir Giles Gilbert Scott's modern 'cathedral' of industry.

Bankside in 1970, by Trevor Chamberlain. The infrastructure was still, just, in place, though commerce by then was rapidly disappearing.

Cross and Waterloo too were connected to this hub, which swept St Thomas's Hospital away from its ancient site. The result was that old Bankside, which also suffered the Metropolitan Board of Works' divisive construction of Southwark Street in the mid-1860s, was now riven with railways trundling at rooftop level. The most damaging was the line that curved round from Blackfriars to London Bridge, carefully skirting the Anchor Brewery to avoid paying Barclay Perkins hefty compensation, but removing in its path the old Cure's College almshouses and graveyard, and rumbling above the Borough Market and the remains of the Bishop's palace to join the tracks from Cannon Street, before snaking round the south front of St Saviour's church as if it would throttle it.

Antiquarian interest in what had come to be known as 'Old London' was well established by the 1860s, but its influential followers failed to protect Southwark's venerable parish church. It was just as well the old pile had managed to get itself rebuilt a generation before: had it still been as ruinous as Edward Sells proclaimed it to be in 1836, the power of the railway interests would surely have swept it away entirely. It is perhaps a measure of how far Southwark had fallen socially thirty years later that greater efforts were not made to route the railway further from the church. But it is also the case that in this same decade the view of St Paul's from Ludgate circus was defaced (for the next hundred and thirty years) by a railway viaduct, and that St Pancras old church very narrowly missed being demolished for the convenience of the Midland Railway's coaling yards. Progress, it was believed, must not be thwarted. The coach-routes had all been dismantled, and many of the old inns along with them; the last of the turnpikes were following them into oblivion. The old, all-purpose hackney carriages were replaced by the purely urban hansom cabs, and soon, where cattle had recently been herded, horse trams would come.

As if to distract attention from what their lines were actually doing to the old Borough, the L, C & D Railway

Company made much of the large new hotel they were building at London Bridge. They were under the optimistic impression that there was an urgent need for accommodation in Southwark much grander than was supplied by those of the High Street inns that still survived. The planned Terminus Hotel had a hundred and fifty bedrooms, with bathrooms and water closets on each of its five storeys, lifts, restaurants, a Ladies Only coffee room separated by the library from the general coffee room, and – in a separate block – smoking and billiard rooms, which may have been more suited to the real needs of the typical customer arriving at London Bridge.

Too close to the City and to London as a whole to be a necessary staging post, too much surrounded by rough streets to attract the politer class of visitor come to stay for several days in the capital, the hotel never really flourished. It had descended in use to railway offices long before a bomb demolished it in the Second World War. The conception and building of it were redolent of the last era in which it was still imagined that railways somehow had a beneficial effect on the districts through which they passed. *The Builder*, which had written effusively about the plans for it in the summer of 1861, wrote in November of the same year and in the same enthusiastic but vague tone about the 'many changes' scheduled for the Lambeth waterfront, which was a prolongation of Bankside:

'... when the Main Drainage and embankment plans have been completed, rendering that which was in the memory of some few living a dreary and, in part, impassable marsh, dry and wholesome. The increased bridge and railway accommodation will also confer benefits . . . the locality will become more suitable for healthy dwelling and for the purposes of various descriptions of industry . . . wharfs [for] coal, stone, wood and many other materials crowd the once unprofitable land; shot and other factories . . . and matters too numerous in brief space to mention give employment to thousands.' (One senses that the writer had no real idea what he was talking about.) 'The main thoroughfares are swarming with life, omnibuses, cabs and carriages . . .'

Three years later, the *South London Press*, Southwark's now-flourishing local paper, was extolling the newly opened Southwark Street (which cut a direct route from Borough High Street to Blackfriars Bridge Road) in similar if more focused terms. The Hop Exchange was then being erected, on what was predicted to become 'one of the handsomest thorough fares in the metropolis . . . The frontage is of stone, with well-executed carvings, and the whole is being carried out by Mr Davies, builder of Union-street, at a cost of £10,000. A little distance further, on the right, we come to a building which, although plain in design, has a deal of interest attached to it, being the improved industrial dwellings for the working classes. This has been erected by a company, whose offices are at Carpenter's Hall, London Wall, and is now fully occupied by mechanics and their families. Each floor is almost like a house itself, and is furnished with every convenience. It is hoped, while ground remains to be disposed of in this street, that more of these dwellings will be established, giving, as they do, so great a boon to the working classes, hundreds of whom, through the improvements in Southwark, and the requirements of the various railway schemes, were forced to leave their dwellings . . .' And the rest of the column is about the numbers of warehouses, of similar dimensions to the industrial dwellings, newly built nearby.

Over the following twenty years many blocks of industrial tenements went up in Southwark, filling the censuses for the later decades of the nineteenth century with hosts of undifferentiated names and numbers. Most of them have now gone again, destroyed by bombs or by planners with other and different visions of socially desirable working class existence. One example of an early (1860s) block still stands, with its characteristic open stairs and iron balconies, cherished now again with paint and geraniums. It is just off Southwark Bridge Road in Redcross Street, not a stone's throw from where the supposed dust of the medieval Single Women lie beneath the Cross Bones ground.

But whatever the good intentions of housing philanthropists such as George Peabody and Octavia Hill (who was responsible for the erection of some more attractive, cottage-type workers' homes in the same street) there were many members of the Victorian working classes who did not earn steadily or respectably enough to aspire to the relatively high rents of Model housing. Or maybe they just preferred the old, familiar, individual courts, yards and alleys, even when these had trains lumbering overhead. They went on living their own lives on now-unregarded Bankside, in what seems to have become to official eyes little more than a series of spaces between 'commodious modern blocks' and 'fine new warehouses'. These remnants of lanes that were old when Shakespeare, Henslowe and John Taylor were young was the space left to them.

These people were not newsworthy, nor the subject of any plans: they were just there, in their own busy world, as the working classes of Southwark had been for centuries. They were lighter-hands, wharf-hands, coal-porters, rabbit-skinners, street-sellers, char-women, public-house pot-men, labourers, boiler-stokers; they were minor wage-earners in the breweries, the hop warehouses, the foundries, the soap works, the hatters, the tanneries. Chronically short of money but not destitute, as distinct from the 'wretchedly poor' as they were from the respectable shop-keeping and clerking classes, they were much as they always had been. The only difference was that, by the mid-Victorian era, the immediate district of Bankside had been vacated by almost all those who had earlier provided an articulate, respectable, monied presence as counterweight and support: the Thrales, the Barclays, the Hornes, the Shalletts, the Potts, the Sells.

What had gone with them was a world of social cohesion, which had existed in spite of substantial class distances. It had been a world in which wholesale dealers in coals, potatoes or rice could see for themselves on their own door-steps the hardships that a bitter winter could bring and were prepared to foregather in cold churches to make immediate plans for practical help – a world in which the coal-porters living in Cardinal Cap Alley and the Skin Market knew the current Mr Sells or Mr Horne as a neighbour and might rely on regular work from him. Indeed, at the beginning of the 1830s, Thomas Horne had tried without success to get a standard pay rate fixed for the porters so that they would not have to compete against one another when work was scarce. On the subject of this particularly illiterate and vulnerable class of worker, Henry Mayhew later wrote, 'Of the kindness of masters to men, of discouragement of drunkenness, of persuasion of the men to care for the education of their children, I had the gratification of hearing frequently.' But he adds that there was no general structure of provision for these labouring men, when their muscle-power declined through age and when the copious draughts of beer that they all believed to be 'strengthening' no longer had an effect.

After the middle of the century the masters, kindly or otherwise, even if still involved in Bankside industries, were more distant both geographically and socially. The old quarters of the metropolis were no longer a shared, familiar habitat: they were turning into 'the slums', into 'darkest London'. When interest was shown in 'the plight of the poor' – which it increasingly was, as Victorian consciousness of the subject increased – it was the almost anthropological interest of the concerned outsider, writing as if bringing back despatches from another continent. 'Missionary' societies were set up by clergymen to take religion, but also practical help and advice, to the less fortunate classes: exactly the same principle that was being applied in the burgeoning British Empire.

The mantle of Dickens who, in his early novels, had specifically shed light on some of the more oppressed corners of London, was taken on by journalists such as Mayhew and Hollingshed. Henry Mayhew's wonderfully comprehensive, deadpan articles were first written for the *Morning Chronicle* around 1850, and were published in book form some ten years later as *London Labour and the London Poor*. John Hollingshed's articles appeared in the *Morning Post* that same year, 1861, when the winter was particularly hard, and were eventually turned into a book called *Ragged London*. More of an indignant polemicist than Mayhew (he was particularly strong on the moral evils of over-crowding), he too provides valuable detail on everyday lives that would otherwise have gone unrecorded. Here he is on the houses immediately behind 49 Bankside, where he was taken by a local clergyman, secretary of the South London Visiting Relief Association:

'Some of the houses in the courts about the Skin Market . . . have been built within the last twenty years. There is Pleasant place, where the rooms are only about 3 yards wide, the back-yard about 3 foot square, and the windows not more than 2 foot and a half square. The court or passage in front is in exact proportion to these dimensions, and the houses stand in 3 parallel rows with their faces to each other's backs . . . Each lets for about 4/- a week, and contains 2 of these confined rooms. In White Hind alley, near this place, there is a row of old black, rotten, wooden dwellings, chiefly rented by river thieves . . .'

Hollingshed's personal obsessions with Vice and Bad Air (as if the two were inextricably connected) can become wearisome, but he had a strong sense of place and accurately perceived the historical sequence by which old areas such as Bankside had reached the state they had by 1860. Under the heading 'Mistaken Charity' he inveighs against the preservation of ancient almshouses, since 'the field or country lane of the sixteenth, seventeenth or even the eighteenth century in which [the inmates'] original hermitages were built, has become a close street of busy warehouses, if not an alley of dirty hovels . . . Let anyone, in passing over London Bridge, towards Southwark, look down upon a squat row of cottages lying between St Saviour's church and the wharf warehouses of Messrs. Humphrey and others . . . New London Bridge and its approach from the south have raised a noisy roadway high above their heads, and wharf buildings, Bridge House hotel, and other places have towered up round them, until they seem now to live at the bottom of a deep brick well . . . huge packages seem always hanging over them at the end of cranes, threatening to fall and crush them.' Such buildings should be sold off, he declared, and the money used to maintain the old people elsewhere, where there were no passing costermongers or boatmen to call them 'witches'.

Unlike some other writers of his time, who were content to emote and make their readers in Camberwell or Kensington feel guilty, Hollingshed understood that increasing charitable awareness of the great city's multiform social problems was providing only panaceas, not adequate solutions. England, he pointed out sardonically, spent more on charity than anywhere else in the world — 'Nearly a million "cases" receive free medical advice and assistance in London alone every year. The hat is always going round. The first stone of some benevolent building is always being laid. We dine, we sing, we act, we make speeches in aid of a thousand institutions . . . Casinos, harmonious pot-houses and pugilistic exhibitions catch the benevolent infection and work like mill-horses to aid noisy soup-kitchens . . .'

The wheels of the world's greatest industrialised capital system turned, producing more spare wealth for more people in Britain than ever before, but the very nature of competitive trade was that some people got ground up in it or were simply left out. There was also the paradox, familiar already from the eighteenth century and the earlier part of the nineteenth, that social evils were spoken or written of in scandalised terms as if they were something new, whereas really they had always been there and the fact that they were now being discussed was an indication that something was beginning to be done about them. People who were old by the mid-century, such as the radical working-class reformer Francis Place, were in no doubt that, as compared with the days of their youth, ordinary London people were far less likely to be scrofulous, rickety or lousy, far more likely to be wearing shoes and stockings and to be able to read. Fewer babies and children died. There was an abundance of cheap food and a whole network of soup kitchens, dispensaries, night shelters and Ragged Schools: many fewer poor people succumbed to absolute want. There was also generally agreed to be less roughness, violence and street theft than there had been a generation earlier: the establishment of the Metropolitan Police in the 1830s had been more successful than most people had expected. (Although not yet officially part of London, Southwark had had to accept the police.) These positive trends continued throughout the rest of the century and into the next one, when such wonders as free, compulsory schooling for all and old-age pensions began to be established.

Nevertheless, and perhaps necessarily, the note of shocked revelation continued to be sounded through the decades. It was as if the more comfortable the proliferating middle classes became, living in miles and miles of stuccoed, porticoed villas ('bran-new people, in a bran-new house in a bran-new quarter of London' in Dickens's words),[3] the more they wanted to be regaled with horror stories from the hidden, parallel world. In 1883 a twenty-page pamphlet written by the clergyman who was Secretary to the London Congregational Union, *The Bitter Cry of Outcast London*, produced an effect quite disproportionate to its real content. At the same time George R. Sims, a successful journalist, was playing the by now familiar explorer role in a series of articles called *How the Poor Live*, taking his readers on a journey into 'a dark continent that is within easy walking distance of the General Post Office'.

Hollingshed, Sims and others shed light on the chronically deprived section of society, or on those who had been more or less respectable members of the working classes till a sudden misfortune had tumbled them 'into the abyss'. How far did life on Bankside exemplify this? Had it become a sinister, exotic place where decent Londoners would hesitate to go? Well, hardly. It is true that Dickens's last completed novel, *Our Mutual Friend*, written in the 1860s, begins with the furtive snatch of a dead body from the river, and that this takes place from 'a boat of dirty and disreputable appearance . . . float[ing] on the Thames, between Southwark Bridge which is of iron, and London Bridge which is of stone, as an autumn evening was drawing in'. But the sinister Jesse Hexham, the depraved waterman with his trade in the dead, actually lives much further downstream, beyond Wapping. Bankside is simply the almost incidental site of this particular expedition – though no doubt Dickens chose this spot, right opposite the City, to emphasise the alien and secret nature of the world or worlds he is going to reveal.

When the last of the Sells's households had moved out of Bankside in the 1850s, leaving the house at 49 simply as the business address of the firm, there were still a few genteel neighbours. In 43 was a long-established sail maker, Joseph Sutton, with his wife, one teenage son still at home, two servants and his wife's elderly aunt. With the coming of the steam-vessels, sail making cannot have been quite the rock-solid, prestigious trade it had been for hundreds of years, but no one yet seriously thought that commercial sailing ships would disappear entirely. The old, elegant Horne house, number 44, where the Reverend Mann had lived with his numerous daughters, was let to yet another coal- and coke-merchant; while 47 was occupied by a paint manufacturer and his wife, with two children down as 'scholars', an unmarried brother described as an 'agent', one living-in servant and, on (Census-night) two visitors, one a 'Provision broker' from County Down and the other a tea-merchant who had been born in Bombay and was noted to be blind. (These sound potential characters for minor roles in a novel by Dickens or Thackeray.) At 48 lived a Lieutenant in the Royal Marines. Aged fifty-seven and employing one servant, he had presumably retired, after a not particularly illustrious career, to gaze out over the water.

Number 53 was, as it had been a decade earlier, a small shop, apparently the sort of all-purpose general supplier of dry groceries, soap, candles, patent remedies, clothes pegs, sewing thread and the like that was then known as a 'chandlers'. It was kept now by a widow of forty-two with a daughter in school. In the same house lived a man of fifty-four whose occupation is illegible, and his own daughter of twenty who worked in the drapery business. I would like to believe this to be evidence of a happy if irregular relationship, but it may merely be a sign of the social descent into multi-occupation of one-time family houses, that was going to overcome Bankside in the decades to follow.

At the next Census in 1861 the principal working occupant of number 49 was a young wharf clerk called William Tuckfield, whom I assume was employed by what had then become Charrington, Sells, Dale & Surtees. I think that it was at this time that the ground-floor room over-looking Bankside was partitioned to create a narrow passage from the front door going towards the central hallway and the stairs. The doorway into this room from the passage was placed next to the front door, which suggests that this room was now to be an office more readily accessible from the quay rather than from the rest of the house. The partition remained for the next hundred-odd years before the house was restored to something nearer its original state, and the mark of it is still visible today on the old floor-boards.

Listed as the head of the house was William Tuckfield's widowed mother, aged fifty. William was only twenty-three, but he had on his hands several younger brothers and sisters. The youngest boy was still at school, but the three teenage girls were all down as 'military embroideresses', and an eighteen-year-old brother as a coppersmith. The Tuckfields had in fact done well to launch William into the responsible job of wharf clerk, for they can be glimpsed elsewhere on the Bankside in the Census of twenty years before in a humbler situation, when Joseph Tuckfield the father was down as a male servant. Like most of his kind, Joseph had been born somewhere in the country, but his wife was a girl from Limehouse, and in the intervening years of their married life they had, judging from the birthplaces of successive children, moved about quite a bit but remained faithful to the Thames shores. In 1861 the Tuckfields had no servant living in, but they would almost certainly have employed a housewife in a sacking apron from one of the alleys round about for a few hours a week to do 'the rough': blackleading the kitchen stove, scrubbing the floors and in particular the front step, since no woman with any pretence at refinement could be seen doing that herself. Anyway, the Tuckfield girls – neat centre partings, slightly greasy ringlets, crinolines when they went out – would have needed to keep their hands smooth for their long hours at the military embroidery.

The neighbouring household across Cardinal Cap Alley in 1861 was in a similar situation, also headed by a widow. Martha Gabb was only forty, but she is described as a 'fundholder': evidently her husband had left her something besides a large family. The three sons, of eighteen, seventeen and sixteen, were all clerks, respectively in engineering, the railway and haberdashery; that is to say, they were white-collar workers, however modestly paid, with the possibility of 'bettering' themselves by and by. Two more sons were said still to be 'scholars': since they were in their teens too, they were presumably at the stage of acquiring a commercial education, perhaps at St Saviour's Free Grammar School, to fit them, too, to wear tight black suits and push pens. Three girls in the family, all younger, were also down as scholars. They had their aunts to keep an eye on them, and possibly to run up their dresses and pinafores on one of the new sewing machines that were just beginning to revolutionise home needlework, for the household was completed by Martha's two unmarried sisters, aged forty-four and forty-two, with no occupations mentioned.

It is clear that the Gabbs, like the Tuckfields, enjoyed a social status which, while considerably below that of the departed Sells, was well above that of the labouring poor. I was a little puzzled to see that all the Gabb children but the eldest two had been born in the Bear Garden, a working-class address, but when I sought them there in the Census of ten years previously it was to find that the late Mr Gabb, eleven years older than his wife, had been the licensed victualler in charge of the White Bear Inn, a hostelry whose origins went back to Tudor times. Publicans were pro-verbially much more prosperous than those who drank in their establishments: evidently it was the proceeds from this business that had secured the boys their clerkly education and were now keeping Martha Gabb *and* her sisters. The sisters, in 1851, had been 'assistants in the business', in other words, bar-maids. It looks as if, with the move to Bankside and the boys' occupations, a greater gentility had now come over the family, at any rate in its public face.

Such were the vast mid-Victorian lower middle classes, impotent as individuals but collectively a powerful force. The poet Matthew Arnold, writing in the 1860s, famously derided this class for being 'dismal and illiberal', in thrall to a 'narrow, unintelligent, repulsive religion' which allowed them no entertainments beyond the occasional lecture on 'teetotalism or nunneries', and of thinking 'it is the highest pitch of development and civilisation when . . . letters are carried twelve times a day from Islington to Camberwell, and from Camberwell to Islington, and if railway trains run to and fro between them every quarter of an hour.' One might note in passing that, while both Islington and Camberwell were now beginning to slip down the social scale, as the green fields receded further from them and the London fogs increased, the railway connection between them was hardly direct. But the overall sense of Arnold's scathing remarks is not accurate either, since huge numbers of this class, including the Tuckfields and the Gabbs, impress one rather by the vitality and determination they must have employed to haul themselves out of the working class and make use of the unprecedented opportunities the nineteenth century offered. For such people, the trains, the steamer trips to the Kent coast, the postal services, trams, gas-light and water on tap, and indeed the whole spread of London with its new plate-glassed shops, public libraries, public baths, institutes, concert halls, evening lectures and church socials, were not the marks of a 'dismal, illiberal life' but of a newly liberated one. And if some of these new middle classes did embrace religious observance and teetotalism too fervently for the taste of the more confident and moneyed upper classes (from which Arnold came), that is hardly surprising when you think that society as yet offered no other safety nets but self-conscious respectability and caution. 'The abyss' – in

Victorian parlance – was always there, yawning in wait for the self-indulgent and unwary. For the earner who spent his wages on drink or gambling, or the woman who deviated too publicly from a strict moral code, a descent to the hand-to-mouth life of the slum and the pawnshop was the all-too-likely fate. In Southwark, you could not fail to be aware of this.

The Gabbs, at any rate, can hardly have been teetotal. I have no idea if the Tuckfields were adherents of the huge Temperance movement that had risen in response to working-class drinking habits, whether they were eager attenders at matins and evensong or at the exciting hellfire sermons of a Dissenting chapel, or whether they went to the popular winter evening lectures at the Surrey Chapel in the Blackfriars Bridge Road – 'Rambles around Italy and the Italian Lakes', 'Sowing and Reaping' by A Clergyman. Maybe they even ventured into the music halls, which were now just developing towards their Victorian heyday. The very first Tavern Concert Room to use the term 'Music Hall' was in the Southwark Bridge Road, and another followed in the 1850s in Union Street. Did the Gabb sisters, having retreated from the bar of the White Bear into unpaid respectability, regard such places as being for the boys only? Or had each of them acquired, like many of their kind, a discreet 'gentleman friend' of a slightly higher social class, with whom they enjoyed outings to places unknown to the wives of clerks in Islington and Camberwell? Were the Tuckfield girls pretty enough to attract young men from similarly obscure but equally energetic families, who would one day take them away from the exacting work of sewing gold thread onto epaulettes and into neat suburban villas of their own?

One would like to think so. By the time of the next head-count both families have vanished from Bankside. The individuals who were momentarily fixed in the copperplate ink of the Census-taker have rejoined the mass of innumerable others, and without any clue to their movements we cannot follow them. They have been absorbed again into the 'vast, immense London, rain-sodden, smelling of heated iron and soot, smoking continuously into the foggy air'[4] that so impressed all foreign vistors.

By the time another ten years had passed quite a few of the old houses along that stretch of Bankside seem, judging from Directories, to have become primarily wharf-offices rather than residential property, but number 49 still retained its status as a one-family home. We know that it and its immediate neighbours on the other side of Cardinal Cap Alley were now in the possession of Moss Isaacs, iron-merchant, who would buy the freehold outright in 1873. During the sale, the Holditches seem to have been in residence there, but in the Census of '71 the house is lived in by an iron-merchant who was presumably in business with Isaacs. He was oddly, almost wittily, named Urban Gardener. 'Urban' is hardly a standard working-class Christian name, but suggests that, as with the Sells family, there was some French connection. He was born in Oxfordshire by the Oxford Canal, which was by then a main trade link, via the Grand Union Canal, with London. It is tempting to think that the canal played some part in his eventual presence on Bankside, particularly since that same Census lists twenty-six people who were sleeping on barges that happened to be moored that night in the vicinity of Mason stairs.

The Gardeners then had four sons and a daughter, all born in south London, ranging in ages from eleven to one year, and two living-in female servants of eighteen and fourteen. I imagine the fourteen-year-old was there chiefly to mind the baby. Ten years later the family were still on Bankside, but now in another of the Isaacs's houses, number 51. By this time they had had three more sons and another daughter; all nine children were still at home, and the eldest had joined his father in the business. Clearly, the Gardeners were in the same fertile, healthy mould as the Sells of forty years earlier. Number 49 was by then occupied by a 'lighterman and barge builder', as if time were circular and we were back to the days of the first Edward Sells a hundred years before. There had been fears, when the great off-river docks were built earlier in the century, that they would irreparably damage the lighterage trade, but since the lighters were allowed in and out of the docks without paying dues, and the sheer volume of trade had increased enormously, the lighters continued to flourish. The lighterman who was in number 49 in 1881 lived with his wife, an elderly female boarder and one servant.

It is for this same year that I know what this section of Bankside actually looked like, by putting together the small elevation drawings from Flood Prevention plans, as described in Chapter IV. These form a complete single snapshot of a moment when Bankside was into its relentless evolution from pretty residential terrace to working waterfront, but still retained much of the physical structure of its previous life. By this date, some large warehouses have appeared up river of Cardinal's Wharf, at the coal-wharves then in the possession of Hinton & Horne, and at Queen's Wharf, which was the point at which the western end of Bankside veered away from the river to run behind the riverside buildings rather than in front of them.

After this warehouse, coming eastwards, are some more coal-wharves, with Mason stairs alongside, and then an oddly asymmetric house with an archway in it leading into White Hind Alley. Because of its position and also its roof-line, I believe that there may be concealed within it parts of the Tudor 'Fish House', once the entrance to the Great Pike Garden, which survived intact till the late eighteenth century. Across its façade at second-floor level runs the legend 'Meredith's Velocipedes'. The modern bicycle would not be invented till the 1890s. The earliest velocipede was constructed, as the name implies, to be propelled along by the feet touching the ground, but it soon evolved into the pedal-driven 'penny-farthing'. By 1880 go-ahead young men were beginning to charge precipitously about on these machines and enthusiastic cycling clubs had been formed. Next door is the long-established Waterman's Arms ('Meux

& Co's Entire – Wine and Spirit Merchant'), a Georgian building which had replaced a much older ale-house from former times. I think it was probably in the Waterman's Arms that the Bankside coal-porters had traditionally been allocated jobs and received their pay – partly in beer – though this bad old practice, with its cartel of powerful publicans, was dying out by 1880. This public house, and the velocipede merchant alongside, are approximately where the Millennium footbridge stands today.

Imperial Wharf

Britis Wh

Brick face

Next come the two early Victorian warehouses of Crown Wharf, four-storey blocks with ornate iron wall-cranes, one marked 'Henry Sykes Engineers' and the other 'Mitford Slate'. Then comes Moss Alley and then a third, more recently built block. This covers the ground which, a few years before, was still occupied by numbers 54, 55 and 56 Bankside, where several generations of Sells intermittently lived. East of that, however, the old houses are still intact. Here are 50, 51 and 52, with 'Moss Isaacs Iron Wharf' running across them and Cardinal Cap Alley going through the archway, then number 49. This now has the distinction of being the only house along this run whose front does not bear some lettering – testimony to the take-over by industry and commerce. Nos.48 and 47, where curates had lodged,

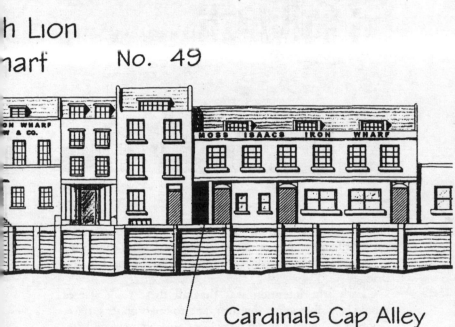

are now 'British Lion Wharf, PR Leeuw & Co'. Numbers 46 and 45 are 'Imperial Wharf', while 44, the house William Horne did up for his own use with indoor plumbing and brass accessories, and where the Reverend Mann lived, is now 'Cantler & Co., Licensed Lighterman'. Next door is the

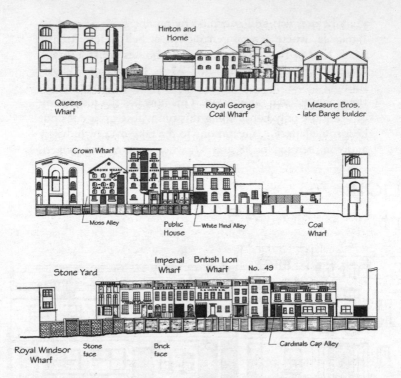

Queens Wharf · Hinton and Home · Royal George Coal Wharf · Measure Bros. - late Barge builder

Crown Wharf · Moss Alley · Public House · White Hind Alley · Coal Wharf

Imperial Wharf · British Lion Wharf · No. 49 · Stone Yard · Royal Windsor Wharf · Stone face · Brick face · Cardinals Cap Alley

long-established 'Sutton, Sail Maker'. Then comes the stoneyard and more new warehouses, but further short runs of old terraces still survive between Southwark and London Bridges.

Clearly, the intention was that all these trade names should be visible across the river, and to boats on its surface. Another of those circular effects of time is present here, summoning from the distant past Stow's waterfront houses of dubious repute that 'had signs on their front, towards the Thames, not hanged out but painted on walls.'

So, by the last two decades of the century, Bankside was simply the works-yard of the great commercial city on the opposite bank and apparently all but invisible to anyone who did not have business there. Books with names like *Living*

London, Wonderful London and *London: Heart of the Empire*, which were beginning to be published, scarcely mentioned London's oldest embanked shore, then or for most of the next century. Only the exceptional commentator had the vision, and the deep-seated knowledge of London, to see beyond 'coils of rusty chain, and bits of rusty machinery . . . cranes for the hoisting of things in or out of the barges . . . planks lying in position for the wheelbarrows'. But such a one was Walter Besant,[5] he who also mourned the transformation of the countryside south of Southwark within his own lifetime from a world of beauty into crowded urban sprawl. From the vantage point of the platform on the water belonging to the Anchor pub by Southwark Bridge, he evokes the sunset scene looking up river:

'Blackfriars Bridge, standing out with sharp, clear lines, as if cut out of black cardboard; above it, the dazzling golden light of the western sky; and below it, the broad bosom of the river at the flood.' There would be fifty or sixty – 'or a hundred' – barges moored, in tiers running half way across the river, some laden, some with sails furled: 'all were painted gaily with streaks of red, blue, yellow and green'.

He characterises the Anchor and one or two other public houses along the river as being 'of a quiet kind' and remarks that after eight o'clock at night all the activity on the quays ceases – 'It is generally unknown who are the private residents of Bankside: if a man wished for perfect retirement, a place where his friends would never think of looking for him . . . he could not do better than to take one of these houses – there are not many – and live in it.'

Upon this, his story, which is a novel, takes off into a happy evocation of whom these private residents might be. He imagines finding 'quite the cleanest and most respectable house on Bankside – it was even provided with a Virginia creeper, now rapidly becoming green with its first shoots of spring'. There he takes lodgings: his landlord wears 'an immaculate frockcoat', works in a lawyers' office and lives with his brother, who is an impoverished poet. The brothers tell him: '"You have done well, Sir, in coming to the Bank Side.

Here we breathe. Here we catch the pure breeze fresh from the German ocean" . . . [The North Sea is what is meant. The use of the older term, already out of date by then, is indicative of the brothers' old-fashioned ways.] "If this place were generally known, those who now live in Eaton or in Berkeley Square would gladly exchange with us who live upon the Bank . . . As for ourselves, we are, I believe, the oldest Family of Bank Side."' They recount that they have been there for the last hundred years, and that their grandfather had run the place as an academy. They still hold meetings for 'The Society of Bankside', in which four eccentric but educated old gentlemen gather for 'Exchange of Thought'. According to another lodger, there is no society in the neighbourhood any longer in the generally accepted sense of the term – ' "There is a clergyman or two – and there are, I suppose, a few doctors – sixpenny doctors."' The first-floor front room in which these antique exchanges of thought are held is furnished with Georgian furniture, family portraits and punch glasses – 'Nothing had been changed in the room for sixty years at least.' The new lodger is put into the best bedroom, which has a four-poster bed and a candle for lighting.[6]

This is, you may say, a romantic evocation, but it is nevertheless a plausible one. Moreover, Besant had the insight, unlike most of his contemporaries, to see beyond the grimy wharves not only the lost past but a possible future to come. In his novel, he lends this visionary imagination to a young girl, Althea, daughter of the house, who takes him on what we would now recognise as a 'history trail' through the old lanes behind Bankside. She evokes for him Paris Garden, the Falcon, Shakespeare and Kit Marlowe, Maiden Lane, scents of flowering honeysuckle and ' "fish quite, quite fresh, dipped in oil rather turned and then imperfectly fried"'. With a nice sense of both the transience and the permanence of things, she assures him, ' "We are ghosts of the future."' He, for his part, begins happily to envisage a future in which just such 'strong and beautiful girls' organise 'West Enders or Americans' into street walks, recounting to them history in return for a fee.

It was to be forty years before another young writer found his own ancient hideout on Bankside for real, but it happened. Sixty-odd years more and Besant's dream of eager tourists following a guide has become a fact too.

In 1891 number 49 was lived in by another lighterman; he is marked as 'employed' rather than as an employer of men himself. He was married, with five children aged from ten down to two. No servant. The whole family were Southwark-born. In 50 was a 'master spectacle-maker', apparently living on his own: a number of the houses that remained seem under-tenanted by this date, no doubt because many of the rooms were occupied by wharf offices. In number 48 was a husband, wife and eighteen-year-old son, all of German origin. Germans, along with Italians and with Russian Jews, were the economic migrants to Britain of that era, the prototypes of many waves to come.

By 1901 number 49 had finally come right down in the world. No longer a one-family house, it figured in the Census of that year as the dwelling place of thirteen people divided into three households. The social distinction that had, in the past, separated the houses actually on Bankside from the tenements in the side lanes was now almost obliterated. Next door in 50 the head of the house was a 'waterfront labourer', and in 51 a 'coalman – domestic', i.e. a deliverer of sacks; 52 housed Moss Isaacs's foreman in the old iron business.

The Waterman's Arms some fifty yards upstream still stood, but on one side of it the velocipede merchant and on the other an early Victorian warehouse had both gone, replaced by the new premises of the City of London Electric Lighting Company. The presence of the Phoenix Gas Company already near at hand made this part of Bankside a natural site for the newer utility. Half a dozen years later the expanding electricity plant, together with that of the Hydraulic Power Company, would finally sweep away the old house that was associated with Sir Christopher Wren.

The principal householder in 49 now was Henry Rolfe, a

heating-furnace worker of fifty-five. He had with him a wife, not in employment, and two sons, both apparently gas-fitters. A daughter of twenty-three was down as a book-binder, a classic Southwark trade. Her younger sister was a 'shirt-maker' and the fourteen-year-old girl a 'stationery hand'. Florence, at ten, did not work: she may have attended St Saviour's parish school, which was still near the old grave-yard. (The eighteenth-century buildings were finally pulled down, and a new school built over the road, in 1908.) Or she may have gone to St Peter's school, which was established close to her home in Emerson Street off Bankside, between Pond Yard and the Bear Garden. The same year, elementary education for all, which had theoretically been compulsory since 1888, was made free, and so at last near-universal, up to the age of eleven or twelve.

The number of adult children at home, and their skilled or semi-skilled trades, would have meant that the Rolfes prob-ably had adequate money coming into the household. The middle-aged parents would have been enjoying their best years, with the expense and strain of bringing up a family almost over and the possible hardship of old age yet to come. Old-age pensions only began to be introduced in 1908 – which probably came too late for the 'heads' of the other two households that were somehow accommodated within 49.

The bare facts of the Census are redolent of much. The Warren household, probably occupying only one room, consisted of a widowed mother of sixty-two, born in Southwark, apparently without occupation, and her daughter of twenty-five who is down as a 'pastry-cook'. There were many food-preparation factories along the river by then, including Sainsbury's rising empire in Stamford Street above Blackfriars Bridge, the large works of Peak Frean, the biscuit-manufacturers, and a nearby jam-factory where women and girls worked with their clothes, skin and hair in a state of perpetual sugary stickiness. If Edith Warren was employed in somesuch place and was the sole support of her mother, how could she ever escape into the alternative labours of marriage, even if the chance came?

The case of the Elliott family seems rather bleak too. I happen to know that they occupied the top floor, that is, the attic, since the Electoral Register for 1901–02, uniquely, gives this kind of information, along with the fact that George Elliott was a registered sub-tenant of Rolfe's and paid him four shillings and ninepence a week. They would have had a fine view over the river, but the reason that attics were traditionally the realm of the poor was that they were hot in summer, cold in winter, and you had to go down several flights to reach a tap or a lavatory. George Elliott had been in the hat-making business, that time-honoured Southwark profession for which the nineteenth century had provided a huge mass market. The bowler hat, designed to withstand wet weather, was invented in Southwark, and Dickens had claimed that 'a smell of hat-making' always hung around the Blackfriars Bridge Road. But, at sixty-five, George Elliott was now retired: his wife was in her sixties also. The third member of the family was a daughter of twenty-five down as a 'sweet-stuff maker', which would seem to indicate a trade carried on at home: probably she supplied a small local shop or street-seller. Poorly paid piecework of this kind was done in innumerable London garrets and basements at this date – creating everything from match-boxes to ginger-beer, clay pipes, ornamental lace doilies and dolls' eyes. Mayhew noted that 'Treacle and sugar are the groundwork of the manufacture of all kinds of sweet-stuff. "Hard-bake", "almond toffy", "halfpenny lollipops", "black balls", and the cheaper "bulls eyes", and "squibs", are all made of treacle.' All Marion Elliott would have needed to start in business, besides a few penny-worth of ingredients, was a stove to cook on and a sturdy saucepan. The family must have lived, eaten, slept and woken each morning in the cloying smell of boiled sugar.

The reason I am fairly sure Marion made her sweets at home is that the Census notes her as being 'crippled from childhood'. In an era when lameness from a dislocated hip or a club foot was too common to cause much comment, 'cripple' indicated a far more severe handicap. She may scarcely have been able to walk at all; she may have been incontinent. The unsuitability of an attic home for someone in this condition is all too obvious. But at least, it seems, she was earning something for herself and her elderly parents. She had something to do all day, from her chair by whatever stove had been installed under number 49's old roof slates.

There was as yet no educational provision for those who could not get to the ordinary schools on their own legs. 'Cripple parlours', which were sheltered training workshops for youngsters, would not be inaugurated for another fourteen years, though, when they were, one was opened in the nearby Union Street. But by the turn of the century a few influential people were concerned about the subject. John Grooms of the London City Mission, founder of orphanages, had a home for crippled girls in Clerkenwell as early as 1880: he had them taught to make artificial flowers, that classically pure alternative to a life of degradation. Dr Barnardo too encountered many disabled children among his destitute charges – and he had had a handicapped child born in his own family. In the 1890s a thoughtful London clergyman called Howatt, who was associated with the Ragged School movement, called attention to the isolation of working-class child cripples and advocated a 'visiting friend' system, since 'their parents, in the struggle to keep a roof overhead, have generally to be out at work most of the day, and normally healthy children naturally do not care to remain long with a sufferer'.

What Marion Elliott's twenty-five years of life had been within four walls, long before wireless or television, when companionship and the activity of the streets were a crucial parts of most people's lives, strains the imagination. How many more years remained to her? An obscurity, even denser than that which will cover almost all of us, envelops such vanished individual lives. Were there elder, healthy brothers and sisters who, before they left home, brought a little animation into her existence? Did the other occupants of the house befriend her, or did the fine class distinctions of lower-class life and the need to preserve privacies within an over-crowded space preclude this? Did she perhaps benefit, while a child, from a rare charity outing or two, such as one reads of in this account of a 'Fresh Air Scheme' for the sickly, run by the Ragged School Union? In this instance the day out was in Folkestone, and the point of departure London Bridge:

'A livery stableman lent a large brake and a pair of greys to take [the children] to the station; women stood at their doors waving farewells; a publican – an ex-pugilist – who contributed to the fund, and put all the fines for broken glasses into the treasury, was active in lifting the children into the brake.' Greengrocers donated fruit; gas workers raised their caps and waved and cheered from the tops of gas-holders. It sounds as if it was happening right in the Bankside area. The day seems to have been a success, but it is a little daunting to find that the narrator (C. J. Montague, in his memoir *Sixty Years in Waifdom*, 1904) regarded its 'greatest value' as lying in the lesson in Christianity and humility it offered to the able-bodied working classes.

By the turn of the century, Bankside was almost entirely working class. It does not figure on Charles Booth's famous 'poverty map' as one of the poorest parts of the district, for obviously it housed a sprinkling of respectably paid warehouse clerks, book-keepers and the like, but here is how the waterfront seemed to a commentator writing in a popular partwork in the early 1900s:

'It is a fine morning in June. We are standing on London Bridge at a very early hour . . . on Surrey side . . . We glide off to our right, by the side of St Saviour's Cathedral[7] through Clink Street, and we find ourselves on Bankside. Here, for a while, we watch the wayside labourers at work. We see them loading a barge with grain. Some of the younger men are of Herculean proportions, and have almost the strength of a Samson. The sacks they carry on their backs weigh, on average, two hundredweight and a half. These men heave them with perfect ease, and run along a narrow wooden plank that bends under their weight. The older men, who have to keep pace with the younger ones in life's terrible struggle, groan and gasp under their heavy burdens, but still stagger bravely on . . .' There is, he explains, no other work they can do.

'We walk on and watch other barges being loaded, but with very different cargo, some of them with heavy bars of iron, others with crates of bottles, others with barrels of grease and fat.

'. . . We pass under Southwark Bridge, and watch yet another lot of waterside labourers at their daily task of unloading barges of coal, and then we turn off into the courts and alleys to see the homes in which many of these toilers live.

'We are in the land of Shakespeare . . . Yet how very unromantic these parts are today! Poor, dilapidated dwellings are the houses in these courts – Moss Alley, Ladd's Court, Bear Gardens and White Hind Alley – which abut on the banks of the river. Hard indeed are the lives of the poor families that dwell therein. From morning to night they hear the ceaseless hum of the great fan at the electric lighting works hard by. At first painful to listen to, it becomes music to them in time, so that they sing and work to its metrical movements.

'The waterside labourer earns a precarious income. Half the year he is without work . . . When he gets any money he often spends it with absolute recklessness . . . In the winter months many of these poor families are on the verge of starvation, and it is a blessing to them that their children are supplied with free meals through the agency of various funds. But for these meals, many of the waterside labourers' children would starve . . .' He goes on to explain that many of the wives and young girls work too, particularly – in the vicinity of the old Skin Market behind Cardinal Cap Alley – as 'pullers', pulling the fur out of rabbit skins, in a haze of fluff that got into noses, throats and eyes. The fur was afterwards spun into fine wool and the skins went to the hatters. Meanwhile the boys were engaged in a different enterprise:

'Along Bankside on a summer's day there are always to be seen a number of boys wading in the mud, and trying to find such treasure as may have fallen into the river during the day or night. Here are a party of lads making their first attempt to swim. Every season a number of them terminate their youthful career in a muddy and watery grave.'[8]

A year or two after that volume was published, a little girl, Grace Golden, was born in a house on the other side of the river at Queenhithe, the old dock below St Paul's. Although the family, who may have been of immigrant Jewish origin, were in relatively modest circumstances (Mr Golden was an electrician), Grace was sent to the fee-paying, academic City of London Girls School. She was good at drawing – she grew up to be an artist, with a scholarship to the Royal Society of Arts, and pictures by her have come to rest both in the Guildhall Library and in the Museum of London.

'I tried my childish pencil', she wrote, 'on drawings of barges clustered amid stream; barges with furled reddish brown sails, and brightly painted houseboats with lace curtains coquettishly draped back to reveal the potted fern standing in the tiny window . . . [from the City side] the narrow alleys opening onto the Bankside looked like black caves, inviting me to explore them.' Explore them she did, as soon as she was old enough to wander about on her own, among the cranes and the dust chutes that seem, by the early decades of the twentieth century, to have become a feature of that waterfront. Later in life she researched, wrote and eventually published a book, *Old Bankside*. While this is fervently anti-Catholic and historically not always reliable, it is written with such passionate feeling for the precise detail of place and for the persistence of the past that no one interested in London's other shore can fail to warm to it. Hers is a lone voice, speaking for Bankside in an era when no one else seemed to care about it at all, indeed hardly to see it.

Chapter X

Doom. And Rebirth

In the rear mirror through which we view the past, the house at Cardinal's Wharf enters a blind spot at the beginning of the twentieth century, for lack of documentation, just as it does in the early eighteenth century at the time of its rebuilding. Under British regulations detailed Census material may not be consulted till a hundred years have passed since its collection. The identities of all those who lived in the house in 1911 and in subsequent decennial years are lying quietly in an archive as I write, but neither I nor any other researcher can access them till the requisite term of years has elapsed.

So, at this point, the procession of individuals we have been able to call up fleetingly from the expended generations – the Sells and then the Gardeners, with their numerous children, the Holditches, the Tuckfields, the Rolfes, the afflicted Elliotts – ceases. For three decades, till other information pours in suddenly from other sources, there can be no speculation as to whether this girl might have managed to marry the white-collared lodger, or if that boy survived the slaughter of the 1914–18 war. The boys, girls, widows, clerks, factory-hands and wharf-labourers who *may* have passed through the house in those years simply do not figure on any reckoning. The street directories list only the commercial nature of premises, if any, or the permanent addresses of established, rate-paying citizens. They provide a useful indication of the increasingly dock-and-industrial, nature of Bankside in the early twentieth century, but nothing further. The Electoral Register, superceding the old rates lists, are by this time a significant source, but till after the First World War they list only men, plus a few widows and the like who were entitled to vote in local elections but not in Parliamentary ones. Of wives, children and other dependants or lodgers, of transitory inhabitants who did not bother to register, of occupations, ages, places of birth and any other personal details, there is no information to be had.

In 1903 the Rolfes, and their tenants the Elliotts, were still living in 49 Bankside, but by the following year they had all moved out, to be replaced by a Henry Hopkinson. The Electoral Register records him as the rate-paying tenant of a dwelling house, but at the same period, in the Commercial Directory, a Mrs Dean is recorded as keeping 'coffee rooms' at that address: presumably Hopkinson sub-let her the ground floor. The coffee rooms (the term of the period for a workmen's café) did not apparently last long, but it is nice to think that the house at Cardinal's Wharf recovered, briefly, something of the role it had had long ago as an inn, before its eighteenth-century rebuilding. At the same time the Waterman's Arms, at number 60, was listed as being run by the 'People's Refreshment House Association Ltd', which sounds like a well-intentioned Temperance initiative to turn an old pub into something more morally desirable. In any case, the building did not survive long after that, being first annexed by the London Electricity Company and then demolished as that enterprise continued to expand.

By 1907 no trade or occupant is listed for 49, which does not necessarily mean that there was no one temporarily perching in the panelled rooms of the by now shabby, disregarded house. Two years later one more lighterman was in occupation, the last in a long tradition, but he soon went again. The place may have been untenanted after that, for fewer and fewer people lived actually on Bankside as the years went by. Although the side lanes were still heavily populated, the waterfront consisted either of commercial premises such as the Isaacs's, using several old houses together for offices and storage space, or, increasingly, of purpose-built wharf-houses that replaced them. Just after the First World War, if not earlier,[1] the houses immediately to the east of 49, houses that had sheltered Hornes and Manns and, long ago, Shalletts and Oldners, and had replaced Henslowe's timbered properties, were demolished. On part of their site a tall warehouse, with an ornate tiled frontage, was erected by Craig & Rose, paint manufacturers: its factory premises ran back alongside the whole length of the garden of 49. 'Garden' one could probably no longer describe it: it had been paved over for the old iron business, but it now had a brick wall looming fifty feet above it.

Isaacs's had for some time been in the control of two of Moss's sons, Moss II and Samuel, with residential addresses in the then-genteel areas of Brixton and South Lambeth. The third generation was to be located in Bayswater and still more exclusive places. Like the Sells long before them, the Isaacs clan had prospered through trade and moved up in the world. For the whole period of their occupancy of Bankside they had had a few people resident in one or more of the houses they owned, presumably either employees in the iron trade or caretakers. The favoured house for this presence was number 50, and for many years a married couple called Mallison lived there. They continued there after the First World War, when an Edward and Ellen Kimpton were installed alongside in 49. This new presence probably signified the moment at which the Isaacs, who were still to own the house till the beginning of the 1930s, let it as a separate premises, without the wharf-space, for £60 a year. The tenants were Elliott, Hughes & Easter Ltd, gum-merchants according to the Commercial Directory. Did they sell glue, which was one of the by-products of the Bermondsey skin-trade?

The journalist and short-story writer, V. S. Pritchett, who was born in 1900 and lived almost until the end of the century, worked in a leather works near London Bridge from the age of fifteen to nineteen. He has left memorable evocations of the Southwark and Bermondsey of the period.[2]

'There was a daylight gloom in this district of London. One breathed the heavy, drugging beer smell of hops and there was another smell of boots and dog dung: this came from the leather which had been steeped a month in puer or dog dung before the process of tanning. There was also . . . the stinging smell of vinegar from a pickle factory, and smoke blew down from an emery mill . . . From the occasional little slum houses [came] the sharp stink of London poverty. It was impossible to talk for the noise of dray horses striking the cobbles.'

The teenage Pritchett, just too young to be conscripted for war service, rather enjoyed his long hours in these busy streets near the river – eight in the morning till seven in the evening and till four every Saturday. For this he earned twelve shillings and sixpence a week, rising to eighteen and six by the time he left, and ate the same meal every day in 'someone's Dining Rooms, a good pull-up for carmen, near the Hop Exchange . . . steak and kidney pudding followed by date or fig pudding . . . the whole cost 8d. but went up to 10d. the following year.'

A few years later, number 49 Bankside harboured such a Dining Room, apparently run by the sub-tenants who were the successors to the Kimptons, a family called Morley. So, once more, as during the brief coffee-room time twenty years before, customers could sit and eat looking out onto the river and the far bank as others had in the seventeenth and sixteenth and fifteenth centuries. But the Dining Rooms did not last long in that economically depressed time (1926, when they figure in the Directory, was the year of the abortive General Strike) and by 1928 the house was apparently the work-address for two other exiguous trades, sign-writing and window-cleaning.

Just how poverty-stricken the residential aspect of the Bankside had become by the 1920s, even though commerce continued to flourish there, is clear from Grace Golden's testimony, both in words and in pictures:

'Samuel Isaacs and Sons, iron merchants, occupied number 52 for many years of the last century, until about

1924 [actually a few years later] when it was used as tenements. In the late thirties candles were still being used to light them.'

Since gas-light was initially regarded as something for commercial premises rather than domestic ones, it is likely the Sells, who were still in residence in that run of houses in the 1840s and early '50s, had never bothered to install it, or at any rate not on the upper floors.

The state of the lanes leading down to Bankside was not helped by the revival, once again, of the plan to build a bridge across to St Paul's. It was shelved at the outbreak of war in 1914 but the ground landlords of much of the property round there, by now the Bridge House Estate, went on hoping after the war that it would go ahead: they allowed the buildings that would be demolished for it to deteriorate. The young Grace Golden explored these lanes, at whose dark entries she had been gazing all her childhood from the house over the water at Queenhithe. The irregular small alleys of the Skin Market held for her the fascination of a strange country. She kept, and quoted many years later, the notes she had written on them at the time:

'On one side, a row of two-storied, jerry-built houses, on the other, the crumbling brickwork of half-demolished dwellings . . . Cats and children are everywhere . . . A child with bare feet and matted hair crawls out of the open doorway up to the level of the alley. The gas-lit interior – there is no daylight except from the doorway – shows a broken brass bedstead and tumbled bedding. A woman pushes aside the torn lace curtain and rubs a broken window pane . . .

'Down a tributary alleyway there are the pathetic remains of a few square yards of fenced-in garden. A shabby bassinet in front of the door which leads straight into the living room. Under and beside the window, fruit and vegetables are stacked against the wall – ready for selling the next day. A wheelbarrow almost closes the passageway.'

On Bankside itself, the evidence was of a slightly less needy existence: not that Grace made the distinction, since it still seemed to her to be located in another time and world from the one she knew on the City side:

'On a summer evening at an open window on the river front, one might see a turquoise blue gramophone horn, wheezily playing "A Bird in a Gilded Cage". Behind the horn can be seen the floral wallpaper, almost covered with velvet-framed photographs . . . We move onto a group of people around their doorstep. Grandmother in a white apron spreads herself over a broken-backed chair; Mother, the line of her corset dividing her torso into planes, squares herself on the doorstep; the children, their mouths and cheeks jammy with the last slice of bread and jam, scream at each other; Father is in the local.'

Other vestiges, too, of the domestic Bankside of Victorian days and earlier still lingered in Grace Golden's youth. At the Falcon Dock, at the level of 79 Bankside, 'fowls took their Sunday morning stroll down the slope to the water's edge. And, on a hot summer weekday, carmen used to drive their steaming horses down to the river where the great beasts stood cooling their hooves in the lapping water.'

However, by the end of the 1920s, the City of London Electric Lighting Company acquired much of the planning-blighted land west of 52 Bankside. The bridge-scheme having been once again abandoned, the land became the site for a more extensive six-chimneyed Power Station, which took in also the old site of the gas works. City money cleared the slum lanes and re-housed the occupants in yet another large tenement block. With their clearance went much old geography, including Moss, Unicorn and White Hind Alleys and the last references to the 'Pye' or Pike Gardens, all perilously close to 49 Bankside. Only the vagaries of chance, the historical accident of the ownership of parcels of land going back over two centuries, kept that house and its immediate neighbours out of the clearance scheme. It was a close call, and one that was to be repeated several times in the middle decades of the twentieth century.

*

By 1931 the Isaacs still owned the run 49–52, but the lucrative old iron business was being consigned to the past: numbers 50, 51 and 52 were occupied by a firm of wharfingers (that is, general waterfront traders). The gum-merchants had given up their tenancy of 49, and no one seems to have been living there. The house, now one of the few remaining survivors in a changed landscape, had reached its nadir – the point in time at which it was not even thought to be worth finding a new tenant for it. I have been told that various cargoes from lighters, including mahogany, were stored there, ships' wood within the wooden, shiplike interior. In the deep cellars a Bankside flood of 1928 (which was to be the last) had left a black sludge on the Tudor flagstones, which no one bothered to clean up. The river rats made a home there. At the top of the house, in the attic under the leaky slate roof where generations of servants had slept, and where the Elliotts and their crippled daughter had once made their home, pigeons got in through a broken window and whitened the wide old boards with their droppings. The house must have seemed destined, like one of Dickens's sooty riverside dwellings of a hundred years earlier, to be pulled down any time, leaving only disturbed air and a fading memory.

But that year a young man called Robert E. Stevenson took to wandering along the river in the evenings. His name, with its echo of the author of *Treasure Island*, was propitious, for he was a script-writer and soon-to-be director attached to Gaumont British film studios. The cinema, which had become a mass industry in the 1920s and was now being given a further boost with the coming of talkies, was reaching its high noon of popularity. Southwark alone had over a dozen 'picture houses' by the 1930s, including a newly built one at the Elephant and Castle that was for a while the largest in Europe. Patient queues for films, almost any film, were a standard feature of the evening streets.

Robert Stevenson came upon 49 Bankside and had the vision to see, through the dirt and decay, that here was a house worth saving. Did he persuade one of the wharfingers to find the key and let him in to wander round its creaking, rat-rustling spaces? Did he take his then-wife, Cecilie, to see the place and manage to infect her with his own enthusiasm? He is long dead, I cannot ask him – but it is evident from documents collected up with the Deeds of the house that by the end of 1931 he was in negotiation with the by now extensive Isaacs clan, and legal wheels had begun to turn.

They needed to. Already, in 1922, after 49 had been let to Stephen Easter's firm of gum-merchants, a tidying-up exercise had had to take place. The original old iron man, Moss Isaacs, had died in 1889, leaving his Bankside properties in equal shares to each of his six children. With the passage of another generation, these one-sixth parts had turned into one-fifteenths. Each of these individual portions must by then have been worth almost nothing, yet various of the descendants were in dispute with one another on the matter. The properties had finally been put into a family Trust, in charge of a solicitor – who then mislaid the Trust document. Statutory declarations concerning it had to be made in 1931, one of them in front of the British pro-Consul in Cannes, to which place one of Isaacs's descendants had wandered. The family names, figuring on the copious documentation of 1931–32, are redolent of cosmopolitan, comfortably-off Anglo-Jewish society: Isaacs, Cohens, Levys, Bensusans and Hakims. They styled themselves 'stock-jobbers', or simply 'gentlemen', variously of Pembridge Villas, Bayswater, mansion blocks in Earls Court and Maida Vale, and Khandala Marine Mansions of Bexhill on Sea with a pied-à-terre in Covent Garden. One or two injected an additional touch of inter-war rackety chic. A brother-in-law lived in the Villa Hakim, rue Puget, Nice, while Ernest David Isaacs, 'late of the Royal Automobile Club, Pall Mall', was attributed to 'the British Club, Alassio, in the Kingdom of Italy'.

It is to be hoped that both these gentlemen had the acumen to settle in England by 1939.

It was Ernest who was finally given, by his quarrelsome cousins, the power to negotiate with Robert Stevenson ('gentleman'), late of Fitzroy Square – then a fashionably bohemian address. Stevenson seems to have moved into Bankside anyway in the meantime. A lease on 49 and its waterfront was at last signed on 10th December 1932, making him 'tenant for life' in consideration of a transfer premium of £600 and an annual rent of £2.10s for 999 years. Two days later the freehold was sold outright to him for £55 (altered in ink from £50), which was the equivalent of only twenty-two years of rent.

Since the freehold had originally been acquired by Moss Isaacs in 1873 for £1300, Robert Stevenson had either bought a heap of bricks from which almost all value had evaporated – or he had got a remarkable bargain.

Robert Stevenson had a new roof put on and enlarged the attic, creating space on the leads at the back of it for a roof-garden. He also cleared the long yard to turn it back into a garden again, and installed French windows in the ground-floor back room which he used as a dining room. As if in ghostly re-creation of a very distant time, he put a small fish pond at the end of the garden. (Subsequent claims that this pond is an actual vestige of the Pike Garden are not valid.) More prosaically, the house got its first bathroom, in the top-floor closet over Cardinal Cap Alley. The restoration was otherwise a matter of stripping out the inner layers the house had acquired during the nineteenth century. Vincent Sells's Regency fireplace was left in place in the first-floor front, but the wallpapered plaster board was taken away, exposing again the early Georgian wood panelling, here and in the stairwell. Victorian fireplaces, probably dating from the tenure of Edward Perronet Sells II or the Tuckfields who came after him, were removed, and Stevenson found to his delight that some original grates were intact behind.

He also removed the sagging crust of sodden and dried-out Victorian ceiling in the basement and discovered the timbers of the Tudor cellars holding the whole thing up. Many of the old beams had to be replaced, but of those that were still sturdy enough to remain several were indentifiable as ship's timbers: the re-use of these well-seasoned bones of old ships was common in past centuries. The idea of an ancient connection between the house and the sea appealed greatly to Stevenson, and it seems to have been during his occupation that a story became current about the house having once been the property of a smuggling sea-captain. A secret passage was said to run from the cellars down to the river, and there were tales of brandy casks. There is no evidence of any such passage having existed: perhaps Stevenson's workmen had lighted on one of the old drainage ditches? In any case, a captain with a line in smuggling would have lived down in Rotherhithe or Deptford, not on Bankside above the constantly observed Pool of London. But if Stevenson made things up, it was also his writer's imagination that led him to discern the house's quality. While living there he wrote an historical novel, his only venture into hard covers, I think, called *Darkness in the Land*.[3] It still reads today as a creditable and well-researched pastiche of an account by a well-born young man of the late seventeenth century. We have the Plague of London, his escape to the country and then to the Dorset coast, an encounter with an 'Aegyptian' (gipsy) princess, and his final escape from England with her to Massachusetts. A make-believe Introduction says that the author died in Boston in 1726.

This book is dedicated 'to Anna, with love'. What had happened, by then, to the shadowy Cecilie Stevenson? In the Electoral Register of 1933 she is there in 49 with her husband, but by the following year her name is replaced by that of a 'Joanna Winifrith'.

Admittedly, information on a first wife transmitted by the second is apt to be faint and partial, but it would seem that either Cecilie never took to the house from the start, or that the Art Deco scheme she imposed on it (all-white walls, divans, a mirror-lined chimney breast) were resented by Robert as inappropriate to the house's eighteenth-century character. Or perhaps it was simply that he fell irrevocably in love with a rising star of Gaumont, Joan Boniface Winnifrith, daughter of a Kent clergyman, who was soon to re-invent herself as Anna Lee.

'He was such a nice man. I should really have stayed married to him.' Anna Lee herself, seventy years on and with two more marriages behind her, spoke to me from the bed on which she lay, in a pink silk robe, fragile but animated, in a pretty house in Beverly Hills. I had travelled across the world to see her, unable to resist the chance of hearing at first hand from someone who had been there at the time of the house's transformation back into a cherished home. In fact, during the few years they lived in it, the new young couple made it not only a home but a famously daring and smart address. The rare tourist boat that went up the Thames towards Richmond or Hampton Court would announce through loud-speakers as it passed, 'That is the home of Miss Lee, the film star.' Over the front door, like a blazon in her honour, Stevenson put the entwined masks of comedy and tragedy. Film stars were the top celebrities of that day, and newspapers were eager to publish accounts and photographs of one living in such an 'amusing . . . original' place – somewhere, in other words, where most moneyed young couples would not have dreamed of living – 'In Bankside, where the very cobblestones have echoed to the tread of Shakespeare, Johnson, and Goldsmith, is the home of a popular new movie star. She's blonde, young vivacious. Her name is Anna Lee and she is one of England's youngest stars, whose current screen appearance is opposite Boris Karloff in "The Man Who Lived Again". Previously she scored hits in "First a Girl" and "The Passing of the Third Floor Back". Shortly after she married Robert Stevenson, brilliant young director of "Nine Days a Queen", she decided to do something about a home where she could loaf in the grand manner or entertain *a la mode*.

'Anna, who loves the bizarre quality of the waterfront and the picturesque oddities of the river banks [read "dust chutes and cranes"] went up the Thames toward the Tower and on the south side of the river found Bankside, with its maze of cobbled alleys, little lanes, old buildings and giant ware-houses . . .'[4]

So Cecilie had been written out of the story. But, in Anna Lee's defence, she really did love 49 Bankside ('more than any other house I've ever lived in') and in California in 2003 was eager to hear what I could tell her about the house's sub-sequent history. She was most disconcerted that a modern photo of the place showed the house and its cobbles in front separated now from the river by a higher walkway: she said, rightly, that the house no longer now seemed to be *on* the water. She recalled for me, as if from another world, as indeed it had been, the dinner parties she and Robert Stevenson had given ('Table-decorations by Constance Spry,' *The Lady* reported). Guests included other stars such as Jack Hulbert, who had introduced her to Stevenson, Jack Buchanan, John Mills, Merle Oberon, Sybil Thorndike, and Jessie Matthews, who was then a dancer long before she became the lynchpin of the BBC radio serial *Mrs Dale's Diary*. Michael Balcon, by then already embarked on his long career as a film producer, came as did the young John Betjeman, who presumably never guessed that he was walking into a house that had once been the territory of 'Charrington, Sells, Dale and Co./ Nuts and nuggets in the window'. The crowning occasion was a Tudor-style water party the Stevensons gave in June 1937 for two hundred people, for which they hired a barge to take them all to Greenwich and back while 'roast swan' – actually goose decorated with swans' feathers – was consumed.

The following year Anna had a baby girl. 'Anna Lee's Baby almost born in House of Commons,' announced the *Evening Standard*, since the baby had begun to make its presence felt while Anna, overdue, was sitting in the Strangers' Gallery with her mother to while away the time. "In those days," Anna explained to me, "very few actresses had babies for fear of hurting their careers." In the course of a long, if chequered, acting career she was to have four more.

In the 1930s married couples anywhere near the Stevensons' income bracket still employed living-in servants.

A Mr and Mrs Poole were incorporated into the house, with a sitting room of their own in the front basement. The kitchen had been established in the old ground-floor front room off the passage, which had earlier been an office. Mr Poole acted as butler and always wore a black leather glove on one hand – "no one dared ask why". Mrs Poole was a good cook but was reputedly fond of the bottle: on several crisis occasions, when she turned out to be incapable of attending to the stove, Anna's younger sister, fresh from a domestic-science course, was summoned to help. This sister recalled for me that as soon as she got over Southwark Bridge "a policeman would appear and would escort me to the door. The area was thought to be dangerous after dark." More exactly, it was thought unsuitable for a middle-class girl to be crossing at night on her own. Married ladies, somehow, were considered more robust – and 'shop girls' were apparently quite safe. In reality, the brutal 'outcast' underclass of the previous century had now virtually disappeared. Between the two wars, London was a safer city than it had ever been before.

When the baby was born a Nanny was added to the household. But in fact the Stevensons' time there was nearly at an end. The collective opinion of their smart friends – "Darlings, you *can't* bring a child up *there*" – must have had some weight, but Anna herself told me that their decision that Bankside was unsuitable was much affected by an event which she situated, in memory, near the end of their stay there, but which in fact took place some eighteen months earlier. Next door in number 50 lived a wharf labourer, with his wife and two little boys. One summer the younger one fell over the edge of the quay when the tide was in and was drowned.

"I felt so for the family. I went to see the mother. The child was laid out there in the front room, washed, with his best suit on, all pale and still. I think we gave them some money to help out. I know that a long time later we had a nice letter from a brother of the family, thanking us."

Anna Lee rather thought the family name had been

Murphy. No one of that name is recorded in the Electoral Rolls in the late 1930s, but a trawl through the Death Registers for the various names that did offer themselves produced a result. An Edward and Annie Crumpton, who had moved into number 50 at about the same time that the Stevensons were married in Marylebone Registrar's Office, lost a six-year-old, John. The Southwark coroner reported 'asphyxiation caused by accidentally falling into the river Thames' on 9th June 1936. Before me as I write, I have a copy of the death certificate indicating this short, lost life, this tragedy that is itself now obliterated and lost. Accidents of this kind must have been happening on Bankside since the very first houses were built there – 'Every season . . . [boys] terminate their youthful career in a muddy and watery grave' (*Living London*, 1901–2).

In spite of this tragedy, Mr and Mrs Crumpton stayed on in the house overlooking the water. Perhaps other work was hard to find. It was the Stevensons who left, for a rented house in Dorset that suited the Nanny better. 49 Bankside was sold by auction: presumably the West End agents had no idea what price to put on such an 'unusual property'. A handsome brochure was produced, with much use of olde-worlde typeface and made-up stories about sea-captains, Wren and others – 'It is believed that Oliver Goldsmith lived there for a time as a doctor, giving his services for nothing to his poorer neighbours.' There were also photographs of various rooms in the house, furnished in disconcertingly sparse, 1930s style, with Anna Lee reclining in daring trousers on a divan, or tending her garden. There were notations such as 'the radio-gramophone in this room is excluded from the sale but can be purchased at valuation if desired'. The front cover showed the house viewed from the water through a picturesque forest of ships' masts.

It fetched £4000, so even with the expense of restoring it, Robert Stevenson had done extremely well out of his bargain. He was also lucky that he sold it then and not at the outbreak of war, when the universal conviction was that the whole of London was due to be flattened by German bombs.

This caused the perceived value of property to descend to a level from which it took many years to recover long after the war was won. But in any case, by September 1939 the Stevenson family were in the United States. They had not run away from the war: they were too heedlessly focused on their own careers and too uninterested in politics to know it was coming. When Robert was offered a commission by film mogul David Selznick, he accepted it, and his wife and little daughter (and Nanny) accompanied him to Hollywood for 'a few weeks holiday'. While they were there war was declared. Much to Anna's surprised annoyance, the British Vice-Consul in Los Angeles refused to deliver the special permit needed for her, baby or Nanny to return to Britain.

As things turned out, she was never to return, except on brief visits. She acted in John Ford's *How Green Was My Valley*, and her subsequent career – and later marriages – evolved willy-nilly in the United States, where she ended her days as the grande dame, wheelchair-bound, of a television series. "I was a star in England," she told me wistfully, as she lay at home in Beverly Hills with old cuttings spread between us. "I never have been in America. Except a soap star." I was the last person ever to interview her. Less than a year later, at the age of ninety-one, she was gone.

It was a Civil Servant who paid the £4000 for the house, now picturesquely referred to as 'Cardinal's Wharf'. Anna Lee could not recall his name, but a chance encounter brought me some information on him. He was William Montagu Pollock (1903–93), younger son of a military baronet, who eventually acquired a knighthood of his own after an ambassadorial career in Scandinavia, Peru, Syria and Switzerland. The fact that he listed his recreation in *Who's Who* as 'washing up' suggests a self-deprecating sense of fun at variance with this august public profile. So indeed does his choice of Bankside as a home. I was told: "at Cardinal's Wharf he once chased a young woman round the dining table. His wife was called Prudence, and when they had a daughter, to patch up some particular misdemeanour, she was christened Fidelity." His son, born in 1935, was a very small boy when the family lived on Bankside, where he dimly remembers his father giving the door a coat of red paint – further evidence of unconventional leanings. This son used to be taken for walks along the quay by his Nanny (another one), nicely dressed as befitted a child of the Nanny-employing classes, and had to be hastily shushed when he remarked loudly that the wharfside labourers were 'dirty'.

At the outbreak of war the family went off to Stockholm in neutral Sweden, to which country William Montagu-Pollock had been appointed Her Majesty's representative. But fears early in the following year that Germany might breach that neutrality sent Prudence Montagu-Pollock and her two small children home to England, on an extra-ordinarily circuitous route through distant parts of Europe that had then not, quite, been invaded. After that, as their son put it, the marriage was over anyway.

When the war, too, was over, mother and children returned to London from the home of country relatives, and a visit was paid to Cardinal's Wharf to see what state it was in. Bankside had been severely blitzed. The bombers had been aiming at both warehouses and railway lines, and in any case the river itself had been an obvious marker and target. On the opposite shore, St Paul's still stood, but acres of roofless, blackened buildings lay between it and the river. On the Southwark side Emerson Street, just down the river from Cardinal's Wharf, had been virtually wiped out, as had Pond Yard and most of the Skin Market. Numbers 50, 51 and 52 Bankside stood, but they had been gutted by small fire-bombs early in the war and were effectively roofless. Number 49, miraculously, was more or less intact, though the back rooms had been badly damaged.[5] To the ten-year-old schoolboy, fresh from the country, with his fading memories of a cheerful family house with a red front door and boats everywhere, the whole place appeared unspeakably desolate, ruinous, fit only (once again) to be swept away. There seems to have been no question of mother and children returning there. They had settled in respectable Eccleston Square, and the visit across the river was probably made only because the house was on the point of being sold.

I had known that the house had been acquired just after the war by members of the part-Swedish Munthe family, and had been puzzled as to how this had come about. No doubt William Montagu-Pollock's presence in Stockholm for the duration of the war provides the answer, for Axel Munthe (1857–1949) was then lodging in the palace as a retired physician to the royal family. He was a Swedish doctor and writer who had lived in a number of European countries. His book *The Story of San Michele*, a memoir centering on the house he had built himself on Capri from the ruins of the Emperor Tiberius's villa, was hugely successful in the 1930s. An extraordinarily self-congratulatory work, stuffed with Gothic fantasies and half-truths, it still has a compelling readability. Munthe married an upper-class English woman thirty years younger than himself, Hilda Pennington-Mellor, though the fact is nowhere mentioned in his memoir. They had a son, Ludvig Malcolm Munthe, a swashbuckling figure who claimed the Scarlet Pimpernel as an ancestor on his mother's side, and who, as a Major in the British army, played a genuinely valiant Resistance role in occupied Norway during the war. It was for him that Cardinal's Wharf was bought in October 1945, but I do not know how much was paid: not much, probably, at that date. Like his father, Munthe had a good eye for remarkable places and their buried history, and, also like his father, he seems to have found fantasy irresistible.

He and his wife lived in the house, at any rate inter-mittently, for several years, figuring in the Electoral Rolls as 'DeMunthe'. The bundle of house Deeds contains copies of laborious letters from a wharf company who, he pointed out, were infringing the wharf rights he had purchased along with the house: '. . . I have had a talk to the Barge Company and they tell me that they are not aware of any breach of the order they have given to their workmen that you shall not have their barges on your wharf. They suggest that the most that can have happened is that they have tied up on their wharf and that the end of their barges have over-lapped, and they point out that this is a thing which always takes place and cannot be altered as it depends on the tide . . .'

It is not recorded, however, if Munthe ever had a boat of his own to moor. Number 49 and its neighbours have no such wharf rights today, but no one seems to know quite when or how these were extinguished. It is possible that, when plans were laid around 1970 for the Jubilee walkway to be added to the quay on the river side, the Greater London Council failed to consult individuals, and that no one at that point with a vested interest in Number 49 thought to raise the matter. (A similar combination of inattention and public-authority high-handedness has also resulted in the loss, over the last twenty years, of a number of ancient rights-of-way between the river front and Park Street.)

The bomb-damaged back of the house had to be repaired, and no doubt also the roof. It seems that Munthe did what was essential but was more interested in décor. On the re-plastered ceiling of the ground-floor back room, the dining room, a large round picture appeared: Neptune, or possibly Father Thames, with attendant Tritons, and old London Bridge in the background. Above the front door onto Bankside, in place of the Stevensons' theatrical masks, went the supposed coat of arms of the Pennington-Mellors. By and by, at the side of this door, a double plaque appeared:

Here lived
Sir Christopher Wren
During the building of St Paul's cathedral
Here also, in 1502, Catherine
Infanta of Castile and Aragon
afterwards first Queen
of Henry VIII took shelter
on her first landing in
London

The writing is curly, in pseudo-ancient style. The whole thing is made out of plaster, probably by Munthe himself. There had in fact been an eighteenth-century porcelain plaque, referring to Wren, attached to the house further up Bankside which was pulled down in 1906. After that, the homeless plaque was apparently put on the boundary wall of the Power Station which had swallowed the site of the house, not far from number 49. Anna Lee recalled seeing it there. When the post-war rebuilding of the Power Station began, Munthe evidently saw no harm in appropriating this small piece of history for himself.

What other embellishments of his own he might have contributed to Cardinal's Wharf, had he lived there more permanently and for longer, one rather dreads to think. Fortunately his attention was absorbed by several other family properties, including a house at Southside, Wimbledon. Here, his fondness for otiose structural improvements-in-the-style-of was given full rein, as was his passion for collecting ancient artefacts without much regard for their provenance or authenticity. That house remains open to the public to this day, a monument to dubious antiquarianism.

But though one must be thankful that 49 Bankside escaped this fate, I have come to feel grateful to Munthe. For in putting up his bogus plaque he may actually, whether he knew it or not, have saved the house once again. In the Brave New World spirit of post-war planning, that now-reviled era that produced the wastelands of the modern Elephant and Castle and desolate housing estates in Bermondsey, Georgian houses were something to be pulverised without a second thought. In the words of one planner extolling the future Festival of Britain site in Lambeth, where the last old houses in Belvedere Road were just being destroyed, 'huddles of mean streets' were to give way to 'the shining architecture of the future'. The Abercrombie Plan for London, which was drawn up before the war was even over, did not spare the riverfront from its good intentions. On its designs, no trace of quays or wharves is to be found on the whole stretch between

Southwark Cathedral and Waterloo Bridge, though this was many years before the great shift of the port away from London began to be seriously envisaged.

One would like to think that Abercrombie and his team were exceptionally prescient (many of the Plan's ideas for integrated road–rail systems and new railway lines to the docks were sound) but I suspect that, for Bankside, vision had simply overcome realities. On the outline design, trees line the Southwark shore, in a way that would have delighted John Evelyn but no one else much in the intervening three centuries. Behind this frill of greenery is an almost unbroken wall of medium-high concrete blocks set at right-angles to each other – 'Offices and flats'. Had this been built, not a trace of Bankside's ancient identity would have remained.

However, the force of existential circumstances is sometimes greater than that of futuristic vision. The old Power Station needed to be replaced by a more modern one with a greater capacity. You might have supposed, given Abercrombie, the new post-war concern for 'zoning' and for the removal of noxious industries from central London, that plans would be made to site the new plant anywhere rather than opposite St Paul's. Certainly, the LCC thought so. But evidently such was the continuing invisibility of the Southwark side of the river, to everyone but the dwellers and visitors at Cardinal's Wharf, that the old site was still felt to be the obvious one. It was as if the City were a house and Bankside was its unregarded back door, necessary but beneath attention – or as if the watery space that separated London from its Surrey side was perceived to be much wider than it was in reality.

There were considerable protests, not so much at the siting of the Power Station as at the size of it. Sir Giles Gilbert Scott, who had designed the coal-fired Power Station at Battersea a few years earlier, and who happened also to be Chairman of the Royal Academy, was asked to design this new one. There were fears that its cathedral-like proportions would dwarf the Wren dome opposite and emit clouds of polluting smoke. But by 1947 *The Builder*'s correspondent was writing sanguinely: 'The station is lower than the original building Allowed under the London Building Act. As you can see, it will be more a question of the other buildings overshadowing the station than of the station overshadowing them.' The *Illustrated London News* of the time was equally soothing – 'The new power station would have only one chimney, designed as a "campanile" . . . Oil-fuel would be used, delivered by underground pipe-lines from barges discharging at a small jetty off-shore. Thus there would be no derricks or coal dumps, nor smoke from the "campanile", which would emit only exhaust fumes which had been cleaned, washed and purified prior to reaching the upper air.' The shining future, evidently, was on the point of arriving.

The debate continued with some fervour, in and out of Parliament, before the project was finally approved by Lewis Silkin, the Minister of Town and Country Planning under the post-war Labour government. Opponents christened it 'Silkin's Folly'. Construction did not start till 1948, and in the several years since the initial proposal for it, the first flush of extremist, money-no-object enthusiasm for a totally replanned London had abated. The Royal Academy now designated the Surrey shore not for anodyne 'offices and flats' but for 'well-designed wharves and warehouses'. No longer was the new Power Station as depicted in artists' impressions flanked exclusively by regimented modern blocks. The magazine *The Sphere* published a mocked-up view which actually highlighted and labelled 'Wren's house' near by, though placing it carelessly on the west side of the new Power Station rather than the east! The *Illustrated London News* paragraph quoted above ends, 'A picture of the Bankside house where Wren lived during the building of St Paul's appears on p.548.'[6]

Evidently something, perhaps indeed Malcolm Munthe's timely and inventive labelling of 49 Bankside, served to make councils, planners and other public bodies shy away from touching it, even while they were reducing to rubble other equally old and beautiful houses both up and down the river.

In due course numbers 50, 51 and 52 were reconstructed

after their fire-bomb trauma, to form, along with 49, a small preserved enclave. But theirs was more of a complete rebuilding than a repair, with some windows altered and the three houses converted into two. They are so changed that the shade of little John Crumpton seems unlikely to linger there. Today, they are in the property of Southwark cathedral and the Provost lives in one of them.

At some point in the later 1940s Malcolm Munthe let his house. In what, by then, was becoming a tradition of distinguished maverick occupants, the principal tenant was Peregrine Worsthorne, then a young leader-writer on *The Times*.[7] Half a century later, in his memoir *Tricks of Memory* (1995), Worsthorne described going to Cardinal's Wharf for the first time with his French wife, Claudie:

'The day chosen was a summer Sunday when the river was looking so beautiful that one scarcely noticed that the house stood alone and isolated amongst acres of post-Blitz desolation . . . After giving us tea in lovely china, Malcolm Munthe showed us around the house, which was full of period furniture. The dining room, too, was ravishing with a ceiling hand-painted, or so we were led to believe, by Rubens . . .'

Once they had moved in, things were rather different. There was also the Power Station, at that date still the old one:

'. . . Not only did it emit an ominous low hum, but, much worse, a steady stream of black smoke which coated everything with sticky grime. Rats from the barges, tied up at the wharf, were also a problem. The basement, which we had not been shown, was infested with them.'

Although the basement had been in use as habitable space before the war, Munthe must have abandoned it. A photo taken in 1949 shows the nineteenth-century pavement grid cemented over again and its railing removed.

'. . . at night [the rats] would invade our bedroom where they had the effrontery to climb up the drapes surrounding the four-poster bed in which Catherine of Aragon was supposed to have rested.'

As for the 'Rubens' ceiling, it was flaking worryingly. *The Times* then employed a museum's correspondent who happened to be a Rubens expert, so Worsthorne asked him if he would mind visiting to give some advice on preservation? It was while the great man was contemplating the ceiling (with some reservations, I should imagine) that Rosie Darc, the char-woman, bounced in. She revealed briskly that Munthe had painted it himself – "Don't you worry. It only took him half a sec to put it there, and he can do it again in no time."

The rats eventually got too much for Worsthorne, who developed a jaundice so serious that he was carried off to St Thomas's Hospital. There, the doctors were puzzled, until the exact nature of the conditions in which the young couple lived was revealed to them. Worsthorne had, apparently, contracted a rat-borne strain of the disease that was 'rare to the point of non-existence, a bad memory from the days of Victorian slums.' The Worsthornes, by then expecting a baby, moved out.

However, the late Michael Oakeshott, then already Professor of Politics at the London School of Economics, who was for a while the Worsthornes' sub-tenant in the attic, seems to have felt nonchalant about the rodents. Their boldness – chewing through a rolled-up carpet to get into the kitchen – amused him. His very young girl-friend, artist June Hooper, who shared the attic, even remembers them with affection – 'I woke up one morning,' she told me, 'to a sort of rustling. And there was this perfectly enchanting black rat sitting on the edge of the waste paper basket.' She was quite unfazed too by the dark quay at night. 'I always felt perfectly safe there.'

In the years immediately following the war, Bankside was a shadow of its former self, with so many of its buildings ruined. But by 1951 Grace Golden could write:

'Bankside today is coming to life. The gloomy fronts of buildings which for years have looked like unburied corpses are receiving fresh coats of paint . . . Cranes, which I thought permanently flattened against a wall, are swinging back and forth . . .'

It seemed then that all the industry and trade that had been traditional there for over two hundred years would pick up and continue as before. For a few years, it did. But this revival in the 1950s was to be a last Indian summer.

Chapter XI

Bad Guys and Good Ones

By the early 1950s the more exotic occupants had departed from 49 Bankside. It was still owned by Munthe, but it once more became a family home and was to remain so for over fifteen years.

Not that the Black family was particularly conventional. Mrs Black had been to Art School, and it was in company with friends from these student days that she found number 49, then untenanted, and persuaded her newly married husband to rent it. Dr Black was then a young registrar at the London Hospital in the East End; he later trained as a psychiatrist at the Maudsley, in Camberwell. Over the next few years three sons were born, including Daniel, the middle one, my informant. The youngest boy had a home birth, probably in the same top-front bedroom where Sells children of several generations had been born into the silvery river light.

For much of the boys' childhood an extra person also lived in the house 'like a sort of permanent uncle'. Geoffrey Davidson, one of the friends of student days, was a dancer with the Ballet Rambert and subsequently a dance-teacher. He inhabited the ground-floor back room giving onto the garden that had been Munthe's elegant dining room. The crumbling ceiling painting of a watery deity was still in place. The children were not allowed to go into the room immediately above it in case the vibration of their feet should dislodge further shards of paint, but in any case that room was a repository for Munthe belongings and was kept locked. The little boys liked to think that it was out of bounds because it was haunted.

Some of the Munthe antique furniture was in use in the house, mostly in the first-floor front room, which was Dr Black's study. Dan Black recalls that the other rooms were 'quite austere', with traces of the 1930s minimalistic white décor still in place, and rather antiquated gas or electric fires. No central heating as yet, a quite usual state of affairs in the '50s and '60s. The kitchen, in which they ate and which they used as 'a general family room' since there was no other one to spare, was still in the ground-floor front with the corridor running alongside. It had an old-fashioned coal range as well as a gas cooker. The cellars were still 'ruinous and full of junk', but the rat problem seems to have abated. The rats were known to be there, but were '*sotto voce*'.

It may be that continuous human occupation was enough to discourage these creatures, but their decline may also have been a measure of Bankside's declining trade. For Dan Black's childhood there, roughly from the late '50s to about 1970, saw the last of Bankside as it had traditionally been. When he was small there was a crane in operation 'about every twenty or thirty metres' and many barges tied up. River craft still hooted and cranes dipped, in the time-honoured way, to mark New Year's Day. There was two-way wheeled traffic along Bankside, as there had been for the last three hundred years. The new Power Station was fully functional and, beyond it, the Blue Circle Cement Company created a white silt which drifted in at windows, competing with the still-ubiquitous London soot. Immediately to the east of 49 the warehouse that had belonged to the paint manufacturer was now occupied by a company making wirebound hoses, and there was other light industry still along the river front towards Mary Overie's Dock. There, 'it was like walking into the nineteenth century', with iron walkways overhead between warehouse loading doors, cobbles underfoot, and a smell of spices, bacon and fish. There were still warehouse men around in suits and caps, and foremen wore bowlers –

locally made. But they were the last of their kind. Already, by the 1960s, many warehouses were empty.

Like the trade, the industry of Southwark was not what it had been. Most of the firms whose premises had been flattened by bombs had either gone out of business entirely or had moved out of London. When the war was over and the blitz-dust had settled, they never moved back. A works near a major road, where the new articulated lorries could get in and out, was more attractive. The Skin Market, directly behind 49 Bankside, was a case in point. In the late nineteenth century, apart from a jam factory, this had been full of small houses that supplied the army of labourers needed to manhandle goods on and off barges. By the 1930s, with greater mechanisation in use on the wharves, many of the houses had been supplanted by an extended factory, now making soap, perfume and patent medicines. But by the time Dan Black and his brothers were running down Cardinal Cap Alley to what had been the Skin Market, it was to play on a mound of bomb debris, sprinkled with the rosebay willowherb that was known as 'fireweed', devastation which no one seemed in a hurry to rebuild.

There was in any case, in the planning ethos of those years, a persistent prejudice against industry, even light industry, in districts that were also residential. The fact that this logically led to a net loss of jobs for local people was not, somehow, as apparent to planners as it should have been. Or possibly, if it was apparent, for years it was vaguely thought to be a Good Thing. As the current archivist of Southwark put it to me with restraint, 'Local authorities at that time were often remarkably anti-commercial in their attitudes.' More specifically, perhaps, too many of those who went into local government at that time had a bred-in-the-bone mistrust of small businesses, as incarnating the bogey of capitalism.

It was as if they also failed to realise, at the most basic level, what urban areas are and what sustains them – as if townscape were simply a stage-setting, to be manipulated and renovated at will. The two twin planning obsessions of the time, that industry should be 'got out of cities' and that 'huddles of mean streets' should be demolished to make way for 'tree-lined boulevards', worked together to fatally accumulating effect. The Abercrombie Plan, with what now seems an almost Stalinist lack of regard for democratic independence and human preferences, had proposed as a target that Southwark's population should be fifty per cent lower than its pre-war figure. In the words of two local historians:[1] 'To begin with, population reduction happened naturally – if being unable to return to a bombed out home can be called natural.' But through the '50s and the '60s it went down and down, far below any target, as on the one hand local jobs were discouraged or folded and on the other people were 'decanted' out of the borough in ever more megalomaniac council building schemes undertaken in the name of progressive policy.

The local authorities of both Bermondsey and Southwark, and also of the LCC, bear a heavy responsibility for the cavalier way in which they treated the venerable districts under their charge, but the collapse of water-borne trade along the river was not mainly their fault. The root of the matter was the decline, and then the closure, of London's extensive dock system.

The docks had seemed, superficially, to recover well from the blasting they had had in the Second World War. In an illustrated book called *London Perceived*, published in 1962, V. S. Pritchett, who had known Thames-side life intimately as a young man, could still write about the docks and wharves all along the Thames in the pride-of-our-great-City way that had been traditional for the last hundred years: 'We have passed miles of cranes, forty-six miles of them to be exact, if we reckon both banks of the river. They are thickest in the Pool, like an infestation of grass-hoppers sticking an articulated limb, with an insect's unknowable intention, into the sky . . . to drop a bale into a lighter, dead straight and suddenly, like a spit . . . At London Bridge they suddenly thin out. By Blackfriars, they have vanished. Trading London ends, ruling London begins.'

The last stretch described is, of course, Bankside, with the cranes stopping logically at the new Power Station that did not need them. But there must have been some warning voices by then, for Pritchett wrote on the same page, 'Some say that in fifty years half the area will revert to what it once was: a pleasure ground.' But 'fifty years' in prospect is a misty vista. There is little sign that he realised he was describing a riverscape that was, even then, barely intact, and on the point of passing into history. Down on the river's estuary at Tilbury a port was being built for huge new container ships which did not need unloading in the traditional way. This had its effect on the docks, this in turn affected the Pool of London, and this affected the function of the riverside above London Bridge.

Whether the coming of containerisation was the single, overwhelming reason that London's docks were put out of business is a huge subject in its own right. Some would say that the failure to construct better road and rail links to dockland in the post-war period played a part. Others would also point to the dockers' own intransigent refusal to adapt their working practices. All one can say is that it happened, and that no one, laying visionary plans in 1945, seems to have foreseen it, any more than they foresaw the arrival of the jet plane, or cheap mass travel, or the growth in car ownership, or indeed many of the other social changes of the 1950s and '60s.

The first dock to close, in 1967, was the East India Dock. Built for sailing ships in 1806, it had no space to accommodate the container trade. St Katharine's Dock, by the Tower, and the London Dock at Wapping, which had both been losing money hand over fist, followed two years later. The others went the same way in the 1970s. About half of the trade went to Tilbury, but the rest went to other coastal ports in the United Kingdom or indeed to Rotterdam in Holland. London's long history as a leading world port came to an ignominious end.

Along with the docks and the Pool, the lighterage and river-wharf trade, which depended on these sources of work, declined sharply also. In the 1930s there had been some 9000 lighters on the Thames at London, often moored many deep in the centre of the river waiting for tugs and the tide. 'They are ubiquitous,' wrote a journalist in *The Evening News*[2] in the approved telling-readers-in-Kensington-about-working-London style of the times: 'They are as plentiful as lorries in the streets of dockland; indeed, they are the lorries of the river, which is the biggest street of all.' By 1963, already, the number of lighters had been halved to 4600 and was going down all the time.[3] In 1974 an *Evening Standard* journalist interviewed a group of lightermen at length and quoted one of them as saying: 'Only six years ago the few wharves at Bankside that remained from the original thirty-two were moving 150,000 tons of cargo a year. And now this great God-given east–west highway has been allowed to die.' The journalist described the empty warehouses rising 'sheer and bleakly deserted from the river . . . only the names remain emblazoned proudly, like that of Ozymandias.'[4]

By 1983, when the last dock, at Millwall, had been closed and the Isle of Dogs was beginning to be turned into a district of glass office towers, there were under a thousand lightermen left. By then, the identity crisis being suffered in riverside boroughs had well and truly come home even to the most bone-headed local authority. Already, six years before, the Borough of Southwark had had to admit that it had more than a million square feet of warehouse and manufacturing space standing empty. And, to add to the problem, a programme of office-building had been undertaken, there as in several other boroughs, which bore no relation to actual demand.

The closure of businesses on or near Bankside was piecemeal, and not always directly or obviously related to the ending of water-borne trade, but it was inexorably part of the same general change. Post-war LCC plans had promoted these closures, but when the Greater London Council took over in the mid-'60s some attempts were made to revive the riverfront, with talk of 'rebuilding the past'. In practice, this led to a narrow, local focus on light industry, often of a rather transient and uncertain kind, with old, large works being pulled down and replaced by smaller, flimsier constructions. Jobs were 'created' in the 1970s and early '80s, none of which existed by the following decade. Because of this belated preoccupation with shoring up a way of life that had been allowed to collapse, ironically, planning permission was refused at this time to convert industrial buildings into offices, that is, into businesses of another kind. Handsome, solid Victorian manufactories and warehouses were thus destroyed without another use being sought for them, sometimes even in the teeth of well-informed and influential opposition. Neither the local MP nor John Betjeman was able to save the finest building at Mary Overie's Dock.

The centuries-old hat trade collapsed because people stopped wearing hats, but it would have been driven out of Southwark anyway by post-war restrictions on noxious industries, as was the equally ancient tanning trade. Many printing firms moved elsewhere, reputedly because printers were now a well-paid lot who tended to want to live in green suburbs. A worse loss to Southwark's economy, and one that might well have been avoided, was that of the flourishing hop trade which had, for hundreds of years, linked Southwark with a rural heartland. After the war the traders found the local authority was making it too difficult for them to rebuild their warehouses, and so they relocated to a vast new structure in Kent. Fortunately the splendid Hop Exchange in Southwark Street just managed to escape demolition and now houses offices and a restaurant. The great Anchor Brewery, with its dray-horses and its yeasty smell, that had been such a feature of Bankside since the early eighteenth century, shut down in stages after Barclay Perkins merged with Courage in the 1950s. It became merely a bottling plant in the next decade, with some of its buildings let off for other uses. Someone who was a trainee engineer then at the Power Station recalls that there was 'an egg-breaking plant' there (which smelt just as much as the brewery had) and was staffed entirely by women. No doubt that too shut when the great food-distribution wharves folded below London Bridge, as did the Sainsbury food-processing works above Blackfriars Bridge. In the 1980s the whole large brewery area was cleared, for what was supposed to be new 'workshops' but which became a housing estate and offices. Fortunately, by that time, the Anchor pub, which had been scheduled to be demolished as 'slum clearance' after the war, was prized as a relic and was allowed to remain.

Nearer to 49 Bankside, the City Lead Works by Southwark Bridge, with its tall chimney, had been derelict for years when it was finally demolished in 1981. Blue Circle Cement went too. The London Hydraulic Power works, next to the Power Station, shut in 1977. Blocks of unremarkable flats were built on the site and were named 'Falcon Point'. As to the Power Station itself, for all its impressive presence and its much-advertised modernity, it turned out to be a white elephant of major proportions. It had to be built in stages so that the old one could be gradually phased out, and was not complete till well into the 1950s. Finally modifications were made in 1963, by which time Gilbert Scott's 'brick cathedral' approach already seemed out of date. Ten years later the oil crisis drove up the international costs of petroleum, and an oil-fired power station became uneconomic: from then on it was doomed. In 1981 the plant was shut down. The Electricity Generating Board proposed selling the site for redevelopment, but no firm plans were made.

For twelve more years it stood empty, its machinery rusting inside the great turbine hall, visible through the huge but dirty mullioned windows. Rain found ways to infiltrate and left puddles on the floor, birds got in too and colonised the interior, depositing their droppings and flying about as if in an enormous, dim aviary. It looked as if the place were only awaiting its end, just as the equally huge and unwanted hulk of the Albion Flour Mills had stood near by for eighteen years before finally being demolished, almost two centuries before.

*

By the 1970s, when Bankside was reaching its lowest ebb, derelict, silent and largely unfrequented, the Black family were no longer at number 49.

They had flourished there for many years. Dan had suffered from asthma (one wonders if the Cement Company was partly to blame?) and spent some time in the Evelina Hospital for Sick Children, on the site of the mid-Victorian workhouse that St Saviour's parish had shared with St George's. But he remembers his childhood as happy. What would have been their nearest primary school, in Emerson Street,[5] had been bombed during the war, along with St Peter's church to which it was attached, so the boys went to St Saviour's Parochial School. Now on the opposite corner of Union Street from the Cross Bones site, it was essentially the same school of which Edward Perronet Sells had been Treasurer over a hundred years before. Their mother went there too, as a teacher, for a number of years. Their father's career advanced. The Blacks were a sociable couple, in the effervescent 1960s. Once more, as in the Stevensons' day, the old house resounded with parties to which 'everyone came. Tony Armstrong-Jones came.' But at the end of the decade the marriage was more or less over. By 1971 the whole family, including their confidant, the 'permanent uncle' Geoffrey Davidson, had moved out of Bankside.

Davidson went to teach dancing in Turkey. Three years later Mrs Black flew out there to see him to 'give herself the strength to get a divorce'. On the return journey the Turkish DC10 airliner stopped off at Paris Charles de Gaulle airport. When it took off again it was to crash into nearby woods, killing all on board.

Dan Black, living elsewhere in south London, used to check up on his childhood home through the years. Every so often he would ring the bell, and talk to whoever answered it. But the place was to go, initially, through a very bad time.

The general abandonment of Bankside seemed to mean that even the house at Cardinal's Wharf, which had been rescued and admired, and photographed for posterity by a local antiquarian, was temporarily abandoned also. Even though GLC plans were afoot for the 'Jubilee Walkway', which would make its way gradually along the south bank of the river from Hungerford Bridge over the next twenty-five years and would eventually be extremely popular, for the time being Bankside seemed to be off nearly everyone's mental map, disregarded and vulnerable.

Malcolm Munthe had by then impoverished himself trying to maintain his various houses around Europe, and 49 Bankside had been placed in a Trust. One letter that has finished up in the bundle of Deeds, written by a Trustee to the Town Clerk of Southwark in 1970, suggests that the lease (presumably then still in the name of Dr Black) might be given up at the end of the year. The Trustee was enquiring about the possibility of a local authority grant for 'redecorating those parts of the house that are of historic interest'. Not only were Wren and Catherine of Aragon offered as reasons, but Henry VIII himself and also Shakespeare were added to the optimistic list of former occupants. It was also hoped that money might be forthcoming to 'mount exhibitions' and 'to open certain parts of the house to small parties of students and historians for whom the interior of the property would be of considerable interest . . . Without proper and interested care, this property might fall into an even worse state of repair than it has already.'

There is no record of a satisfactory reply to this letter. Given the attitude of mind that prevailed in Southwark Council at that period, and the fact that Rennie's London Bridge was even then being removed in favour of a pre-stressed concrete replacement, the Trust's quest probably had no chance of succeeding.

At all events, the house fell empty. It was then squatted – this was also the time of triumphalist and destructive student sit-ins – and vandalised. Some of the original panelling was destroyed, cannibalised as fuel in the house's own fireplaces, and so were most of the doors and the barley-sugar banisters. Their removal, and that of some of the stairwell panelling, left the staircase effectively floating, anchored only to the remaining newel posts. By the time the intruders had been evicted for the third time late in 1972, the Munthe family felt desperate for a solution. It was Guy Munthe, Malcolm's son and Axel's grandson, who took the place on.

Many years later, Guy was described by a journalist writing an article about the house as 'sometime merchant banker, waiter, poet, actor, film director and Afghan *mujahidin*'. The last term apparently referred to a fleeting role, in disguise, as an Afghan war-correspondent. Guy always claimed to have received a 'war wound' there which had damaged his health, though those who knew him well thought that his declining health was due to a quite other cause. An eventual obituarist wrote: 'He was a frequent escort of Princess Margaret and sex-change model April Ashley, as well as being the lover of gay mass-murderer Michael Lupo . . . A virtuoso on the musical saw, Munthe occasionally dressed as a tramp and made £40 or so a day, with his renditions of Vivaldi, Chopin and the Beatles . . . [He used] to be found circumnavigating Chelsea on his ancient motor cycle with pet parrot Augusta gripping the handle bars . . .'[6]

But it is clear from the skill with which he rescued the house (its third rescue in forty years) that he had a core of taste and determination not apparent from the above description. It was, he recollected later, 'in a ghastly condition . . . the curtains were so revolting I had to take them down with tongs'. His first action was 'to clear the decks, paint everything French grey, and then start piecing the house together again'. He scoured London for replacement doors and for old pine packing cases he could use 'faked up' to replace the missing panelling. He salvaged some suitable banisters from another old house. By and by he hung hand-blocked wall-paper and reassembled a collection of fine furniture. Over the years he installed another bathroom, in the first-floor closet beside the lavatory; and re-organised the attic to create a separate flat there which eventually harboured a man-servant. He extended the back of the house slightly, putting in new 'Queen Anne' windows in the first-floor back room. He barred the old door into the alley and removed the corridor partition, restoring to its full dimensions the front room that had been the Blacks' kitchen, which he opened up to the lobby by the stairs through an archway. He tackled the cellars, moving the kitchen down there as it had been in the nineteenth century. The part that had been the Pooles' hidden sitting room in the Stevensons' time became a display place for his collection of skulls. This included a begging bowl made out of the cranium of a Tibetan monk (according to him) and also some Maori shrunken heads. In the same idiom, he had the ground-floor dining room (which had in any case had to be largely rebuilt after the war) re-decorated by a French painter, André Dubreuil. Flaking Father Thames disappeared: instead were *trompe l'oeil* effects of ruined, vaguely Pompeian walls, broken pediments, urns, a guttering candle or two, creepers, and a very realistic key on a hook. Guy's own comment on all this was "*I'm* not real. At least, not in everyday terms."

A good many visitors, chiefly male, passed through the house during Guy's time there. Dan Black called once, when he happened to be on Bankside, and was hospitably invited to stay the night, an invitation he declined.

Guy left some time in the 1980s. It is not quite clear when, since for a while he seems to have alternated between London and Italy, where he wanted to breed Welsh ponies. He said that he was sick of London, which now had 'no society . . . [just] millions of bloody people'. He told a journalist then that a house was 'like a self-portrait; when you've finished it, you can hang it on the wall and look at it, or you can flog it and get on with the next'. He also claimed that he'd 'never achieved a thing in life'.

On the contrary, the repair and preservation of 49 Bankside after the ravages it had suffered was a considerable achievement, and monument enough. When he finally succumbed to his 'war wound', in Italy, the obituarist quoted above remarked, 'Society will be the poorer for his passing.' The obituary appeared under the title 'The Death of the Good Guy'.

While Guy Munthe was living in his self-created world, things were at last stirring on Bankside.

The Jubilee Walkway was being constructed bit by bit. A replica of the *Golden Hind*, the dauntingly small ship in which Sir Francis Drake circumnavigated the world, was installed as a tourist attraction in Mary Overie's Dock. But a much bigger initiative was the plan to rebuild a 'Globe' theatre on Bankside. The idea had long been cherished by the actor and director Sam Wanamaker. An American, who left the United States in the repressive McCarthy era, he became passionately attached to things British. The artist Geoffrey Fletcher, who was publishing books in the 1960s with drawings of buildings and corners that were soon to be extinguished (an invaluable record), was dismissive of Wanamaker's dream. 'I had a fear,' he wrote in 1966, 'that someone would build a replica of the Globe to mark the Shakespeare celebrations of 1964, a fear fortunately not realised.'

One understands what he meant. The term 'heritage industry' had not then been invented, but he had sensed, rightly, that something of the kind was coming – had to come, to fill the emptiness left by the retreat of real industry. Fletcher, with his acute eye for genuine, overlooked remains of old London, was wary of the bogus. But the Globe vision was more durable than he supposed, and the architect who became principally concerned in the project, Theo Crosby, did much to redeem the fantasy element in the reconstructed theatre by his meticulous concern for authentic building methods. When you look at the poor-quality modern blocks, bearing no relation to site, that were by then spotting London, and at the later wave of over-sized private developments that now crowd Bankside, the Globe scheme seems an unqualified achievement.

A money-raising Trust was established. It appeared that Southwark Council would look favourably on the scheme, and agreement was reached that in due course the Trust should be able to buy a riverside site – which happened to be almost next door to 49 Bankside, where the Royal Windsor Wharf and Sutton, Sail Maker had once been. A development company was involved, and money was invested in the drawing up of plans. However, in 1982, the Old Left councillors who had seemed a fixture were replaced by a younger generation with a keener vision. Under their auspices, a body called the North Southwark Community Development Group took the view that building a new Globe would be contrary to the needs of 'the traditional working-class community of North Southwark'. Phrases such as 'elitist tosh' and 'Shakespeare is overrated' were also bandied about. They had apparently failed to notice that two-thirds of the working population had already moved out to places further south such as Eltham, Penge and Merton, and that any further threat to the borough would not come from history-lovers but from private property developers with their eyes on waterfront sites. They could not, they said, give planning permission for the new Globe after all, because the space was currently in use as a Council yard and store where street sweepers kept their barrows and brooms.

The Globe Trust and their development company took the Council to Court for reneging on their previous agreement. Very substantial claims for compensation were now being made, including one from a property company with whom the Council had made a separate agreement. Eventually, in June 1986, the matter reached the High Court, who found in favour of the Globe Trust. The Council talked of a further appeal, but then backed down. They had to spend some millions of rate-payers' money on the cost of the case and on appeasing the various claimants. They also presumably realised that their belief that they were acting in the interests of 'the traditional working-class community' was fatally undermined when a local poll revealed substantial support for rebuilding the Globe.

Three years later, the foundations of the original Globe were verified as being on the ex-Anchor brewery land, and those of the Rose were revealed beside Southwark Bridge. All those who supported Wanamaker made the most of these discoveries, which were one happy consequence of the wholesale destruction of the Southwark townscape that had got under way by then. Wanamaker and Crosby both died in the early 1990s, but they knew that their dream was going to be realised. The Globe, which had further extended its site over that of the warehouse standing right up against number 49, was triumphantly opened in 1997. The reformed Council were by then assuring everyone that their 'commitment to heritage was ongoing'.

The transformation of the Power Station into the Tate Modern gallery was not a simple matter either. Up to the early 1990s, it looked as if the site would be sold off for development. But what development? Through the '80s various ideas were suggested, including an opera house. Theo Crosby (again) produced a splendidly operatic design, reminiscent of a *schloss* overlooking the river Rhine. His scheme also resurrected the endlessly postponed St Paul's Bridge, but this time as a slim pedestrian link with the other shore.

But the conservation movement was now well under way and many voices were raised against the demolition of Gilbert Scott's building. The Twentieth Century Society was campaigning to get the place listed, and a BBC programme was being filmed there with this intention, when it was visited by Nicholas Serota, the Curator of the Tate Gallery. The site had been suggested to him as a suitable place for a new gallery of modern art, but after his visit he became a fervent convert to the idea of turning the existing building into a gallery – which, after a great deal of effort and money-raising, was what eventually happened.

As late as 1993 some sections of Southwark local authority were opposed to this. In the November of that year, the director of the Southwark Environment Trust was writing to *The Independent*: 'It [the Power Station] presents a vertical acre of the ugliest ever bricks to the City and to the river, unredeemed by any masterful detailing . . . the building still casts a miasma of depression . . . Its construction was a disaster in urban planning, which its retention perpetuates . . . How backward-looking, how necrophiliac.'[7]

In essence, this was just the same sort of confrontation as had taken place in the 1830s, between those who wanted to restore St Saviour's and those who jeered at them as 'refined gentlemen belonging to the gothic interest' and wanted the place pulled down.

As had happened a decade before during the Globe saga, when 'the ordinary people of Southwark', who had been invoked so often in the past as a pretext for municipal vandalism, were asked in the 1990s if they wanted the building kept and turned into a gallery, they said yes. Southwark contributed a substantial sum of money. The footbridge idea was re-launched, and at last built to a design by Norman Foster. Today, the whole complex has proved popular beyond anyone's expectations, and for the first time in centuries the Southwark shore seems to have been drawn near again to the centre of London.

This had been an aspiration for a long time. When the Waterloo Bridge was built, the idea of colonising Lambeth Marsh as an integrated part of London was in people's minds, and the same effect was hoped for thirty years later when Waterloo station began to be built. Neither construction really achieved this end, and nor did the deliberate siting of the 1920s County Hall on the Surrey shore. 'South London' remained obstinately other: it was even said to have its own accent. In 1951 the Festival of Britain site, at Waterloo, brought large numbers of outsiders to that part of London for the first time, but it was regarded as an oasis of light and futuristic fun in a nowhere of blitzed townscape 'ripe for removal' (Abercrombie language). Similarly, when the South Bank arts complex began to go up on the ex-Festival site, it continued to be perceived as an outpost of London proper, fortunately accessible by an *ad hoc* plank footbridge stuck to the side of Hungerford railway bridge, rather than in a wider London context.

Even when the walkway was constructed all along the shoreline from Lambeth to below London Bridge, for a while much of it was little used. Around 1990, I often had occasion to walk up river along Bankside in the late afternoon. Once London Bridge, with its newly converted Hay's Wharf was passed, old London, vestigial London, set in. Borough Market, by Southwark Cathedral, seemed to be in decline – a process today, happily, reversed. In Clink Street, my feet trod deserted cobbles. Like Grace Golden in the 1920s, the Stevensons in the 1930s and the Worsthornes in the 1950s, I felt I was venturing into an unknown land.

Now people walk by the river morning, noon and night, and there are new cafés and restaurants in abundance. The great change has not been due to any structured plan. It has been pointed out to me, by someone who has spent a lifetime observing London, that all the earlier attempts to draw the Surrey shore into the metropolis were official attempts, or at any rate conscious schemes to that end undertaken by public bodies. Yet what has finally made the whole hazy vision of regeneration coalesce at last into working reality has been the two quirky projects which would never have seen the light had it not been for the enthusiasm and determination of a few dynamic individuals. I refer, of course, to the Globe and to the Tate Modern.

People like them. And, because they like them, they come to Bankside and wander along, and then they prolong their stroll, under Blackfriars Bridge and towards the previously isolated South Bank Centre, and so eateries have sprung up to serve them. And, at the South Bank Centre, human serendipity has again played a role, for though the concrete buildings are wretchedly unattractive externally, by today's more glamorous standards, the otherwise pointless underpass of the Hayward–Queen Elizabeth structure has proved a haven for skateboarders. Similarly, the immovable bulk of Waterloo Bridge, which appeared a tiresome obstacle on the Festival of Britain site and again when the arts complex came to be built, has turned out a haphazard advantage. One span of the bridge makes a ready-made space, outdoor but sheltered from the rain, for the National Film Theatre café and for the stalls of book-sellers. The 'pleasure ground' that

V. S. Pritchett hinted at in 1962, like the historical tours that Walter Besant fantasised about in 1889, has come about.

It is, however, far too early to assess this take-over of the Surrey shore by arts-and-heritage concerns. Will this prove a long-lasting enhancement of London life? Or will it, along with that fragile south-sea bubble known as 'the tourist industry', seem to our descendants to have been a relatively brief Indian summer before the setting in of a new economic Great Frost? Will future slumps, wars, global disasters make the early years of the twenty-first century on Bankside appear a time of luxury preoccupations and lotus-eating innocence? Or will our great-great-grandchildren be grateful to us that we saved and conserved and re-created attractive buildings, even as we are grateful to those who conserved the last vestiges of the Archbishop's palace or the George inn, or stopped the railway viaducts from strangling St Saviour's entirely. And grateful, of course, to those who saved the house at Cardinal's Wharf from disappearing into rubble, splintered wood and plaster dust like almost all its fellows.

After Guy Munthe's departure, 49 Bankside was sold on twice more. Today, neither slum nor rich man's palace, it is safe and well cared for in private hands. The high, creeper-covered wall of the neighbouring warehouse, the rest of which has been pulled down to accommodate the ancillary buildings of the Globe, still shelters its hidden garden on the east side. On the west side, Cardinal Cap Alley still runs towards the one-time Skin Market, but the right-of-way has been effectively lost, either during the Globe building works, which occupied a large part of the Skin Market, or when the Midland Bank built a computer centre on another part of it. The ancient alley is currently a dead-end, and to avoid what are politely called 'nuisances', the present owners of number 49 have put a locked gate across it at Bankside. You cannot walk into the past that way.

To the east of the Globe, a procession of new blocks of flats and offices, twinkling with lights at night, line the river, just as they do now down the Rotherhithe reach and across the water at Wapping and on many other stretches. The social geography of several boroughs, including Southwark, has been turned back to front. What were originally the 'mean streets' and 'dark dirty alleys' of waterside Thames are now extremely expensive real-estate, a cosmopolitan ribbon worlds away from the drab hinterlands behind them. In this ribbon, 49 Bankside, with its old-fashioned lamp, stands at night like a forgotten cottage in a children's story.

Below the raised walkway and the fairylike Millennium Bridge, the dark tides come and go as ever, now largely unregarded. Here and there, at the sites of a few of the old water stairs, concrete steps descend to the river floor, but they are little used. Sometimes, when the water at Bankside is very low, it uncovers the foundations of ancient wooden jetties, places where boats tied up on the gravelly strand before the Cardinal's Hat was even rebuilt into number 49. Every so often another find – a handmade nail, a copper coin, the sole of a medieval leather shoe – is dredged from the mud where it has been lying while generations came and went above.

London Bridge, as ever, is one of the busiest, in spite of all the others that have been built to relieve it. Every weekday morning a great tide of people comes out from the railway station and flows across it to the City, and every evening the same tide goes back again. '*I had not thought*,' wrote T. S. Eliot of them, echoing Dante, '*that death had undone so many.*'

Since he wrote that, another eighty years of London workers have passed into the dark. They have joined the Browkers, Henslowes and Taylors, the Fritters, Shalletts, Thrales, Hornes, Sells and all the others who have briefly walked through these pages, along with the innumerable unnamed poor. When I am crossing London Bridge one winter evening my male companion is accosted by another man, with the gaunt face of an old labourer – 'Can you give me something, Sir? It's a very cold night.' The voice, the manner, does not seem so much that of a modern beggar as to belong to a long, long line of earlier, shadowy figures on the bridge at this spot.

*

In a house that was part of a new street in fields north of the City when the railway viaducts were cutting across the old lanes of Bankside, I am moving about in the kitchen. The young child on an upper floor of the house is in my charge: a baby-alarm speaker stands on a shelf. At first, I just hear the faint snuffles and thumps of a cot-sleeper settling to rest. Then a silence. Then, out of the air, it seems, out of a dateless past, comes a small, clear voice singing:

'*London Bridge is falling down, falling down, falling down –*
London Bridge is falling down, my fair la-dy . . .
. . . *Sticks and stones will wash away, wash away, wash away* . . .'

The song was old already when the first of the Sells children were growing up within sight of the old bridge. An earlier version of it was already current when Hugh Browker rebuilt the Cardinal's Hat, and when the fish ponds were made, and even when old London Bridge itself was built at the end of the twelfth century. Its earliest origins date back to the destruction of a wooden bridge by the Vikings, two generations before the Norman Conquest.

I like to think that small children will still be singing about London Bridge, and even that the house on Bankside will still be standing, long after I have joined the crowds walking away into the unknown.

Notes

Chapter III

1   *London and the Country Carbonaded*, Donald Lupton, 1632.
2   By tradition spelt thus to this day, but sometimes in the intervening centuries called 'St Saviour's Dock', although great confusion can be caused since there was another creek to which that name was applied, down river in Bermondsey.
3   *The Description of Britain 1577–87*, William Harrison.
4   Robert Crawley, 1550.
5   Horatio Busino, chaplain to the Venetian ambassador, 1617.
6   I am indebted to the theatre director Gregory Doran for pointing this out.

Chapter IV

1   Widely varying estimates based on different pieces of evidence have been made for London's population c.1700, but if one includes all the outlying districts counted 'within the Bills of Mortality', five to six hundred thousand seems about right.
2   I am indebted for this point to Peter Guillery, whose seminal book *The Small House in Eighteenth Century London* appeared while this book was in preparation.
3   *Accounts of St Saviour's*, M. Concanen and A. Morgan, 1795.

Chapter V

1   I am indebted to Dan Cruickshank for this and several

other salient points.

2   I suspect that exploration might, even today, uncover within what is now London further surviving houses whose basic structure is older than their apparent Georgian origins. A house of similar date to number 49, also built at right-angles to Bankside, with a fine central staircase and a handsome doorway on its west side, used to be number 74, also known as Honduras Wharf. It figured, like 49, in the LCC *Survey of London* volume for the district (1950) as being worthy of note. This, however, did not save it from being swept away a few years later in a development scheme.

3   *Mémoires Faites par un Voyageur en Angleterre*, Henri Misson, 1698.

4   William Harrison, ibid.

5   Eventually the lighter became a sail-less or 'dumb' barge, which could be manoeuvred with the tides by the use of a special long oar in the hands of a skilled lighterman, but earlier the word was applied to the barges equipped with sails that were the workhorses of the river.

6   Quoted in *The Story of the Charringtons*, Elspet Fraser-Stephen, 1952.

Chapter VI

1   *Charrington, Gardner, Locket and Co. Ltd – Two Hundred Years in the Coal Trade.*

2   *The Story of the Charringtons*, ibid.

3   *Anecdotes of the Manners and Customs of London during the Eighteenth Century*, James Peller Malcolm, 1810.

4   J. R. Hammond.

5   Later the site of the Bethlem Royal Hospital, the domed building that is now the Imperial War Museum.

6   It was to finish its days in the twentieth century as a well-known centre of boxing – The Ring.

7   I am indebted for this insight to Peter Ackroyd.

Chapter VII

1   Figures from Henry Mayhew's *London Labour and the*

London Poor, collected 1850–60.

2 Not the obscure village of Walworth in County Durham, as another current website misleadingly suggests.

3 *Letters to the Foundling Hospital: Tracts on Nursing Children 1721–54.*

4 *Hints Designed to Promote Beneficence, Temperance and Medical Science*, Dr Lettsom, published in 1801 and re-published in 1816 after his death.

5 *South London*, Walter Besant, 1898.

6 Southwark Vestry's organisation was untypical, in that the parish benefited from several substantial charities set up in past centuries (i.e. 'Cure's Gift') which were used to finance almshouses and charity schools. Therefore its various parochial functions tended to be cloaked in names such as 'Commissioner', 'Warden', 'Keeper of the Estates', etc.

7 Newspaper cuttings, not all of them attributed, in the collection of Southwark's history archive.

8 Zanna Milford, to the *South London Press*.

9 An oil painting probably by Thomas Miles Richardson senior.

10 Vestry meetings in St Saviour's parish could be attended by any parishioner who wanted to, and the vestrymen were appointed by a general vote. The parish had had a 'closed vestry' – a self-perpetuating clique – up to 1730, when they had been forced by Parliament into the 'open vestry' system.

11 In a collection of papers relating to St Saviour's made by two successive nineteenth-century worthies, which is now in the British Library.

Chapter VIII

1 Called thus because it was discovered in the 1950s, rolled up and filthy, in an attic in Rhinebeck, New York State – taken there originally, no doubt, by someone carrying the old world to the new.

2 *Days in the Factories, or the Manufacturing Industry of*

Great Britain Described, George Dodd, 1843. He was assistant engineer to the Rennie family, the bridge-builders.

3 Quoted by Lynda Nead in *Victorian Babylon*, 2000.

4 Dickens, the famous opening to *Bleak House*.

5 They cannot, at that date, have been buried elsewhere. Nunhead Cemetery, which was to become the great out-of-town resting place for people south of the river, did not open till 1840.

6 Till it became two LCC boroughs in 1900 it was administered, with some difficulty, from the City.

Chapter IX

1 Quoted by John Pudney in *Crossing London's River*, 1972.

2 *The Mystery of Edwin Drood*.

3 *Our Mutual Friend*.

4 *A Rebours*, J. K. Huysman, 1883.

5 Walter Besant, journalist and man of letters, founder of the Society of Authors, 1836–1901.

6 *The Bell of St Paul's*, 1889.

7 A new diocese had been formed, and the church was therefore given the status of a cathedral in 1905.

8 Arthur B. Moss, a contributor to *Living London*, first edited by George R. Sims, 1901–02. There were numerous subsequent editions.

Chapter X

1 No Directories or Electoral Registers appeared during the two world wars.

2 The old Borough of Southwark had been split down its central High Street into two LCC boroughs.

3 Heinemann, 1938.

4 Unattributed cutting from Anna Lee's own file, dated October 1936.

5 Oddly, the official war-damage map of the time marked the other houses as mildly damaged and number 49 as so damaged as probably to be fit only for demolition, when

the reality was the other way round. But the survey was carried out at speed.

6 From a collection of incomplete cuttings in Southwark's history archive.

7 He was eventually to become editor of the *Telegraph* and to receive a knighthood.

Chapter XI

1 Leonard Reilly and Geoff Marshall.

2 James A. Jones, 1935.

3 Figures from the files of Southwark's history archive.

4 The reference is to Shelley's well-known poem about an ancient Egyptian statue, with an inscription referring to enormous power, standing fractured and tumbled in an empty desert.

5 The street – originally Thames Street – was named in belated recognition of one of Southwark's Elizabethan benefactors, William Emerson, whose memorial is still in St Saviour's church. He 'lived and died an honest man' until the age of ninety-two, extremely old for that time. Beneath a miniature effigy of him in death are the words *ut sum sic eris* – 'As I now am so shall you be'.

6 From an unattributed cutting in the possession of the house's present occupants.

7 Quoted by Frances Spalding in *The Tate: A History*, 1998.

Bibliography and Sources

Printed works
For a book such as this there are two essential published works which provide the starting point for all other research These are the Bankside volume (Vol. XXII) of the admirable *Survey of London*, published by the LCC in 1950, and the relevant Surrey volume (Vol. 4, part 1) of the extensive *Victoria County History*, published in 1912. In addition, there are the invaluable series of old maps reproduced by the London Topographical Society, namely:

The A–Z of Elizabethan London, Introductory Notes by John Fisher, 1979

The A–Z of Georgian London, Introductory Notes by Ralph Hyde, 1982

The A–Z of Regency London, Introduction by Paul Laxton, 1985

The A–Z of Victorian London, Introductory Notes by Ralph Hyde, 1987

It would be difficult to cite every book which, over the years, has nourished my view of London, but here follows a fairly comprehensive, if heterogenous, list of those works that have contributed to the present book. All are published in London except where another provenance is given. Where they have been produced by organisations that are not essentially publishers, their names are given.

Ackroyd, Peter, *Dickens' London, an Imaginative Vision*, 1987
—— *Blake*, 1995
Acorn, George, *One of the Multitude*, 1911
Anon., *Grey & Martin – City Lead Works*, GLIAS

Newsletter No.79, 1982

Anon., *Southwark Past and Present*, Southwark Borough Council, 1932

Anon., *Tracts on Nursing Children, 1721–53*

Aubrey, John, *Brief Lives*, edited by John Buchanan-Brown, 2000

Barker, Felix and Hyde, Ralph, *London as it Might Have Been*, 1982

—— and Jackson, Peter, *London: Two hundred years of a city and its people*, 1974

Besant, Walter, *The Bell of St Paul's*, 1889

—— *South London*, 1898

—— *London South of the Thames*, 1912

Bodger, Charlotte G., *Southwark and its Story*, 1881

Booth, Charles, *Life and Labour of the People of London*, 1902–03

Boulton, Jeremy, *Neighbourhood and Society in a London Suburb in the Seventeenth Century*, Cambridge, 1987

Bowers, Robert W., *Sketches of Southwark Old and New*, 1905

Burford, E. J., *London: The Synfulle Citie*, 1990

Capp, Bernard, *The World of John Taylor, the Water-Poet*, Oxford, 1994

Carlin, Martha, *Medieval Southwark*, Hambledon Press, 1996

Carson, Neil, *A Companion to Henslowe's Diary*, Cambridge, 1998

Clayton, Antony, *Subterranean City; Beneath the Streets of London*, 2000

Concannen, M. Junior. and Morgan, A., *The History and Antiquities of the Parish of St Saviour's, Southwark*, 1795

Croad, Stephen, *Liquid History, the Thames Through Time*, 2003

Cruickshank, Dan and Burton, Neil, *Life in the Georgian City*, 1990

—— and Wyld, Peter, *London: The Art of Georgian Building*, 1975

Darlington, Ida and Howgego, James, *Printed Maps of London c.1553–1850*, 1964

Darwin, Bernard (as told to), *Two Hundred Years in the Coal-Trade*, privately published, 1931

de Maré, Eric, *The London Doré Saw: A Victorian Evocation*, 1973

Defoe, Daniel, *Journal of the Plague Year*, 1722

Dickens, Charles, *Little Dorrit*, 1857

—— *Our Mutual Friend*, 1865

Dodd, George, *Days in the Factories, or the Manufactury Industry of Great Britain Described*, 1843

Dyos, H. J., *Victorian Suburb*, Leicester 1974

Earle, Peter, *The Making of the English Middle Classes: Business, Society and Family Life in London 1660–1730*, 1989

—— *A City Full of People: Men and Women of London, 1650–1750*, 1994

Evelyn, John, *Fumifugium*, 1661

—— *Diary*, edited by E. S. de Beer, Oxford, 1959

Fletcher, Geoffrey, *London's River*, 1966

Foakes, R. A., editor, *Henslowe's Diary*, Cambridge, 2002

Fraser-Stephens, Elspet, *The Story of the Charringtons: Two Centuries in the London Coal Trade*, privately published, 1952

Geijer, Eric Gustaf, *Impressions of England 1809–1810*, introduced by Anton Blanck, 1932

George, Dorothy M., *London Life in the Eighteenth Century*, 1925

Gilbey, Elizabeth W., *Wages in Eighteenth Century England*, Cambridge, Mass., 1934

Glanville, Philippa, *London in Maps*, 1972

Golden, Grace, *Old Bankside*, 1951

Guillery, Peter, *The Small House in Eighteenth Century London*, New Haven, 2004

Hall, P. G., *The Industries of London since 1861*, 1962

Halliday, Stephen, *The Great Stink of London: Sir Joseph Bazalgette and the Cleansing of the Victorian Metropolis*, Stroud, Glos., 1999

Halton, Edward, *A New View of London*, 1708

Harrison, Shirley and Evemy, Sally, *Southwark: Who Was Who*, London Borough of Southwark, 2001

Harrison, William, *The Description of Britain 1557–1587*, edited by Ernest Rhys, 1876

Hayward, A., editor, *Dr Johnson's Mrs Thrale*, 1910

Hollinshed, John, *Ragged London*, 1861

Humphrey, Stephen, *Southwark, Bermondsey and Rotherhithe in Old Photographs*, Stroud, Glos., 1995, a Second Selection 1997

—— *Southwark, the Twentieth Century*, Stroud, Glos., 1999

—— *The Cuming Family, and the Cuming Museum*, London Borough of Southwark, 2001

Inwood, Stephen, *A History of London*, 1998

Jackson, Peter, *London Bridge*, 1971

—— *Introducing Tallis's London Street Views 1838–40*, London Topographical Society, 1969

Jephson, H., *The Sanitary Evolution of London*, London County Council, 1907

Jones, Jennifer, *Southwark: a History of Bankside, Bermondsey and 'The Borough'*, South Thames Training and Enterprise Council 1996

Lambton, Lucinda, *Temples of Convenience and Chambers of Delight*, 1995

Layton, Walter T., *The Early Years of the South Metropolitan Gas Company*, 1920

Lettsom, Dr, *Hints Designed to Promote Beneficence, Temperance and Medical Science*, 1801, edition with introduction by John Cookley, 1816

Luckin, Bill, *Pollution and Control: a social history of the Thames in the nineteenth century*, Bristol, 1986

Malcolm, James Peller, *Anecdotes of the Manners and Customs of London during the Eighteenth Century*, 1810

Mayhew, Henry, *London Labour and the London Poor*, Vols 1–4 (especially Vol. 3), 1861–62

Misson, Henri, *Mémoires Faites par un Voyageur en Angleterre*, 1698

Montague, C. J., *Sixty Years in Waifdom*, 1904

Morton, H. V., *The Nights of London*, 1926

Mould, R. W., *Southwark Men of Mark*, Borough of Southwark Libraries, 1903

Nead, Lynda, *Victorian Babylon: People, Streets and Images in Nineteenth Century London*, New Haven, 2000

Nef, J. W., *The Rise of the British Coal Industry*, 1932

O'Connell, Sheila, *London 1753*, British Museum Press, 2003

Olsen, Donald J., *The Growth of Victorian London*, 1976

Orrell, John, *The Quest for Shakespeare's Globe*, Cambridge, 1983

Pepys, Samuel, *Diary*, edited by Robert Latham and William Matthews, 1970

Picard, Liza, *Restoration London*, 1997

Pierce, Patricia, *Old London Bridge*, 2001

Pike, E. Royston, *Human Documents of the Industrial Revolution in Britain*, 1966

—— *Human Documents of the Victorian Golden Age*, 1967

—— *Human Documents of the Age of the Forsytes*, 1969

—— *Human Documents of the Lloyd George Era*, 1972

Platter, Thomas and Busino, Horatio, *The Journals of Two Travellers in Elizabethan and Early Stuart England*, Ipswich, 1995

Porter, Stephen, *The Great Fire of London*, Stroud, Glos., 1996

—— *The Great Plague*, Stroud, Glos., 1999

Pritchett, V. S., *London Perceived*, 1962

—— *A Cab at the Door*, 1968

Pudney, John, *Crossing London's River*, 1972
—— *London's Docks*, 1975

Reilly, Leonard, *Southwark: an Illustrated History*, London Borough of Southwark, 1998
—— and Marshall, Geoffrey, *The Story of Bankside*, London Borough of Southwark, 2001
Rendle, William, *The Inns of Old Southwark*, 1888
Richardson, A. E., 'London Re-Planned: The Royal Academy Planning Committee's Interim Report', *Country Life*, 1942
Richardson, Rev. J., *Recollections of the Last Half Century*, 1855
Rudé, George, *Hanoverian London 1714–1808*, 1971

Sabaag, Karl, *Power into Art*, 2000
Saint, Andrew, 'The Building Art of the First Industrial Metropolis 1784–1873', chapter in *London – World City 1800–1840* edited by Celina Fox, Yale, 1992
Sala, George Augustus, *Gas and Daylight*, 1859
Schwartz, L. D., *London in the Age of Industrialization: Entrepreneurs, labour force and living conditions 1700–1850*, 1992
Seymour, Claire, *Ragged Schools, Ragged Children*, Ragged School Museum Trust, 1995
Shelley, Henry C., *Inns and Taverns of Old London*, 1909
Shepherd, Thomas, *London in the Nineteenth Century*, 1829
Sims, George R., editor, *Living London*, 1901–2
Spalding, Frances, *The Tate: a History*, 1998
Spence, Craig, *Atlas of 1690s London*, 2000
Stamp, Gavin, *The Changing Metropolis, Earliest Photographs of London 1839–1879*, 1984
—— 'Giles Gilbert Scott and Bankside Power Station', chapter in *The Building of Tate Modern*, 2000
Stow, John, *The Survey of London*, 1598

Tames, Richard, *Southwark Past*, 2001

Waller, Maureen, *1700: Scenes from London Life*, 1988

Wagner, Gillian, *Barnardo*, 1979

Weinreb, Ben and Hibbert, Christopher, editors, *The London Encyclopaedia*, 1983

White, H. P., *A Regional History of the Railways of Great Britain*, Vol. III, 1969

Worsthorne, Peregrine, *Tricks of Memory*, 1995

Wright, Lawrence, *Clean and Decent: The fascinating History of the Bathroom and the WC*, 1960

Unpublished and other archival Sources

The London Borough of Southwark has a rich collection of archival material amassed over many years, thanks to bequests from several nineteenth-century antiquarians but also to the initiative and care of individual archivists. In the **Southwark Local History Library**, therefore, I have been able to consult Census returns; St Saviour's parish records of marriages, baptisms and burials (from 1653 to 1835, with a few gaps); Rate books (from 1748); and a collection of miscellaneous house Deeds. I have been able to consult London Street Directories (various different publications) from 1790 onwards, and the Electoral registers for the twentieth century for which the Census returns are not yet accessible. I have also availed myself of the Library's extensive files of cuttings, photographs, handbills, advertisements, correspondence and other ephemera, dating from the eighteenth century to the present day; also of the MS. book on the early history of the Union Street parochial schools compiled by Sylvia Morris, the present head of the Cathedral School of St Saviour and St Mary Overy; also of the Archivist's own extensive list of Southwark's one-time cemeteries. I have studied the Library's collection of maps, especially insurance maps for the late nineteenth and early twentieth centuries. I have also made use of the microfilms of the *South London Press*, especially for the 1860s and '70s.

In **The Family History Centre**, London EC1, I have obtained various Death Certificates and Probate records referred to in this book.

In **The Metropolitan Archives**, London EC1 I have been able to consult further documents relating to Bankside, in particular the Vestry Minutes books of St Saviour's parish from 1670 to 1738, and from 1788 to 1824, also a parish Land Valuation of 1807–8. I have made extensive use of their collection of Metropolitan Board of Works archives, expecially the papers of 1856–7 and 1861–3 and 1867 relating to Bazalgette's plans for the London sewer system, and also the Thames Flood Prevention Maps of 1880–86. Also their files relating to the life and work of John Grooms. I have availed myself of the Library's copies of the 1945 Bomb Damage Maps, and of their extensive photographic collection, originally in the possession of the Greater London Council.

In **The British Library**, as well as consulting many of the printed books cited in the preceding section, I have been able to work my way, in the Rare Book Room, through two volumes entitled *St Saviour's Illustrated: History and Antiquities of the Parochial Church of St Saviour's, Southwark.* These are compendiums of printed church records and engravings to which have been added notes, memos, plans, pamphlets, letters, handbills, photos and press-cuttings. The initial volume was compiled for subscription circulation by W.G. Moss and the Rev. J. Nightingale in 1818, and the much-expanded second volume was produced by W. Taylor in 1840. (Unamplified, printed-only versions of both volumes are in the possession of the Southwark Local History Library.)

In **The London Library** I have consulted bound volumes of *The Builder* and *The Times*, particularly for the 1860s.

In **The Guildhall Library** I have been able to consult the records of the Watermen and Lightermens' Company, and also to make use of the Picture Library's extensive collection of London paintings, prints and panoramas.

The Museum of London possesses, among very much else, a Grace Golden Archive of that artist's prints, drawings and personal papers, which were made available to me.

In addition, the present owners of 49 Bankside have

inherited from previous occupants of the house a file of Deeds, a few letters and a number of twentieth-century newspaper cuttings, which have been put to good use.

Acknowledgements

I am particularly grateful to certain people without whom this book could hardly have been written in the way it has. Chief among them are the present owners of 49 Bankside, who have shown unstinting kindness, co-operation and interest in the project and have welcomed me, and others connected with me, into their home on numerous occasions. I also owe a considerable debt of gratitude to various present-day members of the Sells family, especially to Andrew Sells, who generously loaned me privately printed material I would have had great difficulty in finding elsewhere and shared with me his informed interest in his forebears.

Several other previous occupants of the house in the middle decades of the twentieth century have generously shared their memories of the house with me, especially Dan Black but also Peregrine Worsthorne, June Plaat and Hubert Montagu-Pollock. Also the late Anna Lee and her sister Ruth Wood. My thanks, too, to Anna Lee's son, Jeffrey Byron, who helped to organise my meeting with her at what turned out to be only a few months before her death.

All the staff of Southwark Local History Library have provided courteous and friendly help, but I would particularly mention the Archivist Stephen Humphrey, whose very extensive knowledge of the area and its history has been placed at my disposal. The staff of the Guildhall Library, particularly John Fisher and Jeremy Smith in the Prints and Maps section, have also been extremely helpful and understanding. My thanks too to the Museum of London, especially to Mark Bills, Julia Cochrane and Emma Shapley. My thanks also, as often before with earlier books, to the well-informed staff of the London Library, to the Metropolitan Archives and to the Family History Centre.

At different stages in the book's preparation, a number of individuals have been helpful with recommendations, contact addresses, suggestions, advice on sources, reminiscences, references, the loan of material and other forms of support and encouragement. These include Adam Bakker, Peter Barber, Paul Barker, Colin Brewer, Roger Cazalet, Dan Cruickshank, Sara Davies, Nicholas Deakin, Richard Dennis, Tony Flower, David Goreham, Nicholas Hale, Simon Jenkins, Thomas Kirby, Nick Lacey, Richard Lansdown, Fred Manson, Nicholas and Elizabeth Monck, Adam Pollock, Mike Shaw, Gene Simons, Gavin Stamp, Colin Thubron, Nicholas Tindall, Al and Martha Vogeler. Also Douglas Matthews, champion indexer. My gratitude to all of the above, for their time and interest – and also, especially, to two architects: Jon Finney, who took an interest in my self-compiled panorama of Bankside in 1880, and Chris Oliver, who took a great deal of trouble revamping my drawings to his own professional standards and lettering them.

Particular thanks, also, to Colin Mabberley, in his capacity as Grace Golden's executor; to Alan Runagall, the present owner of Trevor Chamberlain's painting *Bankside 1970*; and to Cordelia Stamp, the copyright holder of Albert Pile's work.

Permission to quote freely from his poem *Parliament Hill Fields* was given to me almost thirty years ago by the late Sir John Betjeman, in a personal communication. My gratitude now, as then: my only regret is that he is no longer here to be amused by the discovery that he had himself visited the long-term home of the family whose name formed one of his childhood memories.

Part of the family tree of the Bankside Sells

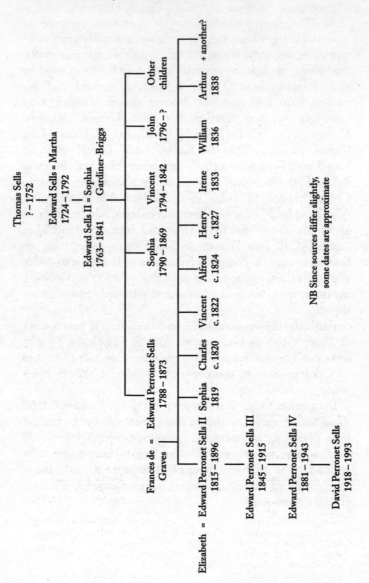

Thomas Sells
? – 1752

Edward Sells = Martha
1724 – 1792

Edward Sells II = Sophia
1763 – 1841   Gardiner-Briggs

Frances de = Edward Perronet Sells
Graves   1788 – 1873

Sophia   Charles   Vincent   Alfred   Henry   Vincent   Irene   William   John   Arthur   + another?
1819   c. 1820   c. 1822   c. 1824   c. 1827   1794 – 1842 1833   1836   1796 – ? 1838

Sophia
1790 – 1869

Other
children

Elizabeth = Edward Perronet Sells II
1815 – 1896

Edward Perronet Sells III
1845 – 1915

Edward Perronet Sells IV
1881 – 1943

David Perronet Sells
1918 – 1993

NB Since sources differ slightly,
some dates are approximate

250

INDEX